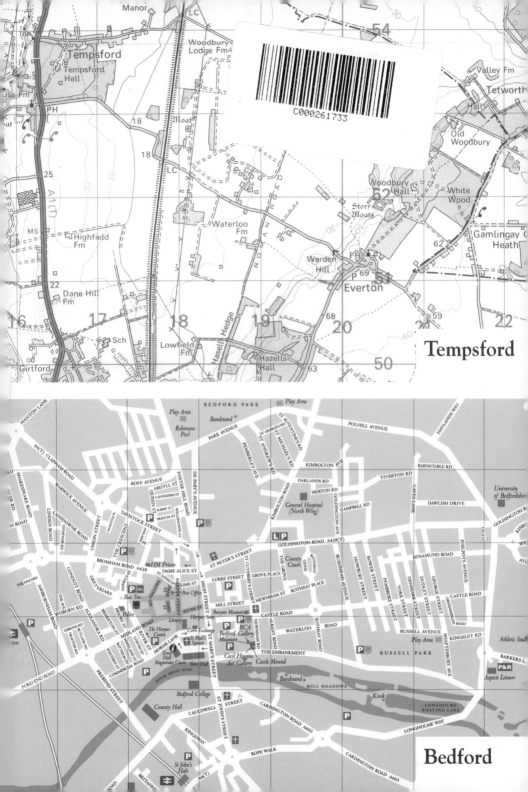

C000261733

Tempsford

Bedford

THE
SPY CAPITAL
OF BRITAIN

For Tom

THE SPY CAPITAL OF BRITAIN

BEDFORDSHIRE'S SECRET WAR
1939-1945

Stephen Bunker

BEDFORD CHRONICLES

First published in 2007 by Bedford Chronicles, an imprint
of Bedford Borough Council Town Hall, St Paul's Square,
Bedford MK40 1SJ, England.

ISBN 978-0-906020-03-06

Layout design by Bluegreen Design Consultants,
The Old Mill, 34a Gladstone Street, Bedford MK41 7RR.
www.bluegreendesign.co.uk

Jacket design by Jeremy Duncan

Jacket montage depicts Violette Szabo, Winston Churchill,
Denis Sefton Delmer, communications room, Met Office,
Dunstable, German Enigma machine, black propaganda
radio transmitter, Potsgrove, black propaganda newspaper
Nachrichten.

Printed and bound in England by Biddles, Kings Lynn.

Contents

Glossary

BBC. British Broadcasting Corporation. Responsible for, amongst other functions, 'white' propaganda. Although not directly controlled by a government department, the BBC was subject to censorship and, by 1939, had already refined the technique of anticipating government demands.

Department EH. The original Department of Propaganda to the Enemy, formed in 1938 (when there was no enemy) and replaced by SO1.

DNB. *Dictionary of National Biography.*

MD1. Originally Military Intelligence Research, abbreviated MI(R), this was moved away from the War Office to the new Ministry of Defence. In fact the 'Minister' was Winston Churchill, and there was no real ministry. This obliged MD1 to dangle administratively as part of the Ministry of Supply.

MEW. Ministry of Economic Warfare. It had three ministers: Ronald Cross (1939-40), Hugh Dalton (1940-42) and Roundell Palmer, Earl of Selbourne (1942-45).

MoI. Ministry of Information.

MB. The usual abbreviation for the 'black' propaganda broadcasting station in the village of Milton Bryan.

PID. Political Intelligence Department. A sub-department of the Foreign Office that established itself at Woburn in 1939.

PWE. Political Wartime Executive. The name was apparently proposed by David Bowes-Lyon.

NID. Naval Intelligence Department, based in the Admiralty but with a critical outlet in Bedfordshire.

SCU. Special Communications Unit. A sub division of the Royal Signals, this body drew the enlistment of many radio amateurs.

Section D. A sub-section of SIS, the forerunner to SO2 and later SOE.

SIS. Secret Intelligence Service. A Foreign Office department, otherwise known as MI6. This had various sub-departments, including 'Section D'.

SO1. The propaganda department created in replacement of Department EH.

SO2. Short lived successor organisation to Section D, also supposed to take over the work of MI(R).

SO3. The ill-conceived administrative leg of the SO operation, and one which Hugh Gaitskell failed to get moving at all.

SOE. Special Operations Executive. Created under Dalton's over-arching Ministry of Economic Warfare, it eventually absorbed the SO departments.

STS. Special Training School. SOE operated a number of these around the country, each with a specific function such as survival, parachute training or explosives.

WAAF. Women's Auxiliary Air Force.

List of Illustrations

Acknowledgements

With the passing of the years since the end of World War Two, there have been an increasing number of books devoted to different aspects of covert operations, and this volume seeks to make a small contribution to this canon by highlighting a number of these that were undertaken in one of Britain's smallest counties. It cannot claim to be a comprehensive account as, aside from the shortcomings of the author, the very nature of a 'secret' war, as well as the passage of time, have served to obscure matters from the researcher. Much knowledge resides with private individuals who have built up a considerable reservoir of information through dedicated research, whilst others have acquired their knowledge through direct, contemporary experience. In this respect I would like to extend my gratitude to a number of individuals for being so generous with their time, their information and frequently with their material. In the early stages of the research Colin Burbidge provided some observations and leads in connection with both RAF Tempsford and the contrived mystery surrounding the death of Glenn Miller. Thanks must be expressed to John Clarke for taking a day out of the maintenance of his Cornish estate in order to illuminate the life of his remarkable father, and a most enjoyable day was spent with Denis Dolton, who kindly showed me around many locations in the Bedfordshire countryside that were familiar to him in his capacity as a driver based at Woburn Abbey. At this juncture, indirect thanks ought to be extended to all the following motorists for being so understanding of our abrupt halts as the memories came flooding back to Dennis. A special appreciation should also be extended to Pamela Emms for kindly passing to me the recollections of her late father, Doug Scales, and particular thanks is due to Kevan Fadden for shedding some light on the Eversholt side of things. Pat Hawker MBE provided critical pointers into aspects of covert operations in Czechoslovakia, whilst Michael and Richard Ingrams both helped to shed some light on the activities and character of their talented, if enigmatic father.

Sadly, there are few around today that were closely engaged in the Secret War but two who were are Jiří Louda, from whom came detail on his time at the Czechoslovak radio station at Hockliffe, and Phil Luck, with whom it was a pleasure to spend a fascinating evening as he provided an insight that simply cannot be gleaned from the written page. As all good policemen should, Tom Madigan quickly pointed me in the right direction (not the first time that he has done that in my career) and I would like to express my appreciation to Mary Neal for sharing her experience of working for some fascinating characters (and for the shortbread biscuits), as well as Yvonne Jones for a splendid evening's hospitality. Again, in the early stages of research, a debt of gratitude immediately became owed to John Pether, one of the team closely involved in the Bletchley Park Trust, for generosity with his time, knowledge, contacts and materials. Few, if any, know more than Neil Rees about the role of the Czechoslovakian contribution to the Allied war effort, and I wish to record my appreciation for his hospitality and crucial pointers that he was able to provide. Much the same expertise lies with Lt. Cdr. A. Struan Robertson with respect to the Norwegian forces in the UK, and I am grateful to him for sharing the information that he possessed. Thanks also to Roy Tink for his recollections of his work in the GPO's engineering unit. One half day in the courteous company of Dafydd Williams served as a reminder of what a cosseted life we now lead thanks to the courage and sacrifices of earlier generations, and a special appreciation is due to Marion Whitehorn, one of the last of the black propagandists for sharing some of her wartime experiences. Last, but only in the alphabetical sense, many thanks to Peter White and Heather Woods for making available the material retained by their respective fathers. This book cannot pretend to provide a comprehensive account of Bedfordshire's Secret War but perhaps it will serve to prompt others to come forward and provide posterity with the benefits of their knowledge.

In addition to the above, I'm indebted to a number of individuals who have given great help in providing the photographs that illustrate this book. Crucially, a number have also endeavoured to source any copyright that may still be attached to some images. Whilst such an attempt has been made for every image, should anyone feel that copyright has been incorrectly attributed, or can prove ownership in the few instances where it has not been established, we will be happy to make the changes in subsequent editions. In the meantime, thanks are due to Bob Body, Dave Cutts, Herb Friedman, Murray Greeman, Hans Moonen, Yvonne Oliver of the Imperial War Museum, and Rosemary E. Rigby MBE of the Violette Szabo Museum. I would also like to thank the family of Jaroslav Bublík for permission to reproduce the picture of the Czechoslovak personnel at Hockliffe.

A number of staff and institutions have also been immensely helpful and I wish to acknowledge the assistance provided by Dr Elizabeth Adey and Chris Grabham at Luton Museum; Bill Lash, Comptroller at Woburn Abbey; the Luton and Bedfordshire Record Office – especially Martin Deacon who suggested the identity of some of the locations of the Research Units; Jon Baker (Archivist), Helen O'Hara (Curator), and Major Alan Edwards at the Military Intelligence Museum at Chicksands; Jean Yeats at South Bedfordshire District Council; David Fowler of the Bedford Association of Tour Guides; Ian MacGregor and his colleagues at the Meteorological Library and Archive; the archivists of Churchill College, Cambridge; the Imperial War Museum, the British Library and the National Archives.

In the early stages of the research, both Ingram Murray and Felix Delmer kindly read through the text and made some helpful (and encouraging) comments. A bigger task awaited Mike Read and the copy editor, Simon O'Brien, who each read through the text as it approached its finishing stage. Particular gratitude is due to the pair of them for undertaking such a task and the invaluable contributions that they made, as well as to Anja Kwambana for proof reading the work. Additional thanks is also due to Jeremy Duncan for unfailing diligence and attention to detail.

Nobody, however, including the author, has been more closely associated with this book than the person who commissioned it in the first place, Joanne Moore, Tourism Development Officer for Bedford Borough Council. It was Joanne who recognised the need to draw together all the odds and ends of information about Bedfordshire's wartime operations that were floating around, or were hidden just beneath the surface. It was also Joanne who remained the constant driving force, guide and encourager as a short research project grew and grew into this account of the Secret War that was based in one small English county.

Commissioning Editor's Preface

'Spy capital of Britain'.... those few evocative words became etched in my mind during the course of a casual conversation whilst touring the grounds of RAF Chicksands with the Base Commandant, Brigadier, Chris Holtom back in the spring of 2000. Brigadier Holtom was very knowledgeable, not only about Chicksands Priory and the Intelligence Corps but also the wartime history of the surrounding area. He remarked that during World War Two, the area had so many 'spooked houses' that it should be known as the 'Spy Capital of Britain'. The idea fascinated me and though I wasn't entirely sure I knew what the Brigadier meant by 'spooked', his words planted a seed in my mind that was to lay dormant for more than a year as work and family commitments each dictated their own priorities.

When in late 2001 I took up the post of Tourism Development Officer for Bedford Borough Council, those dormant seeds began to germinate into ideas of how to develop a unique identity for Bedford and north Bedfordshire to attract visitors.

Over the next couple of years along with supporting the opening of two new museums, The 306th Bomb Group Museum and The Glenn Miller Museum, I was involved with producing a trail guide to the World War Two airfields surrounding Bedford. It was Alan Goodale with whom I worked closely on this project who introduced me to many of his contacts, and they in turn who helped inspire the 'Wartime Bedford' initiative.

I owe thanks to Connie & Gordon Richards, David & Liz Wooding and Ralph & Daphne Franklin, Chris Chandler, Gerry Darnell, Jim O'Connor and Peter Tipping, all of whom helped in the early stages, giving their time freely and sharing their knowledge

On my own journey of discovery it quickly became clear that Bedford's wartime story was unique. As I began to gather information, a picture emerged of a slumbering provincial county town awakened by the sudden influx of British and American airmen from surrounding airbases, spending their liberty time in Bedford and making a huge impact on the town and indeed the surrounding villages.

Much of their daily entertainment was provided by the stars of the day courtesy of the BBC who had evacuated to Bedford in 1941 and performed and broadcast from several local venues including the Corn Exchange. It was a natural move therefore when Glenn Miller and the Band of the Allied Expeditionary Forces arrived in England that Bedford was chosen as their base. With actor David Niven as his British Army liaison, Miller's presence attracted other American greats including Bing Crosby and Bob Hope. Bedford became a centre for not only the nation's entertainment but also for the whole of the Allied Forces as their special programmes were broadcast across the whole theatre of operations.

But that was not all that made the story unique; there was much more to it than at first met the eye. There was a whole sub-text to the story, another layer, more than one could see in the air or on the ground, an 'underground world' of secret activities that had taken place of which I could only get a hint. Like panning for gold; sifting through the silt occasionally there would be the glimmer of something precious.

A chance conversation with Colin Burbidge revealed what he called 'Churchill's Magic Toy Shop' and 'The Spy School' while Bernard O'Connor was a mine of information about the movement of secret agents from RAF Tempsford. A back issue of *After The Battle* provided by magazine editor Winston Ramsey, included a lengthy and informative article about Denis Sefton Delmer and the black propaganda activities centred in and around the Duke of Bedford's Woburn Estate.

So there were famous names and spies, secret radio stations and a 'magic toy shop'; what an intriguing mixture! I wanted to uncover the real face of Bedford and the surrounding county during WWII, but where to start? It was like having the pieces of a jigsaw puzzle without the picture. I wasn't a historian and the task seemed too huge for just me; time to call in the professionals. Research began in earnest in 2005 with seed funding from Home Front Recall (part of Heritage Lottery Fund) and Dr Stephen Bunker was commissioned on behalf of Bedford Borough Council to complete the research.

Like detectives reviewing a 'cold case' we set to work and as such the going was tough; few had survived who could give an eye witness account and even those that could were often only able to offer a small piece of the jigsaw. Historical accounts, biographies, the most recently released papers in the National Archives and various private papers helped to add flesh to the bones. Sometimes the research meant separating fact from fiction and sometimes a lead would take us up a blind alley; to our frustration we found that few if any records had been kept of certain clandestine activities and elsewhere records had been deliberately destroyed or had mysteriously disappeared. To reveal the true face was not going to be easy; it had been masked and disguised, denied and disfigured, maybe it was too tall a task, maybe the true face was too elusive and an artist's impression was all we could hope to achieve.

The project took on a life of its own and before we knew it we had enough material for a book but to publish was a scary prospect. There are probably few periods in history that have inspired the written word more than the Second World War and with so many publications on the bookshelves by noted historians along with first hand accounts by the people who lived through it all, would this be worthy enough to stand alongside them? But nowhere, it seemed was there an account of one small county's contribution to clandestine operations, indeed maybe the biggest single contribution to the Secret War. It would not be another local history book; we wanted to stake our claim as 'Spy Capital of Britain' and what the heck, we had a great title!

Joanne Moore
Bedford Borough Council

Foreword

It was May 2000 and I was in the final stages of planning to host 500 American veterans who had served at Chicksands during the Cold War when Joanne Moore from the Bedford Tourist Information Centre came into my office offering support for the US Reunion. It was during that conversation with Joanne that I described Bedfordshire as riddled with ex 'spook' sites which probably made it the 'Spy Capital of Britain' and how that must have some attraction for tourism.

At that time we were creating the Museum of Defence Intelligence at Chicksands and I needed all the help I could get to run a museum in a secret site that was difficult for the public to enter. The interest in the Chicksands site was underlined very strongly when ten thousand people came into the camp the first day we opened the gates to the public. Suffice to say the US Reunion went very well and thanks to Bedford Borough Council's website a great number of American veterans keep in touch with each other and continue to visit Chicksands to the present day.

Six years later I was surprised and delighted to be asked to write a foreword to this fascinating story of Bedfordshire's substantial contribution to the secret war against Nazi Germany. Reading it through I am struck by the parallels that currently face this country and our allies. Terrorism is Total War. It plays to the weakness of all the traditional rules and behaviour of a democracy. It exploits the frictions between politics, civil servants, police, the military, business and public perception. The neutralisation of terrorism requires the same resolve, courage, cooperation, imagination and ruthlessness that was necessary to build up the remarkable capabilities of organisations such as Bletchley Park, the Political Warfare Executive and the Special Operations Executive. But the success of an organisation lies in its people and this book is full of well-researched descriptions of quite exceptional people acting out their covert roles in the misty Bedfordshire countryside.

I am struck by one thing in particular; the rivalries between covert agencies. My own experience of thirty five years in Defence Intelligence is full of frustration caused by those same corrosive characteristics.

However, the example of Denis Delmer of the Political Warfare Executive recognising the need to cooperate with secret intelligence services and managing the personalities so well is a timely reminder of the need today to bring some strange bedfellows together and make them cooperate to head off the latest threat of terrorism. Selflessness, vision and energy are prime constituents of good leaders and while all the people described in this book have some of those characteristics, only a few such as Sefton Delmer, Edward Yeo-Thomas, Robert Bruce Lockhart, Cecil Vandepeer Clarke and Vera Atkins appear to have them all.

I can report that Chicksands continues to play its part in creating the conditions for cooperation between agencies and allies, hugely encouraged by the support it receives from the Bedfordshire community.

Chris Holtom CBE
Director Intelligence Corps 1997–2001

Introduction

To pick up from Brigadier Holtom's foreword, Bedfordshire's claim that its role in World War Two makes it worthy of the title as the 'Spy Capital of Britain', does so due to its intimate association with a new phenomenon in warfare – the Secret War. To understand what we mean by 'Secret War', it is useful to start by appreciating that World War Two of 1939-45 (like World War One of 1914-18), was designated 'Total War'.

The advent of Total War meant that now *all* the resources of the combatants, each and every individual, every possible means and stratagem, were deployed in support of achieving the nation's war aims. Warfare was no longer principally the preoccupation of armies at the front line; everyone and everything was utilised: military and civilian, young and old; men and women. Neither were the activities of the fighting services – the army, the navy and (a recent innovation), the air force – the only strategic consideration. Propaganda, psychology and behind the lines covert operations (three notable features of the Secret War in Bedfordshire) were amongst those aspects that were now to be integrated – with varying degrees of effectiveness as it turned out – into the war effort.

The importance of these changes were firmly summarised by the man who had more responsibility than virtually anyone for harnessing this combined effort, Allied Supreme Commander Dwight D. Eisenhower: 'In this war, which was Total in every sense of the word, we have seen many great changes in military science. It seems to me that not the least of these was the development of psychological warfare as a specific and effective weapon.'[1]

Broadly speaking, British secret operations fell under the following services: the Special Operations Executive (usually just known as SOE); MI5 (the internal security service); MI6 (responsible for intelligence gathering and operations as part of its wider policy

---

[1] *Psychological Warfare Division SHAEF, An Account of its Operations in the Western European Campaign, 1944-45* (1945). Quoted in James M. Erdman 'Leaflet Operations in the Second World War' (Unpublished typescript, 1969).

requirements of its parent Foreign Office); MI9 (working with allied personnel behind enemy lines); the Political Wartime Executive (PWE); the Government Code and Cipher School; Radio Security Service; London Controlling Section. These services possessed various sub-departments and, naturally enough, organisations came into being during the course of the conflict as strategy or expediency dictated whilst others merged or lapsed. It is also worth adding that the branches of the Armed Forces also ran their own intelligence gathering and covert operations. Never, at any stage of the war, was any single individual responsible for all covert operations and the outcome was a bewildering array of units and sub-units that frequently overlapped one another, resulting in departmental squabbling and petty empire building to a degree that has been roundly excoriated in subsequent histories.

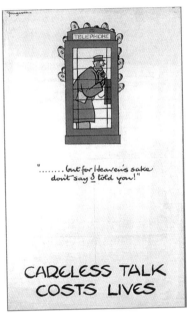

"........ but for Heaven's sake don't say I told you!"

CARELESS TALK
COSTS LIVES

Fougasse cartoon
(*Imperial War Museum, PST01442*).

In an era of Total War, discretion was more important than ever. Viewed like this, *all* aspects of World War Two, in Bedfordshire as elsewhere, were secret. Through radio, in magazines, on advertising hoardings, people were exhorted to 'Keep Mum' because 'Careless Talk Costs Lives'. Cartoons by 'Fougasse' were everywhere warning that 'You Never Know Who Is Listening' or even that 'Walls Have Ears'. Individuals were cautioned to be wary of any slip in conversation that might inadvertently reveal details of troop movements or convoys. Censorship and self-censorship was universal in newspapers, broadcasts, official documents and personal letters. Signposts were removed, names of bombed towns often only referred to obliquely, the identity of individual ships or army units were hidden (telltale insignia in published photographs were deliberately – and often crudely – obscured).

Glenn Miller and David Niven. The published version of a photograph taken at this event had the word 'Bedford' blacked out of the banner in the background for censorship reasons.

So secrecy was all pervasive in World War Two. At least, that was the theory – but it was not clear cut. Classified and open, public and private became intermixed. Whilst 138 and 161 Squadrons were certainly involved in clandestine operations, their location at Tempsford in the east of the county could hardly be entirely hidden. As M. R. D. Foot (one of the most eminent historians of the covert operations) noted, the 'airfield, though heavily camouflaged, was somewhat public – it was sandwiched between the main railway line from London to Edinburgh and the Great North Road; but the Germans never seem to have spotted it.'[2] Perhaps Tempsford was assisted by its low lying position at the foot of the hills at Everton and Sandy, and its tendency (like much of the upper Ouse valley) for fog. Although bombs did fall in the vicinity this was perhaps because Tempsford lay in the line south from one of the *Luftwaffe's* marker point at Little Barford's power station for turning south towards London, and may have been a case of jettisoning remaining bombs. Rather than firing and missing (thereby alerting the

---

[2] Foot, M. R. D. SOE. *The Special Operations Executive 1940-46* (UPA).
See also *SOE in France* (Frank Cass, 2004) by the same author.

RAF Tempsford during World War Two *(Luton and Bedfordshire Archives)*.

passing *Luftwaffe* to something interesting below), the base's defensive gunners held their fire.

Britain entered World War Two under-prepared. It had to catch up with an enemy that had cultivated a militaristic culture over many years and make rapid readjustments to the requirements of Total War. It is a tremendous testimony to the character of the realm that it was able to adapt so quickly and draw upon the full depth of its national resource. In doing this, a remarkable degree of improvisation was called for and was nowhere more amply demonstrated than in gearing up for the Secret War. As the biographer of James Bond author Ian Fleming (who was to make a contribution to Bedfordshire's Secret War), noted, 'London was full of secret organisations. Private armies were forming everywhere. The geniuses and the crackpots were getting their chance at last.'[3] A fair number of these geniuses and crackpots as well as dogged, unsung heroes, found their way into Bedfordshire's clandestine operations.

Challenges

There are intrinsic elements of the Secret War that present challenges when presenting an account of its operations within one county. Although there is a striking array of examples of covert warfare that centred upon Bedfordshire, it is still not entirely satisfactory to concentrate upon events that occurred in one place to the exclusion of elsewhere, just because they were based in adjacent counties, as this obscures the various connections that were an integral part of the same operation. On the other hand, this has also been a blessing as a wider account would have to embrace the immense work that was carried on at Bletchley Park in Buckinghamshire, also known as 'Station X'. Bletchley Park comprises an important background element to this account of Bedfordshire's Secret War, as does Harrington Airfield (base of many American 'carpetbagger' operations), Whaddon Hall (headquarters of the Special Communications Unit) or Chicheley Hall, near Newport Pagnell (one of a number of SOE's Special Training Schools). Because they were respectively situated in Northamptonshire and Buckinghamshire, however, this particular narrative does not focus directly upon them. Additionally, although much of the work might have a Bedfordshire dimension, parts of it would be conducted elsewhere. The operations that ran to and from RAF Tempsford are an obvious example of this, which explains why accounts of their activities by some celebrated agents provide little or no additional detail on Tempsford, the location of which had been kept secret and, in many cases, they may only have seen in the dark.[4]

---

[3] Pearson, John. *The Life of Ian Fleming* (Arum, 2003).

[4] In a recent publication devoted to Edward Yeo-Thomas, *Bravest of the Brave. The True Story of Wing Commander 'Tommy' Yeo-Thomas* (Michael O'Mara, 1997), author Mark Seaman, for example, makes no mention of Tempsford.

There is one other aspect that it is significant: much of the Secret War was kept separate from Bedfordshire life. This means that this was a war where many elements were kept hidden from the home population, as well as from the enemy. The personnel who were recruited to do this work were often not from the locality, a factor that applied to many of the civilian workers as well as the more obvious military component. The telephonists and typists recruited to Woburn's propaganda and intelligence facilities were brought up from London, for example, and the extent of their segregation can probably be understood by the fact that even letters could not be posted locally, but had to be taken to the capital for mailing. Return correspondence was addressed to New Oxford Street in London and then forwarded to Bedfordshire.

Even where locals were involved there was a universal and (perhaps to modern eyes) exemplary level of prudence. Ernest Palmer, a foreman in the stable of Luton print workshops that produced much secret propaganda observed this:

> *I have wondered if the man next door – my neighbour in the bus – or for that matter any man in the street, bothered himself as to what I did or was doing during the war period. We met the same old faces, got on or off at the same stop each day, yet seldom enquired what each was doing.*[5]

This was partly because even those who were directly close to Secret War operations often had only a limited knowledge of what was going on. They had familiarity, expertise even, within their specific field but this was understandably quite narrow. This was necessary from the perspective of operational security, but it is something that makes it harder to join the threads together more than 60 years on. Phil Luck, for example, served as one of the key sound engineers in the broadcast propaganda services, being based at the transmitting stations at Potsgrove in the south west of the county and nearby Gawcott in Buckinghamshire.[6] Although he had heard of Sefton Delmer, the master

---

[5] *The First Daily Newspaper in the World. Being an account of its production by Home Counties Newspapers Ltd., Luton and Gibbs, Bamforth & Co. (Luton) Ltd., The Leagrave Press, Luton.* (Produced privately for the staff of the companies c. 1946.) Of the special editions of leaflets concerning D-Day Palmer added 'and if we chose we could tell the man next door a piece of news the painter bloke himself hardly knew.' (The 'painter bloke' was Hitler.)

[6] Phil Luck had been trained by the BBC upon leaving school. He was invited to join the work at Potsgrove & Gawcott in 1943, when in his late teens.

of black propaganda and the man whose work he was transmitting to Europe, he never, ever met him. Neither did he ever travel the short distance to the broadcasting unit at Milton Bryan, let alone 'Aspidistra' (the huge transmitting station in Sussex), although he did meet Harold Robin, the engineering genius behind its development.[7]

The derelict Milton Bryan studios photographed before the Ampthill and District Scouts took over the tenancy of the site (*Courtesy of Felix Delmer*).

Even at the little transmitting stations in Beds and Bucks individuals worked in what Phil Luck described as their own 'cells – like an egg box', knowing little of what went on in the next compartment. Doreen Purnell worked at Chicksands, forwarding coded messages to the decoding centre a few miles away at Bletchley Park. She later recalled 'I didn't know what Bletchley Park was.' Even closer to Doreen was RAF Henlow where Leonard Tancer worked engineering the components for the first jet engine. According to his wife, he did not talk to her about his work until after the end of the war.[8]

It is also clear that most people instinctively followed the advice to 'Keep Mum'. In the late summer of 1944, for example, radio operator Dafydd Williams was posted to Tempsford to test a new air to ground communication system, working in Lockheed Hudsons. In the two weeks that he worked there Dafydd did not mix with any other personnel at Tempsford other than those he was working with. He was driven up in a ministerial Packard motor car from his billet in Bletchley to his base at Gibraltar Farm, taking sandwiches to avoid the necessity of having to mess with anyone else.[9]

---

[7] Dafydd Williams recalled that he was a man who 'got things done' (interview 8 September 2005).

[8] See the *People's War* section on the BBC's History website (story id. A5090546 & A4376306).

[9] Interview with Dafydd Williams, 8 September 2005. Dafydd signed the Official Secrets Act in 1942. He was spared Tempsford's notorious fog, recalling that the days were bright and sunny.

Dennis Dolton, who served as a dispatch driver in the Woburn/Aspley and Milton Bryan area, could not remember any of his passengers ever speaking to him, including Sefton Delmer (the only one that he recognised).[10] Again, this reflected security concerns as Standing Orders prohibited any of the foreign nationals based in this area from even travelling unless accompanied by one of their supervising officers. Naturally, given the multiplicity of nationalities that came to live in south west Bedfordshire, language would have presented a further barrier between passenger and driver, something that applied to the sound engineers working with the transmission of propaganda broadcasts to occupied Europe.

Phil Luck was initially billeted at Potsgrove in the far south-west of the county with the local Estate Manager, and then in Gawcott with an elderly couple, Mr and Mrs Hicks. Phil recalled that the old man served as the village carpenter and undertaker but neither set of hosts ever knew about the nature of the work in which their tenant was engaged. Phil didn't tell them and they didn't ask. The same applied when he was moved to a hotel at Bletchley where many of the fellow guests worked at Bletchley Park's vast complex (somewhere else that Phil never got to visit). It was not until post war reunions many decades later that they were able to discover what each had really done. Having signed the Official Secrets Act and being paid through the Foreign Office (despite carrying the uniform and pay book of the Royal Corps of Signals), Phil was instructed not to talk to anyone about any aspect of his duties.[11] Needless to say, this prohibition extended to taking photographs and this reticence persisted through the decades after the war.

Even those who were not obliged to sign the Official Secrets Act, such as the Duke of Bedford's domestic staff who served the psychological

---

[10] Interview with Denis Dolton, 26 August 2005. The son of an estate worker, Denis Dolton was taught to drive by the Duke of Bedford's chauffer. When, one night, the need suddenly arose for a driver, the sixteen year old Dennis 'just slipped into it' and, until he joined up two years later, proceeded to drive as required around the Woburn area, to London and to Bletchley Park as a number of the WRENS who worked there were billeted in the Abbey. As the junior driver on hand, however, he suspected that he had some of the less important figures as passengers.

[11] Interview with Phil Luck 23 August 2005. Phil worked in shifts. Three nights (23.00-08.00), three days (08.00-17.00), three evenings (17.00-23.00), with two days off a fortnight and seven days leave every three months. Despite the restrictions and the inconvenient working hours, Phil found his work stimulating.

warfare units based around Woburn, were still sworn to secrecy. Winston Churchill famously referred to the work of the Bletchley Park operatives as 'the goose that laid the golden egg but never cackled', but even cursory research swiftly demonstrates that this discretion was observed far beyond the perimeters of the famous 'Station X'. Some chose to speak of their work as much as three, four or five decades after the close of the war; others never did. Even those who did publish accounts in the immediate aftermath produced carefully edited pieces of work, deliberately obscuring names and locations. The fact also remained that, in certain official circles, elements of the Secret War was regarded as just 'not cricket'.

Many documents were destroyed almost immediately after the end of the war. The passage of time has been unkind in other respects (Luton Borough Council's Emergency Committee minute book covering the key 1940-42 period has been mislaid since it was last seen in the 1970s). Only a small fraction of PWE's papers survived the immediate post- war destruction or the beady gaze of subsequent censorship to be released for public access at the National Archives ('545 messy files' in the opinion of Ellic Howe). M. R. D. Foot and Charles Cruikshank were amongst writers who faced similar problems in producing their accounts of the Special Operations Executive. Foot suggested that 'as a rule, documents written down at the time make the best sources for history'. Yet a lot of SOE's work was thought to be too secret to be put on paper at all, with Cruikshank adding 'the Political Warfare Executive papers are, perhaps inevitably, in a mess ...'[12]

Foot was also aware that even amongst the small amount of surviving material, there was probably much that was so sensitive that it was kept back from even specialist researchers such as him. A key figure in the 'Secret War' was Lieutenant Donald McLachlan, who was killed in a car crash in 1971. McLachlan's papers are deposited at Churchill College, Cambridge; the relevant catalogue including this cryptic footnote: 'He had promised to deposit more papers in Churchill College, but the promise was frustrated by the Ministry of Defence removing the remainder after his death.'

---

[12] Foot, M. R. D. op. cit. Cruikshank, Charles. *The Fourth Arm. Psychological Warfare 1938-1945* (OUP, 1981).

Politicians and other public figures tend to keep diaries (perhaps with an eye to the publication of future memoirs), but those suddenly thrust in to the front line frequently do not, especially since such documents can be incriminating in certain circumstances of clandestine operations. The surviving papers of Oswald Tuck, who came out of retirement in order to train Japanese code breakers in Bedford, include a run of diaries from the early part of the twentieth century, a habit he briefly resurrected in 1946 but nothing survives from World War Two.[13] It is clear that Sefton Delmer, one of the outstanding figures of Bedfordshire's Secret War, was not the only one who later produced an account that was primarily the product of memory. Even written accounts produced on the basis of contemporary diaries were not necessarily as dependable as one would like.[14] The same faulty memories would have applied to Delmer's other propaganda colleagues, as well as the many unsung heroes of Bedfordshire's covert operations: WAAF girls at Chicksands; the trainee cryptographers in Bedford; the airmen of Tempsford. Ellic Howe, regarded as the unofficial historian of black propaganda, in fact rarely saw Delmer and, although he had access to the surviving papers, as well as key figures such as Clifton Child, he too was also working from memory. 'I find it difficult, if not impossible, to provide an orderly account of what actually happened,' he admitted.[15]

---

[13] The Tuck papers are also located at the archive of Churchill College, Cambridge.

[14] Delmer, Sefton. *Black Boomerang* (Secker and Warburg, 1962). In his entry for Bruce Lockhart in the *DNB*, Michael Hughes points out that his writing was not always factually reliable.

[15] Howe, Ellic. *The Black Game. British Subversive Operations Against the Germans During the Second World War* (Michael Joseph, 1982).

Cast of Characters: Some Biographical Notes

'I got to know them by observation ... these for me were like the characters in a long Tolstoyan novel which I was being compelled to study ...' noted Harman Grisewood, a spectator to some of the aspects of Britain's clandestine warfare, and the colourful array of characters that peopled it. Posterity bestowed fame on some of the individuals who played a part in Bedfordshire's Secret War (or who are otherwise noted in the text), whilst others have slipped into obscurity. Some, appreciating the sensitive nature of their work, would have doubtless regarded that this was entirely desirable.

Antelme, France (1900-1945).
A Mauritian born businessman, Antelme had been part of SOE operations in support of the British invasion of Madagascar in 1942. He was on his third mission to France when captured. The SOE files on Antelme were released at the National Archives in 2005 (HS 9/42-44).

Atkins, Vera (1908-2000).
Born in Romania to Jewish parents, 'a handsome grey-eyed blonde, some 5 feet 9 inches tall' (*Dictionary of National Biography* entry). Changed name from Rosenberg to Atkins upon arrival in Britain in 1937, becoming British citizen in 1944. Became assistant to Maurice Buckmaster, the head of the French section of SOE. Described as the 'heart and brain' of the section, with 'an eagle eye for detail', she was also popularly supposed to have provided part of the model for Ian Fleming's 'Miss Moneypenny' (Buckmaster was one of a number who were reckoned to be the basis for 'M'). She worked long hours in service that took her to Baker Street, Portman Place and various RAF airfields (including Tempsford). As a result she frequently didn't return to the flat that she shared with her mother in Bayswater until breakfast, leading her mother to believe that this was because she was having an affair with a married man. Following the war Vera Atkins endeavoured to find out the fate of those who did not return, interrogating their former German captors in the process, and was successful in 117 out of 118 cases (the 118th apparently being last seen in Monte Carlo with a suitcase

full of cash). Vera Atkins 'kept her upright figure as well as her gracious manner to the end of her long life. Her tremendous personality she kept as a rule, screened behind this appearance of decorum'. She did not publish any memoirs.

Barman, Thomas.

A former diplomatic correspondent at *The Times*, and later the BBC, who worked at Woburn 1939-43. Serving briefly as Leeper's Deputy after Bowes-Lyon was posted to America, Barman worked with Americans assigned to Woburn before making an unsuccessful trip to Moscow in the autumn of 1943 in order to try to establish similar collaboration with the Russians. Following the Russian trip, Barman was assigned to the Anglo-American Psychological Warfare Board at Algiers under the leadership of Harold Macmillan.

Bartlett, Vernon (1894-1983).

A journalist and broadcaster who specialised in foreign and diplomatic affairs, Bartlett served as a correspondent on *The Times*, *News Chronicle* and *Picture Post*. During the mid 1930s Bartlett was a member of the Anglo-German Group, an organisation which possessed a significantly pacifistic element, and partly for this membership Bartlett was dropped by the BBC in 1934 after pressure from the Foreign Office. Bartlett did not sustain this neutral position. Opposed to appeasement, he successfully stood as an anti-appeasement independent candidate in the previously safe Tory seat of Bridgewater in the wake of the Munich agreement, in November 1938. Appointed Assistant Director of Propaganda at the outbreak of war, Bartlett also became a member of the 1941 Committee, alongside a number of individuals that included Ritchie Calder, J. B. Priestley, Michael Foot and cartoonist David Low. The 1941 Committee evolved into the Common Wealth Party, although Bartlett joined the Labour Party after the war.

Bowes-Lyon, David (1902-1961).

The brother of Queen Elizabeth, consort to George V. According to Kenneth Young it was Bowes-Lyon who thought up the title 'Political Wartime Executive', later serving as the Head of its Washington office, 1942-44.

13

Bracken Brendan Rendall (1901-1958).

Minister of Information 1941-45, but rarely visited its Bedfordshire wing and closed down most of the 'white' side at Woburn. One of Winston Churchill's closest supporters, Bracken 'made his way by a quick brain, audacity and turbulent forcefulness' (DNB) but to others he was 'a bully, boor or grotesque'. Regarded as the eyes, ears and messenger of Churchill, 'their midnight bouts of wild talk and hard drinking (often with Lord Beaverbrook) were grist to the mill of Churchill's critics'. Although they frequently argued Churchill always took care to soothe his 'poor, dear Brendan'.

Brooks, Reginald Alexander Dallas (1896-1966).

The head of PWE's military wing, one of Woburn's 'key men' who later served as Governor of Victoria. During World War One Brooks had taken part in the famous raid on Zeebrugge where he showed 'outstanding courage', and later played first class cricket for Hampshire.

Calder, Peter Ritchie (1906-1982).

A Socialist journalist and writer who worked for the Daily News, Daily Chronicle and Daily Herald before being appointed to PWE in 1941, and becoming Director of Plans on 17 August 1942. Calder, who was one of those at Woburn who were keen to co-ordinate with the BBC, became a leading member of CND and was made a life peer in 1966.

Ritchie Calder, photographed at the Aldermaston March of 1961. Over his left shoulder can just be seen 'Nobby' Clarke (Hulton Getty).

Churchill, Peter (1909-72).

A talented linguist and a fine sportsman at Cambridge, Churchill worked with French agent Odette Sansom but both were captured by Hugo Bleicher's Abwehr, initially being detained in Annency, part of the Italian section of occupied France. Surviving interrogation, thanks in large measure to Odette, Churchill was moved from one prison to another, including Dachau, meeting with many German dissidents – such as Rev. Martin Niemoller – on the way. Churchill's experiences as an agent were later told in his book *The Spirit in the Cage*. Leo Marks described Churchill as a 'slender man, coiled in his chair like an exclamation mark with a moustache'.

Clark, F. (Freddie) (b. 1923).

Joined the Air Cadets in 1939 and graduated straight into the RAF in the same year. Served with the Royal Air Force Voluntary Reserve and South African Air Force before joining 138 Squadron. After his Halifax was shot down in 1944, Clark was captured and imprisoned at Fresnes, before being sent to Stalag Luft III.

Clarke, Cecil Vandepeer (1897-1961).

Born in London, 'Nobby' as he was known to his friends, abandoned his studies at University of London at the beginning of World War One, serving in the South Staffordshire Regt. in France and Italy. Awarded the Military Cross for his services in the latter, taking part in the decisive Battle of Vittorio Veneto. Patriot, Land Rover driver, steady smoker, avid reader, member of the Special Forces Club and CND (being organiser for Bedford and District), as well as serving as an Elder of Bedford Presbyterian Church. He worked for several years as a Labour Councillor before joining the Liberals in 1959, possibly over the nuclear weapons issue. After the war Clarke moved to 65 Putnoe Lane where he died suddenly from a heart attack in 1961. A week after his funeral a letter was published in the *Bedfordshire Times* in the name of a number of his friends. It noted that 'his passing is more than just the loss of an individual. To us he was embodiment of an ideal, always in his own way striving after the betterment of society. His vision was broad and embraced all mankind, and he spent himself on its behalf.'

Crossman, Richard Howard Stafford (1907-1974).

A 'hornets nest all to himself' (Barman) who was recruited to MEW by Dalton in order to work in anti-German propaganda, working in both black and white fields. 1944-45 Assistant Chief of Psychological Warfare Division for the allies. 1964 appointed as

Minister for Housing and Local Government by Harold Wilson; Minister for Health and Social Security 1968-70. 'Not everyone liked him or trusted his judgement,' recalled Dalton with considerable understatement, but added that Crossman made an 'admirable contribution.' In his entry to *DNB*, Anthony Howard quotes Robert Bruce Lockhart's assessment of Crossman's contribution: 'I have no hesitation in saying that his virtues greatly outweigh his faults. In other words, if he doesn't win a prize for good conduct, he certainly deserves a commendation for distinguished service.' Even after his death the publication of his diaries by the *Sunday Times* during the 1970s was to cause embarrassment to the Labour government.

Dalton, Edward Hugh Neale (1887-1962).

Privileged upbringing and education at St George's Choir School, Windsor, Eton and King's College, Cambridge, against which Dalton reacted. Joined the Fabian Society with poet Rupert Brooke whilst at Cambridge. Appointed as Minister of Economic Warfare and was appointed President of the Board of Trade in 1942; Chancellor of the Exchequer in 1945 and Chancellor of the Duchy of Lancaster in 1948. Working through a number of carefully cultivated *protégés*, Dalton influenced Labour politics long after his death: 'he played an important part in giving his party the intellectual confidence not only to make it electable, but also to make it effective.' (*DNB*).

Damerment, Madeleine (1917-1944).

Born in Lille, Madeleine Damerment spent the early part of the war helping downed allied airmen escape back to Britain. When this network was exposed in 1942 she fled to Britain and trained with SOE as a courier. Captured in 1944, Damerment was interrogated and tortured but still refused to co-operate. Eventually she was taken to Dachau concentration camp with three other SOE agents (Yolande Beekman, Elaine Plewman and Noor Inayat Khan). There the girls were told to kneel in pairs and, holding hands, were shot in the back of the head by an SS officer.

Delmer, Dennis Sefton (1904-1979).

'The one undoubted genius thrown up by PWE,' (Kenneth Young) was born in Berlin to Australian parents, and attended school there even whilst his father was interned during World War. A man renowned for expensive tastes (reflected in his expenses claims). 'In later life Delmer was a huge Falstaffian figure of benign and monk-like appearance' (*DNB*). According to David Garnett's official history of PWE, 'there can be no question that Sefton Delmer made the biggest personal contribution to Political Warfare during the war'.

Fielden, E. H. (d.1976).

A former commander of the King's Flight, 'Mousie' Fielden took over command of 161 Squadron in 1942 when the Flight was absorbed into that Squadron. Fielden was awarded the DFC in 1943, the citation stating that 'This officer has flown on various operational missions, some of a most hazardous nature.' Fielden was reputedly a master of the back-handed put down.

Fleming, Ian Lancaster (1908-1964).

'This most gifted and brilliant of all my friends' (Delmer), the creator of James Bond used much of his wartime experience at the heart of Naval Intelligence as an inspiration for 007's subsequent adventures. The important difference is that Fleming, a fantasist whose relations with women were often difficult, conducted a war that despite its considerable contribution to clandestine operations, was largely desk bound. As Delmer put it, Fleming 'never, never lived the kind of life or had adventures of the kind he later invented for James Bond. He never killed or spied, or infiltrated into enemy occupied territory.' The two men became friends on a working visit to Moscow at which Fleming, who knew the city, played host to Delmer. On the return journey Fleming saw Delmer tearing up his notes as they approached the Russian border: 'You should swallow them. That's what all the best spies do,' Fleming apparently told him. At the border, Fleming was mortified to find that the Russian guards, upon searching his cases and finding a collection of condoms (ostensibly being brought back in order that their synthetic materials could be tested, although with Fleming you could never be sure), proceeded to open and carefully examine each one in turn. 'You should have swallowed them,' whispered Delmer.

Gaitskell, Hugh Todd Naylor (1906-1963).

An academic at University College London, Gaitskell was appointed as a temporary Civil Servant to serve Hugh Dalton. Followed Dalton into the Board of Trade in 1942. Rose suddenly to become Chancellor of the Exchequer, 1950-51 and became leader of the Labour Party in 1955. Was still serving as the Leader of the Opposition when he died suddenly in 1963.

Gibbs, John (1908-1981).

Educated at Dunstable Grammar School and Bedford School. A Director of Home Counties Newspapers and of the printing firm Gibbs, Bamforth, responsible for the short (three copies) run of the *Daily Telegraph*, designed to fool Rudolf Hess, and for *Nachrichten*, designed to fool the entire German army.

Goring, Marius (1912-1998).

Actor who joined the Queen's Royal Regiment, 1940. The following year he was seconded to the Foreign Office and broadcast to Germany via the BBC and at Woburn. Although he fronted Anglia TV's 1987 documentary devoted Woburn's secret war, Goring appears to have been involved largely, if not entirely, with *white* propaganda.

Greene, Hugh Carleton (1910-1987).

Journalist who was expelled as the Berlin correspondent of the *Daily Telegraph* in May 1939 and over the next 12 months was to escape first Warsaw, then Brussels, just ahead of the German Army. After briefly serving in the RAF he joined the German Service of the BBC where he was probably the closest to being the 'white' parallel to the 'black' Sefton Delmer. In the 1960s Greene was an innovative and controversial Director General of the BBC.

Griffiths, Frank.

One of the most distinguished of pilots, Squadron Leader Griffiths flew through flak on more than one occasion only to have his Halifax shot down by Italian infantry when flying over Annency in France. Breaking his arm in the crash, Griffiths was the only survivor but was able to get back home, thanks to the Resistance's escape networks. Griffiths was told by his Station Commander,

'Mousie' Fielden, 'despite your achievements you are the scruffiest officer on the station.'

Hockey, Ronald Clifford (1911-1992).

Commanding Officer of 138 Squadron for twelve months from April 1942. Prior to joining 138 Hockey was part of a special duties unit (1419) whose task it was to transport VIPs (including Winston Churchill and Charles De Gaulle). Promotions later in the war included taking command of No. 38 Wing and helping to organise the parachute operations for the Normandy landings.

Haugland, Knut (b.1917).

Radio operator with *Operation Grouse*, who apparently disposed of his equipment in an Oslo maternity hospital whilst making his escape. Whilst training in Britain Haugland met Thor Heyerdahl, after the war being part of Heyerdahl's 1947 *Kon Tiki* expedition which sailed the Pacific on a balsa wood raft.

Haukelid, Knut (1911-1994).

Born in New York, where his father was an engineer on the subway, Haukelid returned to his native Norway the following year. He was later educated in the United States and, during the 1930s, attended universities in Berlin and Dresden. The twin of Hollywood actress Sigrid Gurie, Haukelid served in the Norwegian armed forces after the war.

Ingrams, Leonard St Clair (1900-1953).

'A star operative' (Delmer) and one of the most enigmatic of the figures who worked in psychological warfare. Possessing a wit that was 'quiet and sardonic' (Harry Thompson), as a long jumper Ingrams was a member of the British 1924 Olympic team. He worked for Barings Bank before the War, and was nicknamed the 'Flying Banker' because of his habit of flying himself around the continent on business. His secretive work within the Ministry of Economic Warfare, as well as his intimate

Leonard Ingrams
(*courtesy of Richard Ingrams*).

knowledge of the pre-war German banking system, earned Ingrams a place on the Nazi hit list of Britons to be dealt with in the event of a successful invasion. In 1946 he attended the Nuremburg war crimes trial (interviewing the senior Nazi prisoners), which formed the basis of an unpublished book. Awarded the OBE in the same year.

Jebb, Gladwyn (1900-1996).
CEO of SOE. Immediately after the war Jebb served as acting Secretary General of the United Nations (1945-46), later becoming Britain's Ambassador to that organisation, and then to France. Jebb became politically active once in the House of Lords from 1960, serving the Liberal Party.

John, Otto (b.1909).
An 'anti-Nazi from the beginning (or almost the beginning…)' in the words of Bruce Lockhart, to whom John was recommended by 'C'. Lockhart routed him to Woburn to work with the black propaganda teams. Assisted the Allies at the Nuremberg trials and was later appointed the head of West Germany's police security service. Disappearing in mysterious circumstances in 1954, John resurfaced in 1955 claiming that he had been kidnapped and taken to the Communist East Germany. This was not accepted by the Federal German authorities and John was sentenced to four years for defecting, being released in 1958.

Leeper, Reginald (Rex) Wildig Allen (1888-1968).
An anti-appeaser, Leeper was openly talking about the possibility of Germany attacking Britain as early as 1934. He was appointed Assistant Under Secretary at Foreign Office (August 1940), heading SO1 1940-41. Director of Country House HQ at Woburn, 1941-43 but this 'very quiet, shy' man (Mary Neal) found that his 'uneasy relationship' with Dalton 'eventually disillusioned and exhausted him,' (DNB) and Leeper was apparently relieved to be made Ambassador to Greece in March 1943. It ought to be added, however, that he had outlasted Dalton and was equally disappointed to lose the tenure at Woburn. Leeper's belief in the significance of what he described as 'cultural propaganda' had led him to become a central figure in the establishment of the Cultural Relations Committee in 1933, in collaboration with representatives

of other government departments. A year later this body was to evolve into the British Council, Leeper becoming an honorary Vice President from 1948 until his death.

Lockhart, Guy.

A man with a reputation as being a skilled card player and gambler, Lockhart was 'a striking looking, slim young man' as recalled by Hugh Verity. As well as his RAF wings, he also wore French military wings on his right breast pocket. After leaving the Lysander squadron, Squadron Leader Guy Lockhart was later killed during the war on active service.

Lockhart, Robert Hamilton Bruce (1887-1970).

A 'man of great energy and charm whose open personality allowed him to make friends easily, although he could sometimes be self-indulgent and extravagant'. This latter characteristic meant that Bruce Lockhart was prone to living beyond his means to a degree that obliged him to undertake a number of jobs in the inter-war years to stave off money lenders, and perhaps also led to his occasional bouts of depression. Mary Neal recalled him as 'a real dandy … a lovely man,' impeccably dressed, with oil on his hair, scented baths and, instead of pyjama trousers, a simple silk wrap, like a sarong. Intrigued by this, one morning the female staff at Maryland hid to see whether Lockhart's attire would defy gravity as he made his way to the bathroom. The source did not say whether they were disappointed or relieved that indeed it did. Bruce Lockhart lived a colourful life. Amongst his early adventures he had been caught spying in 1918 during the chaotic aftermath of the Bolshevik revolution in Russia. Luckily for Lockhart his brief imprisonment in the Kremlin was one of comfort as he was able to spend his time reading whilst a former Tsarist servant served him hot tea and newspapers. Appointed as HM Government's representative to the Czechoslovak government in exile in 1940, and a Deputy Under Secretary the following year, eventually becoming the Director of the Political Warfare Executive.

Marks, Leo (1920-2001).

The son of a Jewish bookseller, his considerable talents were first discovered in Bedford at the Inter-Service Special Intelligence

School. Marks was the master cryptographer who revolutionised SOE coding security, and became the head of SOE's Codes and Ciphers – a section with around 400 staff. Nonetheless, his later warnings of the Germans' success in turning SOE's agents in Holland and France were fatally ignored. Marks contributed to the film of Violette Szabo, *Carve Her Name With Pride*, starring Virginia McKenna, but refused to be credited, and his later screenplay for *Peeping Tom* was denounced for its subject matter.

Martelli, George (born 1903).

Former Royal Navy officer and journalist (pre-war writing for the *Morning Post*) and author who was in charge of the Italian desk at PID, and head of the Italian section in SO1. After the war Martelli continued to write and travel, producing works of fiction (*Agent Extraordinary*) and non-fiction (*The Man Who Saved London*). Martelli concluded that 'the rudiments of military intelligence [are] not a matter of individual prowess, producing dramatic coups, but a painstaking labour, the result of teamwork piecing together an infinite number of small facts.'

McLachlan, Donald Harvey (1908-1971).

McLachlan worked at *The Times* after leaving Oxford before joining Naval Intelligence during the war. It was he that tipped off Delmer as to the next day imminence of D-Day, allowing the preparation of *Soldatensender's* scoop of the breach of the Atlantic Wall, ahead of news agencies on either side. After the war he returned to journalism at *The Economist*, *Daily Telegraph* and *Sunday Telegraph* (where he was editor). McLachlan was killed in a car crash in January 1971. The papers of Donald McLachlan are held at the archive of Churchill College, Cambridge.

Mond, Henry (1898-1949).

Son of Alfred Mond, the founder of ICI, eventually becoming its Vice-Chairman. Seriously wounded at Passchendaele during World War One, and dogged by ill health thereafter. Emerged from a *ménage de trios* involving the writer Gilbert Cannan to marry Gwen Wilson, and the pair of them made Colworth House their new home (Cannan ended up in an asylum). Active Zionist. Colworth House was purchased by Unilever in 1947 after Gwen persuaded

Henry to move to Miami for the sake of his health.

Murray, Francis Ralph Hay (1908-83).
Described as one of the 'young Turks' who changed the style of news reporting at the BBC during the 1930s (having joined in 1934), Ralph Murray joined Department EH in 1939. Officially attached to the Foreign Office, Murray ran the black propaganda recording studio at Wavendon, also working in close collaboration with Ivonne Kirkpatrick and Hugh Carleton Greene, and lobbying for Aspidistra. Highly regarded by Dalton, who told Lockhart 'I like Murray, although I am told he doesn't like me.' Transferred back to Bush House in March 1942, becoming Regional Director for the Balkans, and later the PWE representative to the exiled Greek government in Cairo the following year. Post-war worked in Austria and Germany, becoming Britain's Ambassador to Greece in the 1960s. 'His natural reserve and downcast demeanour – dominated by sad looking eyes surrounded by dark circles – made him well suited to this clandestine world.'

Pickard, P.C. (1915-1944).
Born Sheffield. Nicknamed 'Pick' or 'Fred for Freddie' (he appeared in *Target for Tonight*). Usually accompanied by 'Ming', his Old English Sheepdog. Commanded 161 Squadron, 1942-43, before moving to fly the Mosquito aircraft of the 2nd Tactical Air Squadron. On 18 February 1944 Pickard led a precision bombing raid on Amiens prison (*Operation Jericho*) which held 700 prisoners, including some Resistance fighters facing imminent execution. Although many prisoners were successfully blasted free, Pickard was killed in the operation.

Rée, Harry Alfred (1914-1991).
Educated at the University of London. Intelligence Corps/SOE agent who spoke French with a Mancunian accent that was so broad that he had to be passed off as a farmer from rural Alsace. Towards the end of the war Rée re-enacted some of his adventures for a public information film *Now It Can Be Told*, which was released post-war as a feature film *School For Danger*. In it, for reasons best known to himself, Rée drops his Mancunian accent altogether and raises his voice an octave. One of the most

successful of all SOE operatives, a tableau devoted to Rée forms the central part of a display at the Military Intelligence Museum, Chicksands. Returned to university life after the war, becoming one of the leading campaigners for comprehensive education.

Robin, Harold (1911-1998).

A brilliant radio technician, Robin was chiefly responsible for the establishment of the massive 600w MW transmitter, nicknamed 'Aspidistra'.

Ronneberg, Joachim (b. 1919).

Norwegian commando who escaped his occupied homeland in 1941, later becoming leader of *Operation Gunnerside*, as well as other operations. In 2006 Ronneberg told a BBC interviewer of his time as a commando: 'When you go on a job like this where you feel that probably this is the last thing you are doing in your life, you live so intensely that most things sort of sit there as if it were yesterday.' 'We were extremely lucky,' he concluded.

Russell, Hastings William Sackville, 12th Duke of Bedford (1888-1953).

Provided with a very isolated upbringing, Hastings Russell served in World War One but became a pacifist thereafter which he combined rather unconvincingly with pro-German sympathies. Did not live at Woburn following his accession to the dukedom in 1940. In 1953 his body was found in the grounds of his Devon estate with gunshot wounds. Officially his death was recorded as an accident but it was strongly suspected to have been suicide. As his biographer Christopher Trent put it: 'why a sportsman of lifelong experience was scrambling through the undergrowth with his gun unbroken, loaded and cocked was a mystery that has never been solved.'

Russell, Herbrand Arthur, 11th Duke of Bedford (1858-1940).

Served in the Grenadier Guards (seeing action in the Egyptian campaign, 1882), and was also Colonel of the 3rd Battalion, Bedfordshire Regt. Made millions from the sale of estates in Cambridgeshire, Devon and Covent Garden just before World War One. Became estranged from his son, in no small part because of Hasting's pacifism. Recalled as a 'selfish, forbidding man' by his grandson (the 13th Duke).

Spark, Muriel (1918-2006).

Novelist and poet, probably best known for her 1962 novel *The Prime of Miss Jean Brodie*, the film adaptation of which was to earn Maggie Smith an Oscar in 1969. Born Muriel Camberg in Edinburgh. Moved to Africa, marrying young (and disastrously) before leaving her husband and, placing her son in care, returned to Britain. Worked at Milton Bryan ('a concentrated brain tank'), 1944-45. Billeted at Woburn Rectory, the billet mate that she saw most frequently was a switch censor, 'strange, proud' (and doomed) Marcelle Quennell, who was divorced from the writer Peter Quennell. Spark used aspects of this, 'the oddest relationship I had ever known', as well as her own experience in her 1973 novel *The Hothouse by the East River*.

Stuart, Campbell Arthur (1885-1972).

Managing Director of *The Times* during the inter-war period, Stuart briefly served as Director of Propaganda to the Enemy 1939-40, having fulfilled a similar role under his boss, Lord Northcliffe, in 1918. Associated with appeasement due to *The Times'* stance during the 1930s, Stuart was one of the first to be shunted aside by the anti-appeasers Dalton and Duff Cooper.

Szabo, Violette (1921-45).

Daughter of Anglo-French parents, Violette was educated at Brixton Secondary School and was working as a shop assistant at outbreak of war. On only her second mission she was captured in June 1944, tortured and killed at Ravensbruck concentration camp at some point in 1945. Her daughter received her posthumous George Cross and *Croix de Guerre* on her behalf. Violette is forever associated with the achingly poignant code poem penned by Leo Marks.

Tuck, Oswald (1876-1950).

Left school at fifteen and joined the Royal Navy five years later. Tuck served on pre-dreadnaught battleships in the Far Eastern squadron, teaching himself Japanese in his own time whilst on shore leave. Translated the secret Japanese account of the Russo-Japanese War and worked for the Naval Attaché in Tokyo, 1908-09. Worked in the Admiralty (in Naval Intelligence in World War

One), and in the archives during the inter-war period. Brought out of retirement to work in the Ministry of Information, 1939-41 and thereafter to run Bedford's Language School upon the outbreak of war with Japan. Continued with his teaching post-war, running a Japanese Naval course in Greenwich in 1946.

Verity, Hugh (1918-2001).

Born Jamaica, educated at Cheltenham and Oxford. Described as an 'unfailingly courteous, witty and modest' man, Verity sought a transfer after spotting Lysanders on cross channel flights, whilst he was flying Bristol Beaufighters (a specialist night fighter), and making subsequent enquiries as to their role. The other members of Verity's initial flight were John Bridger, Peter Vaughan-Fowler, Jimmy Cairns and Frank 'Bunny' Rymills. Verity made twenty nine successful pick-ups with 161 Squadron based at RAF Tempsford, his passengers including the heroic Jean Moulin. In 1944, Verity was transferred to take charge of clandestine flights in South East Asia.

Five of 161 Squadron's remarkable pilots. From left to right: J. A. McCairns; Hugh Verity; P. C. Pickard; Peter Vaughan-Fowler; Frank 'Bunny' Rymills. The dogs in the foreground are Pickard's sheepdog 'Ming' and Rymill's spaniel 'Henry' (*Imperial War Museum, HU60542*).

White, Harold (1909-1980).

Joined the *Luton News* as an office boy upon leaving school at the age of fourteen. Became a Director of Leagrave Press and also Gibbs

Bamforth, working on the production of *Nachrichten* and other black/grey propaganda. Later established the White Crescent Press. A friend of George Bernard Shaw, Harold White was responsible for working out and printing Shaw's experimental phonetic alphabet.

Whitehorn, Marion (born 1921).

Born in Potsdam, Marion's father was a Jewish merchant banker. Refusing overt Nazi pressure to divorce her husband, Marion's mother took her children out of Germany in September 1937, in the wake of her husband who had been warned not to return to Berlin, whilst on holiday in Italy. Marion Whitehorn moved from black propaganda, to the white side, later being given the harrowing task of working through the captured records kept by concentration camp warders in order to help trace possible survivors. After the war, at the behest of Donald McLachlan, Marion returned to her native country to work on British controlled newspapers for the local Germans. Eventually settling back in the UK she devoted her career to art, sculpture and garden design.

Williams, Valentine (1883-1946).

A journalist who worked on the *Daily Mail* and who won the MC in World War One. During the inter-war period Williams was author of thrillers such as *The Man With The Club Foot*, and became one of a number who fell to Dalton's cull. Later became a Diplomatic Correspondent for the BBC.

Yeo-Thomas, Edward (1902-1964).

Served in World War One (underage) and then with the White Armies in the Russian Civil War, where he was captured and only escaped after strangling his drunken guard. Worked with Pierre Brossolette to try to better co-ordinate the disparate resistance organisations in France. Although he was successful in eventually escaping Buchenwald concentration camp, the dreadful treatment meted out by the Gestapo, and the neglect of kidney stones which developed whilst in captivity, contributed to the shortening of the life of this extraordinarily tough man. The continuing ill health probably also contributed to the powerful sense of disillusion that afflicted Yeo-Thomas in the years after the war.

Part I

The Secret War
Comes to Bedfordshire

World War Two remains the most cataclysmic conflict of modern times. In total terms, in respect of the range of fighting, the scale of losses and, arguably the depth of its depravity, it has no parallel. The series of crises that punctuated international relations during the 1930s meant, however, that when Britain and France declared war upon Germany on 3 September 1939, it did not come as a surprise. Furthermore, unlike the outbreak of World War One in 1914, it was not greeted with rejoicing and scenes of patriotic fervour within the combatant nations.

This was partly because the shocking experience of colossal human loss in what, until then, had been known as 'the Great War' led to a universal assumption that future conflict would be on an even greater scale and appallingly destructive – even to the degree that victory was not possible for either side. In the main this supposition was due to advances in technology, chief amongst these being developments in aerial warfare. In the 1930s, as disarmament and peacekeeping efforts withered, this fear steadily grew. 'The bomber will always get through' was the gloomy prediction of Prime Minister Stanley Baldwin, and this pessimism was universal. In 1936, for example, the film *Things to Come* (an adaptation of the H. G. Wells novel by William Cameron Menzies and Alexander Korda), purported to show the dreadful consequences of modern warfare; obliterating cities everywhere and grinding on for decades. In the same year, the start of a three-year civil war in Spain appeared to bring that future frighteningly close as aerial warfare was launched against civilian targets, most noticeably at Barcelona and Guernica. Ominously, the main perpetrators were seen to be from the expanding *Luftwaffe* of Hitler's Nazi Germany which was giving aid to Franco's forces and acquiring invaluable battle experience in the process.

The impact of all these events and fears were felt at a number of levels. Extrapolation of Spanish civilian losses into the context of a possible Anglo-German conflict revealed a terrifying shortage of facilities in Britain's voluntary medical system, providing one of the antecedents to the post-war foundation of a National Health Service. Elsewhere, other institutions were making plans, or at least anticipating the necessity of leaving London in the event of war. The BBC, for example, whilst assiduously echoing the appeasement policy of the governments led successively by Baldwin and Neville Chamberlain, was simultaneously preparing for the evacuation of many of its services from the capital as early as 1935. This is why parts of it (chiefly those departments devoted to music and religion), came to be relocated in Bedford, an ideal location in many respects and from which ran direct lines to Broadcasting House for the purposes of live programmes which officially still emanated from London. The radio announcer would latterly refer to programmes 'coming to you from somewhere in England'. That 'somewhere' was Bedford. Numerous sites around the town were utilised by the BBC for the duration of the war (longer than this for Sir Adrian Boult and the Symphony Orchestra, which stayed until 1946). In the wake of the V rocket attacks on London, the concerts of the 1944 Prom season, under the direction of Sir Henry Wood, were broadcast from Bedford's Corn Exchange, where incidentally Wood gave his last ever performance. The facilities in Bedford also provided a base for Glenn Miller's famous orchestra when they arrived in the UK.[16]

The Meteorological Office moved its Central Forecast Office out of central London to the outskirts of Dunstable on 4 February 1940 and, as with the BBC, this move was planned on the basis of certain requirements. There had to be easy access to the capital, sufficient housing for personnel, good wireless reception conditions and the site needed to be convenient for Post Office landlines.[17] Dunstable possessed all these features, carrying the additional benefit in that it was close to both Bletchley Park and the RAF Communications Centre at Leighton Buzzard (although the proximity of the former may have been coincidental in so much as it was probably not part of the original

---

[16] Briggs, Asa. *The History of Broadcasting in the United Kingdom. Volume III, The War of Words* (OUP, 1995).

[17] Bilham, E. G. 'The Central Forecasting Office, Dunstable'. *The Meteorological Magazine*, vol. 76, no. 898, (April 1947).

planning). The Forecasting Division made the move via Birmingham as 'much still remained to be done' at their new home in Bedfordshire when war was declared.[18]

For the Communications section, 'the move to Dunstable was made in appalling weather conditions and was a complicated operation … the last contingent travelling by car over roads deep in thawing snow.' This recollection, from station chief E. G. Bilham, highlights that the carefully planned staged operation was carried out in order to maintain a constant service. Bilham was immensely proud of this 'outstanding feat … without a hitch', with the formal switch-over of teleprinter lines taking place between 15.00-16.00 on the afternoon of 4 February. The Met Office site was protected by low level security, also possessing its own modest Home Guard platoon. This was largely comprised of weather forecasters, whose experience on manoeuvres suggested that it was perhaps fortunate that they were never put to a severe test. Also contained within the complex was an IDA (Installation Design Authority) Unit, created in October 1940 with support from personnel at Bletchley Park. This was rather more tightly protected as it served the Ministry of Defence and Intelligence requirements.

Dunstable Met Office.

Dunstable became the centre of a complex network that sent and received weather reports in partnership with numerous agencies, including allied air forces and the BBC. For the RAF alone, there was a meteorological branch at each airfield, these being linked to a further facility at Group HQ, the Groups in turn being linked to the RAF's Central Forecasting Office, serving its four Command Centres. Gradually, its male staff (including a number who had fled Europe, especially from Poland and Norway) found themselves deployed to the expanding number of bases around the country, their places being taken

---

[18] Audric, Brian. *The Meteorological Office Dunstable and the IDA Unit in World War II* (Occasional Papers on Meteorological History, no. 2, published by the Meteorological Society, September 2000).

by women civilians and WAAFs. A constant presence, throughout all developments at Dunstable, was the twin figures of Bilham, and the Senior Forecaster, C. K. M. Douglas. Both were quiet individuals with the 'totally dedicated' Douglas being especially shy, even distant.[19]

That the Met Office evacuation to Dunstable was delayed was indicative of a clear lack of preparedness for the sudden collapse of appeasement, and this was reflected elsewhere. The absence of coherent preparedness for war, manifest in many aspects of public life, certainly applied in the related areas of propaganda, psychological warfare and clandestine operations. In the years after World War One consideration was given as to just why the allies emerged triumphant from so many years of apparent stalemate. For Germany this process embraced a fair measure of consolation and self-delusion, as well as hard analysis. On both sides, the former combatants achieved a consensus that one area in which the British were especially effective was in the use of propaganda and intelligence. In propaganda alone, the campaign had drawn upon newspaper and literary figures such as Lord Northcliffe (the owner of the *Daily Mail*) and the popular author, Rudyard Kipling. This even enabled some in Germany to delude themselves that they had been 'duped' into agreeing to an armistice in November 1918. The eventual entry of the United States into the conflict on the allied side also followed a determined propaganda effort by the British to woo America, something that would make things harder in World War Two as many isolationist Americans felt that they too had been tricked into entanglement in an 'old world' dispute. It had perhaps been forgotten (conveniently so for many embittered Germans), that the effectiveness of the Great War propaganda effort against Germany came late in the war, when the enemy was sliding towards defeat, worn down both economically and militarily.

No-one in Germany better embodied this bitter self-delusion than Adolf Hitler. Determined to learn what he saw as the lessons of the past he established the Ministry for Enlightenment and Propaganda (under Dr Joseph Goebbels), whose job it was to control all aspects of entertainment and the media. In Britain, on the other hand there was,

---

[19] Omer Roucoux 'The Meteorological Office in Dunstable During World War Two'. *Weather*, January 2001, vol. 56, no. 1. Brian Audric's corrections to a couple of errors appear in no. 6, June 2001.

by 1939, an impression that amateurism and slackness had crept in during the intervening period. Against the relentless manipulation as practised by the Nazis, something a little more professional was going to be needed. In his work on the more secretive side of war Ellic Howe quoted an anonymous reviewer who observed that 'the Establishment went to war in the secret services' and that this sector drew upon 'the warrior children of the upper classes'.[20] Whatever virtues these individuals may have possessed, something more ruthless, wide ranging, structured – and a lot less gentlemanly – would be required in the era of Total War.

* * *

A striking feature of British efforts in the sphere of propaganda and information was that at no stage of the war was there a single, over-arching department or office that co-ordinated activity. This was an aspect that was regarded as detrimental in some quarters although, with hindsight, the virtues of such a body might have been more marginal. The Ministry of Information, disbanded after World War One, was resurrected with the possibility of a second conflict and its Director General designate, Sir Stephen Tallents, proposed in vain that there should be co-ordination of information and intelligence across the board.[21] Indeed, although there were examples provided by totalitarian regimes across Europe (especially Germany), nobody much apart from the ignored Tallents seemed to have a real vision of how an information ministry should function in a democracy, other than serving as quite literally a conduit for government information in its narrowest sense.

Inhibited in the early stages of the conflict by an innate and a narrow-minded conservatism, the frequent duplication of effort and wasteful inter-departmental squabbling became a feature of this side of the British

---

[20] Ellic Howe op. cit. Howe produces an excellent introduction to the work of British clandestine operations that will help also make sense of the myriad departments and acronyms that littered this activity, especially in the early stage of the war. Another wide ranging introduction is provided by Martin W. Bowman in *The Bedford Triangle*. *US Undercover Operations from England in World War Two* (Sutton, 2003).

[21] FO 898/1. Garnett, David. *The Secret History of PWE. The Political Wartime Executive. 1939-45* (St Ermin's Press, 2002). Garnett, a Bloomsbury Set novelist who worked within PWE, produced what was supposed to be an official account in 1947. It was regarded as too honest and revealing, and was subsequently suppressed for several decades.

war effort, something that was to impact time and time again on the operations in Bedfordshire. The government couldn't even bring itself to fully trust the pioneering Mass Observation (set up in 1937), an outstanding source of information of people's behaviour and opinions, as it regarded it as too left wing: so it therefore established its own Home Intelligence Unit. There is little surprise in seeing that, in the first 20 months of the war, there were no fewer than four successive Ministers of Information.

Separate from the Ministry of Information, were organisations established by the Foreign Office. This already had its own News Department and in 1938, at the height of the Munich Crisis, the FO established something that was to form arguably the outstanding aspect of Bedfordshire's Secret War. This was the Foreign Office's own private ministry of information, the Department of Propaganda to Enemy Countries, headed by Sir Campbell Stuart, someone who had worked in a similar function during World War One. Tallents was not even informed about its creation. Because its offices were situated in Electra House, along the Victoria Embankment, it became known as 'Department EH'.

The News Department of EH was headed by a foreign office official, Rex Leeper, who also served as a foreign affairs advisor to the department. Although a loyal civil servant, Leeper was known to be critical of the appeasement of the European dictators that culminated in the Munich agreement in September 1938, and it is Leeper that has been credited with another Foreign Office department that was to play a significant role in the Secret War – the Political Intelligence Department.[22] The Foreign Office additionally already had a Secret

Rex Leeper (Hulton Getty).

[22] Taylor, John A. *Bletchley Park's Secret Sisters* (Book Castle, 2005).

Intelligence Service (SIS – or MI6), with its 'Section D' responsible for developing covert operations and sabotage. The War Office had its own sub-department, Military Intelligence Research (MIR), which was to evolve into MD1 and become detached from the War Office.

Because the Munich Crisis did not immediately lead to war nothing much happened beyond Leeper's office in the following twelve months, although plans for evacuation from the capital were made and various individuals recruited, usually personal contacts of Stuart. Amongst those drawn in were Valentine Williams, a novelist and *Daily Mail* journalist with what was described as a 'humorous crinkly red face and laughing blue eyes', and Lieutenant-Colonel Dallas Brooks of the Royal Marines. Also recruited was another journalist, Vernon Bartlett, a foreign affairs specialist who had become a determined opponent of appeasement.

Writing from his office at the *News Chronicle*, Bartlett outlined his thinking in correspondence with Leeper in September 1938.[23] Using his experience, drawing upon his foreign contacts, and arguably influenced by an exaggerated assessment of past performance, Bartlett produced lots of ideas that carried an optimistic view as to the potential impact of British propaganda. He predicted that German refugees would be a potential asset, that the potential of broadcasting ought to be exploited, that 'whispering campaigns' could be surprisingly debilitating, and that a variety of leaflets ought to be deployed. In Bartlett's view '... the German people will be nearly as receptive at the outbreak of this war as they were during the closing months of the last one' and that young people were disenchanted with being over regimented. Furthermore:

> *the older people, having suffered much more during and after the last war ... will certainly refuse to believe in the glories of another war... For these and many other reasons one may take it for granted ... that Germany could be defeated on the Home Front even while her armies were still winning victories over those of less prepared and happy-go-lucky states.*

It is worth bearing in mind that Bartlett's letter was written two days before the signing of the Munich agreement; a treaty that not only sacrificed Czechoslovakian sovereignty in the cause of appeasing

---

[23] FO 898/1. ' Publicity to Enemy Countries 1938-39'. National Archives.

dictators, but also led to an upsurge of domestic support for Adolf Hitler from the German people. Nonetheless, Bartlett, who was to become Assistant Director of Propaganda, also indicates a line of thinking that carried faith in the ability of Allied propaganda to successfully appeal to the reasonable instincts of the rational German, an approach that was to exclusively underpin British propaganda until the spring of 1941.

Even those who were giving serious consideration towards the deployment of propaganda at this stage could not envisage broadcasting being undertaken by anyone other than the scrupulously appeasing BBC, (Tallents wrote 'the broadcast form ... can largely be left to the BBC'). Leeper's office played host to various meetings at which attempts were made to grope towards some sort of policy. Faith was still placed in the residue of German left-wing and religious opposition to Nazism, and it was hoped that they would be receptive to British leaflet propaganda. In the event of war it was even proposed to use this means of issuing regretful 24 hour notices of intent to mount retaliatory bombing raids; again an indication of the naïve assumption that nothing could stop a bomber. As inspiration was sought, the dust was blown off examples of World War One material produced by Lord Northcliffe's propaganda teams; a sign that, on the propaganda as well as the military front, Britain was preparing to fight the wrong war. Already the RAF was showing a marked disinclination to risk their crews on leaflet operations.[24]

The German occupation of Czechoslovakia in March 1939 exposed the folly of appeasement and left British foreign policy in something of a limbo. In the vacuum Lieut. Col. Brooks and Leo Russell, a member of the Duke of Bedford's family, negotiated a 'gentleman's agreement' (probably at some point in the late spring of 1939) with his relative for Department EH to establish its 'Secret Country Headquarters' at Woburn Abbey, an ironic choice of base given the political views of the heir to its estate (see later). In the event it was 1 September 1939, two days before Britain declared war, that the planning, editorial and intelligence sections of EH relocated to a place that Stuart described as:

---

[24] Meetings that included representatives of the Foreign Office (Sir Hughe Knatchbull-Hugesson) and the Air Ministry (Wing Co. A. L. Fiddament) were taking place as early as September 1938. Plans to drop leaflets over Germany at the time of the Munich crisis, assuring the German people of Britain's peaceful intent, were opposed by the RAF who were concerned at German threats towards RAF pilots.

an anachronism even without a Department of Propaganda grafted on to it. The Duke of Bedford was very old and very rich, and had been duke for about sixty years, and, if of late, time had not exactly stood still within his domains, it had certainly moved a good deal more slowly than in most places outside them.[25]

Rex Leeper, who was to have responsibility for the day-to-day running of the Woburn operation, together with his wife, were in the vanguard of the evacuation with Mrs Leeper having a number of the Bedford Estate staff assigned to her. One of these servants was eighteen year-old Mary Neal, whose father also worked on the Bedford Estate, and who had already served at the Duke's other establishments at Battlesden House, Paris House and Maryland (the latter two playing a significant part in events to come). Mary recalled being summoned to what Mrs Leeper called 'a little meeting' at the Abbey in order to have their new duties explained which, in the first instance, was to prepare accommodation for an influx of new residents.[26]

In a cloak and dagger procedure that seems farcical now (and surely not beyond penetration of enemy agents should they had gained so much as a whiff of it), key Foreign Office personnel were instructed to go to the *Sugar Loaf Hotel*, an old coaching inn situated in Dunstable's High Street North. There they were to ask for 'Mr Gibbs-Smith' (Michael Gibbs-Smith, the Administrative Officer for Department EH at Woburn), who checked their ID, whispered 'Woburn Abbey' and provided them with a rough sketch map and a pass onto the Bedford Estate. At a time when Guy Burgess and Kim Philby were already moving towards the sensitive areas of the British security services, this prep school pantomime says more about the unprepared nature of German Intelligence than it does about the sophistication of Britain's internal safety measures. It wasn't that Campbell Stuart disregarded the need for precaution – indeed he apparently had 'a passion for security' – just that he was really quite hopeless at it. Thomas Barman, a former foreign correspondent who had been drafted into the Woburn team, soon discovered that his boss made a point of issuing security warnings at the beginning of each telephone call, just in case anyone was listening who

---

[25] Stuart, Campbell. *Opportunity Knocks Once* (Collins, 1952).

[26] Interview with Mary Neal, 15 December 2005.

shouldn't be: 'I've just been talking with a member of the Cabinet,' he would say. 'He's a Viscount and his name begins with an H. Do you follow?'[27] (The Foreign Secretary at that time was Lord Halifax).

Robert Bruce Lockhart *(Hulton-Getty)*.

By the time that the next wave of staff had been drafted in, the pointless stopover at the *Sugar Loaf Hotel* had been dispensed with. Meeting outside the offices of Electra House, 'a small group … in three or four cars' were taken out of London. 'We did not know our address until we arrived at Woburn Park, although we had our suspicions as we drove through Luton,' recorded Barman.[28] When Robert Bruce Lockhart, diplomat, diarist and former spy, was newly appointed to the Political Intelligence Department of the Foreign Office, he simply travelled out on Sunday 10 September 1939, was met off the train at Dunstable Station by Rex Leeper and driven to Woburn, with Leeper explaining the destination on the way. This turned out to be 'Foxgrove' … 'a small red brick villa situated close to one of the gates', which Mary Neal and her colleagues had hurriedly prepared for them.[29] Not that Lockhart noticed: 'very small house' he sniffily confided to his diary, 'staff not here yet and I have an attic bedroom with no place for my clothes. All slightly comic at present.'[30] 'Foxgrove' represented Leeper's first foothold in the Woburn Estate, its

---

[27] Barman, Thomas. *Diplomatic Correspondent* (Hamish Hamilton, 1968).

[28] Ibid.

[29] Lockhart, Robert Bruce. *Comes The Reckoning* (Putnam, 1947), p.54.

[30] Young, Kenneth (ed.) *The Diaries of Sir Robert Bruce Lockhart. Vol. II 1939-65* (Macmillan, 1980).

former tenant, Lady Ampthill, having moved out. Leeper and a small team of staff, plus families, all crowded in (although Leeper was soon to move out to the 'Old Rectory' at Eversholt). This new team included Lieutenant Commander George Martelli, the designated Italian expert, a journalist who had written on his travels in that country.

The acquisition of 'Foxgrove' was to be swiftly followed by Maryland (initially accommodating the Political Intelligence Department – or PID), on the outskirts of Woburn, and then Woburn Abbey's Riding School with adjacent stable block.[31] Sir Campbell Stuart, a weekend visitor 'in the company of three secretaries and many filing cabinets', stayed at Paris House, originally a half-timbered feature house that had been a display item of the 1878 Paris Exhibition. It had caught the eye of Hastings, 9th Duke of Bedford who had it transported back to his estate (it was assembled with pegs). Stuart described it as 'a nineteenth century reproduction of a sixteenth century style, and successfully combined the worst architectural and decorative features of both periods. It was inconvenient, dark and depressing, and in winter desperately cold.'[32] Considering that Stuart, as boss, could have pretty well stayed wherever he chose for his weekend jaunts, this was a somewhat graceless observation. Meanwhile, radio communications (run under the auspices of the Foreign Office's SIS department), were being thoroughly overhauled and sharpened by two outstanding figures, Richard Gambier-Parry and Harold Robin, based over the Buckinghamshire border at Whaddon Hall and Wavendon Towers. The 'Secret War' had arrived in Bedfordshire.

* * *

The county to which the BBC, Department EH and the Meteorological Office had moved was the smallest of a cluster of counties on the northern side of London. They shared broadly common characteristics: even at the end of the fourth decade of the twentieth century, they remained distinctly rural with their landscape dotted with market towns and villages. Although suburbanisation was spreading, particularly in

---

[31] Section D was originally also scheduled to be housed at Woburn but, no accommodation being available, eventually settled at Hexton in Hertfordshire, a few miles away.

[32] Stuart op. cit. Barman op. cit. Barman liked Paris House.

Hertfordshire, only two towns, Oxford and Luton, could be said to have undergone significant change through industrialisation by 1939. These counties were typically riddled with an array of country houses, and even some ducal palaces, to which a new purpose was to be found during the war. Stockgrove Park Mansion and The Heath, for example, two of the largest houses in the Leighton Buzzard area, were both occupied by the Royal Army Medical Corps. Park House, near Ampthill, was taken over by the military when its occupants moved out, and printing presses installed in its basement, although the rumour that maps for the D-Day landings were produced there has never been substantiated.[33]

Since 1935 one such mansion in the north of the county, Colworth House near Sharnbrook, had been the home of Henry Mond, Lord Melchett. Melchett was the vice-chairman of ICI which his father, Alfred, had founded in 1926. Both father and son had served first as Liberal MPs, and then Conservatives, an experience that they shared with their friend, Winston Churchill (Alfred Mond and Churchill also being fellow government ministers under Lloyd George). Colworth House was to serve a number of separate functions during the war. It was a meeting place for key business leaders (Lord Nuffield of Morris Motors being amongst the visitors), a temporary repository for artefacts from the Imperial War Museum, a nurses' holiday home, a refuge for Jews fleeing Nazi persecution, and a forum for socialising American airman from the nearby Podington airfield. As will be seen in Part III, however, it was Melchett's connections with ICI and Churchill that ensured that Colworth House hosted a particular contribution to the Secret War.[34]

In Bedfordshire, as in its neighbouring counties, a number of the old estates had been broken up after World War One, and the agricultural workforce that had worked on the estate farms had never returned to its pre-war numbers. Some of these country homes were earmarked as reception points for children being evacuated from the blitz threatened big cities, but others in the region were host to a different sort of evacuee. Indeed, it is popularly suggested that one of the reasons that the elderly 11th Duke of Bedford was willing to accommodate the propaganda teams

---

[33] Underwood, Andrew. 'Home Rule for Ampthill' (Ampthill Urban District Council, 1974).

[34] Jones, Michael. Colworth in Context. A History of Colworth Estate, Bedfordshire, 1720 to 1947 (Published by the author, 1997).

that were to become the most striking element of Bedfordshire's Secret War, was so that he didn't have to play host to battalions of juvenile townies. It was also on condition that they kept away from the Abbey proper, restricting themselves to the Riding School precinct (the Duke died in 1940, in any case, and his successor chose not to live at the Abbey).

Bedfordshire was affected by the war in a way that was similar to other shire counties. The county received a number of evacuees (with varying degrees of enthusiasm), with the small market town of Shefford accommodating a Jewish School.[35] Bedfordshire's civilians enrolled in a multitude of services, they queued for rations, supported savings campaigns, gave blood, gazed curiously at the influx of foreigners, queued some more and dug for victory. Local authorities co-ordinated much of this activity, additionally formulating less publicised policies should circumstance worsen: preparations were made in Bedfordshire, as elsewhere, for the dreaded day that German Armed Forces might appear on the doorstep. Bedfordshire was divided into areas under the supervision of civilian authorities whose emergency committees drew up plans to respond to the presence of invaders, both in the maintenance of services and mounting a defence of the community. Pill-boxes, anti-tank obstacles and various homespun means of halting the advance of the invader sprang up around the countryside. Luton Borough Council was responsible for an area that included the neighbouring villages of Streatley, Hyde and Caddington. These were part of an outer ring of defences, surrounding a series of 'Defended Localities', centring upon a 'Keep' that comprised the Police Station, Post Office, the Telephone Exchange and the Town Hall.[36]

As the only large manufacturing town in the county, Luton produced the bulk of the wide range of munitions that were manufactured during the war, although large works were built alongside the railway line near Elstow to the south of Bedford. Luton alone produced an array of war materials that included Churchill Tanks, Mosquito Bombers, Bedford Trucks and key components for other vehicles, planes, ships as well as the

---

[35] Grunfeld, Judith. *The Story of a Jewish School Community in Evacuation* (Sonico Press, 1989).

[36] Luton Borough Council's Invasion Committee papers, like some of its Emergency Committee minutes have not been located, although some of the details of its preparations are outlined in the Home Counties publication *Luton at War* (1947).

Mulberry Harbours that the allies towed over for the Normandy landings in 1944. In total, this meant Luton provided every variety of ammunition in a quantity that ran into millions: it provided mortars, meters, gauges, compasses, ball bearings, parachute ribbons, five million Jerricans, vitaminised chocolate for the children of newly liberated Europe – even 7000 ships' bells.

Many parts of the county were also involved in munitions. Around two dozen were employed at the Flitt Motor Company in the small market town of Ampthill, situated in the heart of the county, and produced some 150,000 small munition parts.[37] At Melchbourne Park, near to the villages of Melchbourne and Riseley, was one of five designated bases in the country built to store lethal mustard gas bombs. Manufactured by ICI, the mustard bombs were never used and the storage was overseen by American personnel. Melchbourne became the depot at which leaky bombs from all five centres were sent for decanting and resealing. The manufacture of all this varied equipment required a high level of secrecy, this being absolutely crucial in the initial research and development, particularly for material to be used in clandestine operations.

There were a number of airfields dotted around the county. Luton already possessed an airport owned by the council and this served as a production and testing centre for a number of aircraft during the war. These were mostly trainers, such as the Percival Proctor and Airspeed Oxfords. The airfield at Henlow, in the east of the county was even older, having been established during World War One and which expanded during the second conflict. Hurricanes, Whitleys and Mosquitoes were based at Henlow, but it was the Parachute Test and Training Section that had been established there since 1925 that was to make a particular contribution to the Secret War. To the immediate south-east of Bedford, lay another air facility, the vast, looming twin airship sheds at Cardington. Home to the development of the tragic airship, R101, the Cardington facility was to also serve during World War Two as a reception centre for recruits. Cranfield airfield was the operational base of 62 Squadron, flying Blenheims, and the base's additional function as an Operational Training Unit (OTU) meant that Beaufighters, Mustangs, Mosquitoes, Typhoons and the later marks of

---

[37] Underwood, op. cit.

Spitfires all were accommodated there.[38] Twinwood Farm, to the north of Bedford was also an OTU, also supporting Hurricanes and Mustangs. Smaller grass landing strips at places such as Barton-le-Clay and Woburn Abbey served as overspill airfields and storage facilities for aircraft.

The bombers were based in the north. Gransden Lodge, near to the Cambridgeshire border in the extreme north west of the county, served as a base for the Halifax bombers – and later Lancasters – of the Royal Canadian Air Force, as well as a Pathfinder Squadron. Airfields at Little Staughton, Podington and Thurleigh hosted the B17s of the 8th USAAF offensive against Germany, with the former also serving as a base for RAF Lancasters, and Mosquitoes of 109 Squadron. This was where testing for the 'Oboe' Precision Bombing System was undertaken. Another airfield at Tempsford, to the east of Bedford, was to play an important part in the Secret War. The RAF station at Chicksands was also to serve on this side of things, but not as a significant base for aircraft involved in covert operations.

In Leighton Buzzard, in the far south-west of the county, was the site of the RAF's central Wireless Station. This was constructed partly underground (utilising the old pits of the Marley Tile works), along the Stanbridge Road which, as one of the main arteries running into town, was closed as a through road to general traffic for the duration of the war. Doreen Luke, who briefly worked there as a Morse Slip Reader prior to being transferred to Bletchley Park, recalled there being a 'comfortable atmosphere on the Watch' although 'the work was very tiring and exacting'. The communications centre was protected by two searchlights and a pair of anti-aircraft guns. As with RAF Tempsford, however, these were only to be used to counter a direct assault upon the station (which never occurred), since their use carried the danger of drawing too much attention to the significance of the site.[39]

* * *

---

[38] Smith, Graham. *Hertfordshire and Bedfordshire Airfields in the Second World War* (Countryside Books, 1999).

[39] Luke, Doreen. *My Road to Bletchley Park* (M & M Baldwin, Kidderminster, 2005). Willis, R. V. *The Coming of a Town. The Story of Leighton Buzzard and Linslade* (published by the author, 1984).

Organised Labour had made very little impact upon the county with Trade Union organisation remaining in a fledgling state even in the two largest towns. The war was to change this, accelerating Bedfordshire's transformation from a primarily agricultural county at the beginning of the twentieth century, to one in which manufacturing employed the majority of its workers by the middle. In 1939, however, the Labour Party was still very much the third force behind the Conservatives and the Liberals, whose decline in Bedfordshire had not yet reached the precipitous state it had elsewhere in the country. The National Liberal MP for Luton, Dr Leslie Burgin, briefly achieved Cabinet rank when he served as Minister for Supply in Neville Chamberlain's short lived wartime administration. Burgin's promotion was rather unkindly described by the historian A. J. P. Taylor as 'another horse from Caligula's well-stocked stable'.

In common with other counties, therefore, Bedfordshire was host to a considerable number of the 'great changes' that General Eisenhower later referred to as being a feature of World War Two. It is worth mentioning, however, one that did not. Although a number of preparations were made in Bedfordshire for the eventuality of a German invasion of Britain, its inland geographical position meant that the county never supported an Auxiliary Unit. These were a network of local resistance organisations that were designed to operate behind enemy lines in the event of invasion but were concentrated in the coastal counties. Innovative guerrilla tactics were, therefore, left to the initiative of local companies of the Home Guard, something that they fully indulged in, perhaps in lieu of conventional resources.

Small transmitting stations ('H Stations') were dotted around the countryside, designed and located in order to stop the *Luftwaffe* using larger radio transmitters as directional aids. One was located near to Biggleswade, on the Bedfordshire border between Wrestlingworth and Tadlow, and further investigation may yet reveal others.[40] In Luton, the crisp, white Portland stone tower of the newly built Town Hall was camouflaged, as was the white lion that had been carved on to the Dunstable Downs near Whipsnade Zoo. Little Barford's Power Station

---

[40] Information from Dafydd Williams, interview 8 September 2005. The original building stood on the site of the 1950s construction.

was also disguised because of its use as a turning marker for *Luftwaffe* on their raids on London, but its now less obtrusive 150 feet high chimneys instead became a potential hazard for unwary pilots taking off from nearby RAF Tempsford. The SKF ball bearing factory in Luton painted a false road (complete with dummy trees) onto the roof of its factory in order to confuse the observers in enemy bombers.[41] One can only trust that this was superior to the Met. Office camouflage at its base on the outskirts of Dunstable. This was apparently more of a marker than a disguise as one woman who worked there was told by a pilot friend, 'it's the camouflaged hill near the Downs, we know it well!'[42] The *Luftwaffe* evidently knew it well enough also as they dropped silver strips of paper in an attempt to distort the radio waves.[43]

Rumour and Myth

A feature of Total War, one that engaged the whole population, was the number of stories that flew around. Some may have had a basis in fact, others were pure fancy. In 1942 Luton's hat manufacturers were thrown into turmoil when communications from the Board of Trade suggested that the hat trade that was synonymous with the town was going to be shifted to the north of England, where the work was needed, and freeing up labour for important war work in Luton. All sorts of meetings were hurriedly raised, condemnatory resolutions passed, and concern turned to fury at such apparent high handed dictatorship from Whitehall. A formidable delegation of twenty one representatives of all facets of Luton, Dunstable and Bedford's businesses and trade unions, descended upon the Board of Trade for a showdown with the minister (an acerbic Hugh Dalton, of whom more later), and his civil servants. Having taken two hours to put its case for keeping the hat trade in Bedfordshire, it received the government's response: notwithstanding all previous communication, suggestions that the hat trade were to be moved north from Luton were just 'a rumour'!

---

[41] German reconnaissance photographs that were published after the war showed SKF being marked out for attention, with nearby Wardown Park being also marked as a landmark to assist the factory's location. See also *A Factory Went To War* (SKF, c.1945).

[42] Audric, op. cit.

[43] Roucoux, op. cit.

It was perhaps inevitable that a war that contained so much that was secretive, should lead to rumours, to legends and to conspiracy theories, some of which have lingered and even been further embroidered long after the conflict was over. In respect of a Bedfordshire connection, nowhere have these conspiracy theories been more prevalent than in the notions that have been touted concerning the fate of two very different men: Glenn Miller, the most celebrated band leader of his day, and Rudolf Hess, Deputy Führer of the German Reich, who made a solo landing in Scotland in an attempt to negotiate an end to the war.

Joining the armed forces, Miller was commissioned a Captain and led the Glenn Miller Allied Expeditionary Forces Orchestra, providing more than 800 performances for allied personnel during the time that he led it. This particular composition was based upon the Glenn Miller Orchestra which, in the early 1940s, had achieved an unrivalled reputation not just for the uniqueness of its sound, but also for the precision of its orchestration. When it moved to the UK in 1944, the enthusiastic reception which the AEF Orchestra received, not merely from Americans stationed there but also from

Glenn Miller fronting his band at the Bedford Corn Exchange (*Luton and Bedfordshire Archives*).

the British and other Allied audiences, was a genuine surprise to Miller who had not hitherto appreciated the extent to which his popularity had crossed the Atlantic. The warmth of the feeling was reciprocated and Miller was even planning to build a 'dream home' in England after the war. From the early summer of 1944 Miller's orchestra became part of some 1.7 million United States personnel based in Britain. With the BBC outpost at Bedford and their attendant broadcasting facilities, the town became the orchestra's natural billet.

By September 1944, with the Allied advance through Western Europe accelerating, Eisenhower moved Allied Supreme Headquarters to its new home at Versailles, just outside Paris and plans were made to vacate as much as possible of the American presence to the European theatre: 'returning Britain to the British' as it was expressed at the time. This included relocating Glenn Miller and the band to France where a six-week tour of American bases and field hospitals and to entertain front-line troops on leave in Paris was planned. The proposed tour during the winter of 1944/45 also included two special broadcasts, one on Christmas Day and the other on New Year's Eve. Miller, by now promoted to Major and Don Haynes his business manager, spent much of November 1944 shuttling between Paris, London and the band's home in Bedford in order to make the necessary arrangements for the orchestra's move. He gave one last live broadcast at the All Services Club, Soho on 12 December before travelling back to Bedford the following day.

Even at this late stage detailed preparation for the band's relocation were still incomplete. Don Haynes had already secured orders for himself to travel to Paris but Miller took the decision to go on ahead of the band taking Haynes' place. On December 14 Miller phoned Haynes, who was lunching at Milton Ernest Hall with Col. Norman F. Baessell, from Bovingdon airfield saying that there was no way he was going to get a flight out that day or indeed soon as all aircraft were grounded due to weather conditions. Hearing this Baessell offered Miller a lift to France from RAF Twinwood (located just north of Bedford near the village of Clapham) the following day.

Baessell, who had been assigned responsibility for establishing and running Aircraft Repair Depots in the liberated areas of Europe, had his own personal aeroplane, a Noorduyn UC-64 Norseman (a Canadian built light transport aircraft). The aircraft was to be piloted by Flight Officer John R. S. 'Nipper' Morgan, based at the 35th Air Depot at Abbots Ripton. The miserable weather, with icy fog and low cloud, made prospective flying conditions none too favourable but both passengers were determined to fly. As he walked out to the waiting plane Miller turned to Don Haynes and said 'Haynsie, even the birds are grounded today.' Major Glenn Miller was last seen climbing aboard the plane on 15 December, on his way to a Paris destination at which he never arrived.

The relative inexperience of 'Nipper' Morgan has been commented upon by some, though Don Haynes recalled that 'he was a wonderful guy, with whom I had flown all over the European Theatre.' Indeed Baessell himself was an experienced flyer and a member of the reserve; but given the conditions it is possible that even the most proficient of pilots would have been hard pressed to cope with circumstances that the tiny Norseman would have faced over the English Channel.[44] Because of the low cloud base (around 2000-2500 feet) Morgan may have selected a cruising altitude of around 1500-2000 feet, but may not have necessarily appreciated that the freezing level would have also significantly dropped as the plane reached the colder continental air. Any such impact upon the plane's fuel supply or engine would have been sudden, giving little chance to rectify or control the situation. A returning RAF Lancaster (NF973) saw a plane below though a break in the clouds, flying at approximately 1500 feet, and one of its crew (who had trained in Canada) positively identified the aircraft as a Norseman. The same crew members also saw that this aircraft suddenly 'dipped its port wing and dived into the sea'. In his meteorological analysis of the circumstances surrounding the disappearance of Glenn Miller, William S. Pike also observed that there was a slight swell in the English Channel and that had the fixed landing gear on the plane's port side made contact with a wave it would have easily flipped over, thus quickly sinking the craft.

As with all accidents in which there are few or no survivors, there remains an element of mystery, especially when a celebrity or public figure is involved. Almost any aspect can then become grist to the mill of conspiracy theorists but it is beyond the scope of this account to wend its weary way through every alternative hypothesis concerning Miller's possible fate, none of which have yet produced utterly convincing evidence.

One of the most intriguing suggestions to be made, for example, somehow connects the British actor, David Niven with Miller's fate, with lurid tales of violence and death in Paris brothels. The two men are drawn together partly because both were stars who played roles in

---

[44] Pike, William S. 'Weather Notes on 15 December 1944, With Particular Reference to the Disappearance of Glenn Miller's Aircraft into the English Channel'. *Journal of Meteorology*, vol. 25, no. 254, December 2000.

providing entertainment for the AEF (Allied Expeditionary Force) in France from 1944 onwards, and partly because Niven was a Rifle Brigade officer assigned to the enigmatically named 'Phantom Squadron' of Commandos.[45] Sheridan Morley's biography also notes that in addition to his duties as an officer and an actor, Niven also undertook some duties on behalf of MI5, the significance of which can be easily overstated. Niven recalled his balloon being somewhat deflated when he first caught a cab to the discrete address given by the security service: 'Ah yes,' said the taxi driver 'that'll be MI5 you're wanting, Mr Niven; all the stars go there in the end.' The taxi driver, at least, was aware that British Intelligence sections directed the service of many 'stars' for propaganda aimed at the enemy, potential enemies, at allies or potential allies – especially the United States before 1941. Niven's fellow actor Leslie Howard (who in 1943, like Glenn Miller, disappeared on a flight over the sea), the director Alexander Korda, writers Graham Greene and George Orwell, and the poet Stephen Spender are examples of prominent individuals who are thought to have served in this capacity during and after World War Two.[46] The Army Lists for the period (the published catalogue of officers and the units to which they were attached) indicate that Niven drew regular service pay, rather than being paid through alternative channels, such as the Foreign Office, as was the case with many service men and women involved in clandestine operations.

---

[45] Morley, Sheridan. *The Life of David Niven. The Other Side of the Moon* (Weidenfeld and Nicholson, 1985). The roving duties of the 'Phantoms' were a response to the new mobility of warfare, involving the linking of the most forward of positions with command centres. They had evolved from the French campaign of 1939-40 and become formally created at the beginning of 1941, when the prospect of a German invasion of Britain seemed a distinct possibility. The elusiveness of their sometimes classified operations would naturally lead to reticence on the part of those who were engaged in them, but in Niven's case this was heightened by his modest dismissal of his work, a reflection of his cultivated habit of trying to appear no more than a light hearted dilettante. This was a guise that didn't mislead his contemporaries at all. Peter Ustinov, then a Private in the Royal Sussex Regiment and posted for convenience sake as Niven's batman whilst the pair of them worked on the film *The Way Ahead*, summed up his officer pretty accurately when he observed 'he was really much more intelligent and profound than he ever let on to being: he would pretend that the superficial cleverness was all, whereas in fact it wasn't even the beginning'.

[46] See for example Cull, Nicholas John. *Selling War: British Propaganda Campaign Against American Neutrality in World War II* (New York, 1995); Lashmar, Paul and Oliver, James. *Britain's Secret Propaganda War 1948-1977* (Sutton Publishing, 1998).

It is unlikely that Niven and Miller had met one another before their paths crossed as part of their AEF duties in 1944. Sheridan Morley attributes their introduction to Cecil Madden, a BBC producer, but is wrong in claiming that this was in 'late 1944'. Chris Way noted that both Miller and Niven visited Bedford on 29 June 1944 to investigate prospective billets for Miller's band and two weeks later, on 13 July 1944, both were present at the Corn Exchange concert broadcast by the BBC (the photograph of which Morley places in London).[47] Although much about the 'Phantom' Squadron remains classified, Niven was doubtlessly being perfectly frank in saying that he didn't know Glenn Miller very well.

One must also be careful in reading too much into Niven's work for the entertainment wing of the AEF either (the award of the American Legion of Merit notwithstanding), since best evidence suggests that Niven was not keen on attending too many meetings: he apparently used to sign in as present, chat to and charm those present, then clear off with a self-deprecatory confession that he probably had little to offer that particular gathering.[48] In any case, Niven was legitimately busy enough with his own military and acting duties: 'A' Squadron of the Phantoms (described as the 'peculiar property' of Niven), served in the operations around Caen in 1944 and although Niven had been 'whisked away' to Eisenhower's staff by then ('where it was thought that his very considerable and particular talents could be best employed'), their former commanding officer suddenly 'appeared, not uncharacteristically, in a battered German car plainly labelled "US NAVY"'.[49]

During his time in Bedford, Glenn Miller and key members of his band became friendly with the Mayor of Bedford who provided facilities for parties complete with alcohol, a privilege that the Mayor enjoyed. A letter from Jerry Gray, Miller's band arranger, to Councillor J. A. Canvin, Mayor of Bedford in 1945 in answer to the Council's letter of condolence, after the disappearance of Miller shows that at this stage the common assumption was that Miller would eventually turn up safe and sound:

---

[47] Way, Chris. *Glenn Miller in Britain. Then and Now* (Battle of Britain Prints/After the Battle, 1994).

[48] Morley, op. cit.

[49] Hills, R. J. T. *Phantom Was There* (Arnold, 1951).

Dear Mr Canvin   *March 14, 1945*

Thank you so much for that lovely sympathetic letter. I know how much you and all like the Major but I sincerely feel that he will be back again with us soon - there is a very good rumour he is a prisoner of war - so we shall know officially within a month. The band's carrying on in true Miller fashion, and I am sure the boys feel, as I, that one day things will be fine again.

Very special regards to Bill and Mrs Canvin.

Sincerely

Jerry Gray

(Bill is Bill Morris, employed by Canvin as a personal assistant).

Although there are no further reports of a landing by the Norseman, on either side of the Channel, speculation has continued to be raised as to the circumstances surrounding Miller's disappearance from those pursuing the case, with each tiny, supposed discrepancy being obsessively alighted upon. Wilbur Wright, for example, draws attention to the absence of official reporting of the missing plane and the failure to launch a search for the tiny craft over the channel.

In defence of the American authorities, it is important to remember that on the day that Miller was reported missing Hitler launched his Ardennes Offensive, a desperate battle that nearly broke the allied lines and involved more than one million men fighting in atrocious conditions (a bitter irony in that the low cloud cover that probably contributed to the death of Miller was simultaneously deemed crucial to the German plans since it nullified Allied air superiority). Even Miller's band members, who had arrived separately and safely in France, later confessed that what was really uppermost in their minds was the prospect of being sent to battle Hitler's last throw of the dice, so perhaps the wider US military can be forgiven for being a little distracted at this time.[50]

---

[50] Bowman, op. cit. Wright, Wilbur *Millergate* (Wrightway, 1990) and *The Glenn Miller Burial File* (Wrightway, 1993).

In fact, William Randolph Hearst, the powerful American media tycoon, drew upon his own considerable resources to pursue his own investigation, but turned up nothing. As to the steady flow of conjecture that has flowed since that time, Chris Way has a pretty blunt assessment:

> Many ideas have been put forward over the years about the fate of the aircraft and Glenn Miller on that Friday afternoon. Some are so fanciful that they are not even worth considering, most of the wild theories appearing to be put forward by those seeking weird publicity for their own ends. This hurts Glenn's family ...[51]

When all has been said and done (and, regardless of the feelings of Glenn Miller's family, quite a lot has been said on this matter), the truth of what really happened to Norseman UC-64 is almost certainly much more prosaic, although nonetheless tragic for all that.

The sad fact is that people occasionally die in transit, (the operational history of RAF Tempsford provides ample testimony of this), and the sixty million recorded changes of postal address in wartime Britain alone demonstrate that there was a lot more transit at this period of black outs and dislocation. Terry Elderton, for example, was a brave and excellent rear gunner on a Halifax bomber who sadly did not survive the war. He didn't die in combat, however – he fell off his bike at the railway level crossing near to his base at Tempsford and died within twenty minutes of striking his head. Terry was capable and courageous but he was not famous, and his body wasn't missing. Doubtless, had either been the case there would have been scope for conspiracy theories but the poignancy of the death of a fighting man in a mundane situation should not detract from the simple fact that Terry Elderton's death was just an accident: so too was that of Glenn Miller.

* * *

The other persistent rumour connected with Bedfordshire that has lingered and grown since World War Two is that Rudolf Hess, Deputy *Reichsführer* to Adolf Hitler, was brought to either Luton or Aspley Guise (or both) for holding/interrogation following his crashed landing

---

[51] Way, op. cit

at Scotland and abortive peace mission. This rumour spread further because of claims made in newspapers in 1990 by a retired Lieutenant Colonel, John L. McCowan, who claimed to have led a force that apprehended three German parachutists at Luton Hoo in May 1941. These parachutists were supposed to have landed under cover of a token bombing raid over Luton. The inference was clear: they had landed to free – or more probably silence – Rudolf Hess.

Rudolf Hess, photographed just after the end of the war as a prisoner of the allies. (*Imperial War Museum, HU26596*).

Intriguing though this prospect is there is no available evidence to support any such claim.[52] Indeed, not only does common sense suggest that there was no point in halting Hess' journey south from Scotland to London, just thirty miles short of it's destination, there seems to be no good reason why information on any such stopover should be suppressed when so much else has been made available, including transcripts of his interrogation. Of course, the Germans may have still believed that Hess was in the area (a number of sites in Bedfordshire and Hertfordshire have been suggested as possible temporary holding centres) but just how three of even the most resourceful and fanatical of Hitler's followers could have tracked him down without arousing suspicion has not yet been explained. Neither is there any record of agents being apprehended in the Beds/Herts area, tried or executed at this time.

---

[52] The available documents on the Hess saga are mainly contained within the Foreign Office papers at the National Archives. This institution has devoted one of its Source Sheets (no.29) to guide those interested in the Hess affair. Through these documents one can see Hess' deterioration from deluded acolyte, through to whinging hypochondriac, and finally to suicidal despair as it dawns upon him that he had committed one of the great miscalculations of the 20th century (although his boss was to make a bigger one on 22 June).

Against a general backdrop of a very real fear of imminent invasion (German parachutists were regarded as the most likely), there was, however, one genuine alert. In May 1941 the Home Guard was given an advance warning that on the night of 27th a German parachutist *would* be landed under cover of a bombing raid over Newlands Farm, on the outskirts of Luton. Units were mobilised, there was 'action taken', but no other evidence of anyone apprehended at Newlands or anywhere else, save for one source: local amateur radio operator, Arthur Roach.[53] Although his memory was hazy by the time that he recorded his memoirs in the 1980s, Roach claimed to have heard via the Radio Security Service grapevine that a parachutist had, indeed, been captured, although he couldn't recall whereabouts this had taken place. He recorded the small pleasure that he took in surprising the Home Guard's Lieutenant Colonel Godfrey a couple of days later with his knowledge of the news when Godfrey (a plait dyer by trade) visited his factory. Recovering his composure, Godfrey confirmed that a parachutist had in fact been captured; if true, an extraordinary and uncharacteristic breach of prudence on the part of two men who in the circumstances should have known better.

The Hess saga did produce, however, one definite Bedfordshire link, and a further example of attempted 'black' deception. After the initial uncertainty had passed, the British decided to encourage Hess to be a little more forthcoming (as well as to elevate his reading beyond *Titbits* and other matter that officials did not think reflected well upon his hosts). In order to prompt Hess, who was already subsiding into depression as he realised the enormity of his miscalculation, into being more talkative it was decided to produce a bogus edition of *Volkischer Beobachter*, the official Nazi newspaper, at the *Luton News*. Knowing to what extent Hess was worried about his family, a small insert was placed into the real copy of the 21 May edition purporting to carry the following clarification: 'Stories in the foreign press to the effect that Hess' wife and 4-year old son are in the custody of the Gestapo are the malicious inventions of enemy propaganda. At the present Frau Hess and her son are in a mental hospital in Thuringia.'

Ellic Howe doubted that the bilingual Sefton Delmer was involved as the headline carried a grammatical error that he would not have made and,

---

[53] WO 166/1260. National Archives. Roach, Arthur. *They Also Serve* (self published, 1987).

in any case, Hess made no comment. In fact there is universal recognition that Delmer, who knew Hess from the early 1930s, was under used in the Hess affair. The groping, even ham fisted response from the British government that is evident in the surviving archive, hint at uncertainty, even fear (the possibility that Hess landed to spark a rising by fifth columnists), rather than any sinister plot on the part of the security services to lure him to Britain, as some have suggested.

A further attempt was made by producing a mock-up of the *Daily Telegraph* edition of 20 June. Again this was produced by the *Luton News*, this time carrying a doctored article from the real edition now hinting that Hess' son was mentally ill, and also that Hitler (who Hess adored) was incandescent with rage at what he saw as his Deputy's betrayal. All but three copies of the print run were apparently destroyed, with one going to Hess.[54] Again, this ingenious effort did not produce the intended result. In any case, Hess' mental state had deteriorated significantly and, six weeks after his arrival, his value to Britain had diminished (the propaganda potential was never exploited, handing the initiative back to Goebbels), especially since the German invasion of the Soviet Union, which Hess had confidently reassured his captors was not imminent (who knew different thanks to Bletchley Park).

* * *

As a counterpoint to the many rumours, some areas of reality were consigned to fading memory, eventually dying with the handful that possessed that intimate knowledge, whilst elsewhere fact, possibility and downright fiction became muddled in fallible minds. Inevitably that leads to stories of tunnels and underground bases. One such rumour was that Stockwood Park, near Luton, contained a local reserve command centre that was equipped to function immediately should the main head quarters be destroyed or over-run. Even into the 1950s, it was said that the air vents could still be seen for an installation that was sealed up, ready for use should the Cold War ever have turned into a hot one. No trace or record exists.[55]

---

[54] The two known remaining copies are in a private collection.

[55] Information from Hedley Lawrence, in an interview with Stephen Bunker, April 1992. Lawrence was a Luton Borough councillor and builder during World War Two. That the Council's Emergency Committee Minute Book for the 1940-42 has been mislaid since it was last seen in the 1970s, can be attributed to neglect rather than conspiracy.

Matters kept secret: morale and protection

'It may be asked, if ARP had been under consideration since about 1935, why so little seemed to have been done, why so much had to be done in a frantic hurry in the end,' summarised Home Counties Newspapers' account of Luton's preparations to protect its population from air raids in the event of war.[56] With around 100,000 people in 1939, and as a principal centre of manufacturing, questions needed to be answered as to the level of protection that could be provided for the people of the town. As early as 1935 Council officials were giving thought to the matter and the town's Borough Engineer, J. W. Tomlinson, together with George E. Scott (Luton's Chief Constable and ARP Controller), seem to have been amongst the first to anticipate conflict, advocating that the town construct a system of tunnel shelters into the hills surrounding the town, following an inspection of the system at Dover.

Vauxhall workers at Luton dig trenches on the outskirts of town, October 1938 (*Luton Museum Service/Luton News*).

Although the tunnel system was not followed through (it was realised that such tunnels were not close enough for the bulk of the population to reach quickly), Scott and Tomlinson worked with a small team of senior officials and councillors to make preparations as they could.

---

[56] (Luton News) *Luton At War* (Home Counties Newspapers, 1947).

Preliminary Air Raid Protection schemes in 'skeleton form' were prepared in order that they could be implemented and expanded should the need arise. ARP wardens were being enrolled in Luton as early as 1937, with other areas of Bedfordshire doing much the same. Although he had turned eighty years of age, Herbrand Russell, 11th Duke of Bedford, showed that he knew the importance of duty and patriotic example by enrolling as an ARP warden in the Woburn district.

The trouble for Luton, as for all other towns, was for 'what they had to prepare was largely guesswork'.[57] No guidance or grant aid for war was likely to be made from a government still wedded to a policy of avoiding it: enrolling would-be wardens was one thing, preparing costly shelters was quite another. As *Luton At War* summarised it:

> *Everyone was in the dark about what ought to be done. Even higher authority dallied in settling a defined policy and, until that was done, what should have been everybody's business was in fact nobody's business. It was a long time before Luton secured freedom to act as it thought ...*[58]

By the spring of 1939 Luton Borough Council were conducting surveys of basements and cellars, as well as endeavouring to calculate the number of Anderson shelters that would be required. By mid May approximately 9000 inspections of premises in the 'congested areas of the town' had been undertaken.[59] For the first half of 1939 most initiative seems to have come from the locality, little from central government (in July the Council was still awaiting information from the Home Office on steel shelters). Whilst giving evidence in the case of vandalism to recently constructed shelters on the part of two ten year-old boys, Superintendent Wood of the Luton Police observed that the 'Chief Constable (was) concerned ... as to whether the shelters will be ready and fit for use by the public if and when we get air raids.'[60]

---

[57] Ibid.

[58] Ibid. p 46.

[59] Luton Borough Council Air Raid Precautions Committee minute book, 1939-40. 20 April 1939, 17 May 1939. From February 1940 this body became reconstituted as the Emergency Committee.

[60] *Luton News* 14.2.1939.

By the time that war did occur, officials were at pains to utter public expressions of confidence in the precautions made. In an interview with the *Luton News* in November 1939 Sir William Spens, Civil Defence Commissioner, Eastern Region, described Luton's provision as 'one of our shining examples. Your local authorities made up their minds what they wanted and acted. The result is that your aid raid shelter provision is very well forward'. For those able to read between the lines, however, the situation was markedly less promising. Just a week previously the same newspaper had carried a report from George Scott, serving in the now twin capacity of Chief Constable and ARP Controller for Luton. Reporting 'much progress ... in the completion of public shelters', Chief Constable Scott stated that there were basement shelters sufficient to accommodate 7090 people.

Scott's publicly optimistic tone belied a very different reality. Although 15,000 Anderson Shelters had been requested, still only 1200 had been sited. Furthermore, protective accommodation for a further 9800 Lutonians amounted to no more than trenches, many of which were of hasty construction.[61] The seriousness of the situation was made starkly apparent in a detailed survey of air raid provision which was made at the same time as Spens' and Scott's observations.[62] Conducted by F. Yates, a member of staff at the Harpenden based Rothamstead Experimental Station, this assessment focused upon the numbers of people who would be likely to congregate at the heart of urban centres in the event of an air raid or warning at various times of the week. The two centres chosen, Luton and Birmingham, represented interesting choices since both were industrial centres (albeit on a different scale), with a high proportion of small workshops (as opposed to large plants such as Kent Meters or Vauxhall Motors where large factory based shelters could be provided).

The survey for Luton made grim reading: if the Munich agreement had indeed bought time for Britain to prepare for war then little advantage had been taken. Furthermore, although Scott may have claimed that 1200 Anderson Shelters had been 'sited', according to Yates only 150

---

[61] Ibid. 9.11.1939; 16.11.1939.

[62] 'Surveys. People in the Open. Luton and Birmingham'. National Archives, HO 338/24. The survey remained closed, under constant review (at any time of which it could have been destroyed), until 1971.

Anderson Shelters begin to be delivered to Luton, October 1939
(*Luton Museum Service/Luton News*).

Anderson shelters had actually been delivered, despite the Borough's efforts. The trench accommodation was dismissed as affording 'practically negligible' protection for the residential population, at best a desperate last resort.[63] It is difficult to imagine a document that, if made public, could have generated more alarm than this.

As for the shelter accommodation, the issue was not the numbers that could be theoretically accommodated, but whether people could actually get to them at certain times. Put simply, the report calculated that 2988 of the 5053 workers in Luton's small factories were completely unprotected.[64] Counting the number of people that congregated in the town's shops, market, pubs, cinemas, shops, cafes and public transport on

---

[63] The report offered this scant consolation: 'Many residents would apparently prefer to be together with their neighbours rather than alone.'

[64] It was recommended that the small factory owners be 'compelled' or guided to group together in order to provide shelters for units of 50 workers.

a Friday night or at the weekend, the survey came to further worrying conclusions, predicting that this 'serious situation' could lead to 'confusion and possibly panic' unless additional public shelters were provided. Its conclusion was blunt:

> The existing shelters are ... just about adequate to deal with the people actually out on the street, but will be seriously overloaded if any of the people in shops, cinemas etc. or even in the market proceed to them.

> In the event of an air raid warning being sounded on a Friday or a Saturday afternoon, therefore, a very serious situation may develop. Undue crowding of the public shelters could only be avoided by locking the doors of all the shops, definitely keeping the audiences of the theatres and cinemas in these buildings, and taking steps to prevent those who work in the neighbourhood from using the shelters.

Locking people into vulnerable sites such as cinemas to prevent 'overcrowding' in air raid shelters of course belied the very reason the shelters were built in the first place. The potential for disaster would be enormous. Fortunately by the time bombing did begin over Luton the four large central public shelters in Gordon Street, High Town, Beech Hill and Albert Road had been completed, with other provision (both public and private) being established elsewhere. The hastily dug trenches of 1938-39 were not much used. In any case, severe though the handful of individual raids were, Luton was never blitzed on a similar scale to similar industrial centres, notably Coventry, a remarkable escape given the war materials that were being produced in the town.

Bedfordshire as a whole escaped heavy damage, not merely its towns such as Dunstable or Bedford, but even key installations such as Chicksands or Henlow. Concern lingered, nonetheless, as to the degree of protection being afforded by the public shelters, especially in the two biggest centres. Following the disaster at Bethnal Green where a stampede on the stairs had killed 178 people (with a further sixty injured), the Civil Defence authorities for the Eastern Region (based at Cambridge) conducted a further confidential survey in the spring of 1943.[65]

---

[65] HO 207/1152 National Archives.

Particular concern was directed at the access points and accommodation of two of Bedford's shelters. 135-139 Midland Road was described as an 'undesirable shelter … and were there no embargo on the building of shelters, I would suggest scrapping the whole of the shelter.' The shelter located at 13-15 The Broadway was simply condemned. For Luton, the worst of the crisis had seemed to have passed during the early years of the conflict. The main problem concerned the cost of reinforcement to tunnels that ran from Gordon Street where the chalk had turned out to be softer than expected. This led to some pretty tetchy correspondence involving the Borough, the regional office and Whitehall.[66] Additionally, the unexpected discovery of a seam of sand caused the digging of the Albert Road shelter to be truncated.

Matters kept secret: morale and fifth columnists

The appeasement of dictators that characterised Britain's foreign policy during the 1930s has to be seen in a wider light. A combination of factors, including pacifism born of a determination not to repeat the carnage of World War One, a resolve not to become entangled in European affairs (for much the same reason), and disillusion due to perceived national decline, were regarded as being elements that had sapped the will of the British nation to seriously contest the will of foreign dictators. The politics of mass democracy was also something that was quite new: the right to vote had only been extended to all men as recently as 1918, with all women having to wait a further ten years after that. Many people flirted with extremist politics on the right and the left, and many who should have known better appeared to condone the supposed achievements of Stalin, Hitler and Mussolini, comparing favourably the virtues of dictatorships that were loudly trumpeted by their respective propaganda machines, with the apparent failings of the democracies. Bedfordshire was no exception to this, with a number avowing support for Communism, on the one hand, or Oswald Moseley's British Union of Fascists on the other. Luton, a town with a tradition of political volatility, experienced disturbances between the BUF and its opponents when Moseley visited the town in 1936, and fighting between supporters and opponents of the BUF in Bute Street resulted in the death of one man.

---

[66] HO 207/1111, HO 207/1360 and HO 207/1137. National Archives.

60

The man who would be the British Führer: Oswald Moseley photographed with local Fascist, L. R. Osgood in what looks like a caretaker's office during a visit to Luton's Winter Assembly Hall, March 1936. Goebbels would never have permitted such a composition *(Luton Museum Service/Luton News)*.

During the Spanish Civil War, one of Franco's Nationalist Generals boasted that in addition to the four army columns that were converging upon Republican held Madrid, a 'fifth column' of clandestine supporters were hidden inside the capital, awaiting his orders to rise and cause havoc within. The fear of so-called 'fifth columnists' and the damage that they could do from the inside, became a European wide concern during the latter part of the 1930s. This fear certainly took root in Britain where, according to police reports, a number with extreme right wing sentiments had infiltrated anti-war organisations. For those who had inclined towards the extreme right, however, the turning point came in the spring of 1939 when Hitler reneged on all previous undertakings and occupied the remainder of Czechoslovakia, in clear breach of the Munich agreement. Appeasement was bankrupt and only die-hard appeasers and pro-Germans did not regard war as almost a certainty.[67]

[67] Griffiths, Richard. *Fellow Travellers of the Right. British Enthusiasts for Nazi Germany 1933-39* (OUP, 1983).

During the 1930s, a fear emerged in the minds of those in authority, perceiving a feeble level of morale amongst the British public. One would have to observe that central government had made a pretty large contribution to this state of affairs but, as things turned out, this turned out to be yet another miscalculation on their part. The British people proved to be a great deal more durable than had been anticipated; whether it was their discernment in dealing with the broadcasts of the traitor William Joyce ('Lord Haw-Haw'), or their fortitude in dealing with privation, or their courage under bombing. Nonetheless, during the early part of the war, when invasion seemed imminent, the fear of fifth columnists was especially high. Some from the extreme right were almost immediately interned, whilst a number of other individuals were identified as being potential 'renegades' and were kept under police surveillance, the records of which were kept secret for more than sixty years.[68] Some were genuinely nasty, others were just plain batty: all were to be immediately detained in the event of a German landing under Defence Regulation 18B.

Of the approximately seventy individuals who are known to have been initially put under surveillance in the east of England, four were resident in Bedfordshire, and their identity bears out most historians' assessment of the rump of pro-Nazi support. Two were recently arrived foreigners, Karl Jorgensen (a Dane) and Jorgen Sohnemann (a German/Dane), and both were doing casual labouring jobs when denounced by fellow workers. Jorgensen, who had arrived in the UK in July 1940 and was lodging at Stotfold, was reported as describing Britain as a 'dirty little country'. A third, Valerie Stockdale, was German by birth. Residing at 'The Meadway', Turvey, Stockdale was described as 'a difficult and disagreeable woman' who had been overheard expressing 'violently pro-German views'.

It was, however, a home grown Nazi that seemed to offer the greatest threat of violent action. Ronald Brewer of 55 Cardiff Road, Luton, was twenty five when Britain declared war on Germany. He had first joined Oswald Moseley's British Union of Fascists in 1932 and was active in Bristol at the beginning of the war. Brewer had declared his willingness to provide food and shelter to German parachutists, had advocated the

---

[68] HO 45/25568 'Detention of suspects in the event of invasion'. (Released 2005). National Archives.

overthrow of the Churchill government and had endeavoured to pass propaganda material on to William Joyce. The principal police informant appears to have been an anonymous 'young woman' who Brewer had advised to listen to the New British Broadcasting Station, a traitorous radio service broadcasting from Germany. Detained in April 1941, he was released in November 1943 (when the threat of invasion had passed), but was retained on the Suspect List for immediate detention should the need arise.

Hastings Russell, 12th Duke of Bedford (*Luton Museum Service/Luton News*).

Britain was spared German invasion so it will never be known whether this motley handful represented the full extent of potential traitors and collaborators in the county, or just how many more would have emerged from under a stone had the fortune of war been otherwise. This cloud of suspicion also hangs over the reputation of Bedfordshire's most prominent enthusiast for Germany, none other than Hastings Russell, Marquess of Tavistock and heir to the Bedford estate to which he succeeded as 12th Duke upon the death of his father, Herbrand, in 1940. Euphemistically described as a 'pacifist', Russell was regarded suspiciously as the sort who cloaked extreme right wing views behind a veil of pacifism.[69] In the desperate period of 1940-41 he was held under particularly close surveillance by the police and MI5, his movements monitored, his speeches noted and his correspondence intercepted. Russell was fully aware that this was occurring, echoing the complaint made at the time (and later) that evidence against himself and others was either deliberately falsified by the authorities, or came 'from

---

[69] The remnants of the security service file on Hastings Russell is held in the National Archives, KV 2/793. Although a minute of the full file still exists, much of the original material was destroyed in 1959.

those whose capacity for forming accurate opinion has been warped by war hysteria'.[70]

In many respects, the position of Hastings Russell, reckoned to be the fourth richest man in Britain, was a complex one. It wouldn't be accurate to regard him as simply a straightforward British fascist, in the black shirted Moseleyite sense of the word. Later it would be alleged that, during an isolated childhood at Woburn Abbey, he had fallen under the influence of a German governess who had previously served at the court of the German Kaiser, and that in 1914 he had been reluctant to serve in his regiment due to a combination of pro-German feelings and physical cowardice (he was supposed to be found hiding in Dover), eventually becoming a pacifist agitator during World War One. Unsubstantiated allegations such as this aside (and the security services were quite willing to use smears), there seem to be particular reasons behind Tavistock's 'strongly pro-German and even pro-Hitler' stance.[71] During the inter-war period the Marquess of Tavistock had developed an interest in pacifism, vegetarianism, Catholicism, flirted with Communism and, above all, became obsessed with the need for fundamental monetary reform. It was Hitler's supposed radical achievements in the sphere of economics that seem to have drawn particular admiration from Tavistock. Even within MI5 Hastings Russell was regarded to a certain extent as 'a disinterested crank and not a clear headed political intriguer', the uncertainty in the assessment of him reflected in another report that described him as operating 'wittingly or unwittingly, wickedly or in child-like innocence of purpose' as 'an instrument of Nazi propaganda.'

There was enough, however, to warrant a close watch. Openly anti-semitic, the Marquess of Tavistock was contributing to right wing journals such as Action during the late 1930s, arguing in one that 'there is little evidence that he (Hitler) would engage in an aggressive war with neighbours of a non-German origin who did not treat him unfairly'.[72] In February 1939 he attended a BUF luncheon and sustained close contact

[70] Letter to Sir Norman Birkett who chaired the Advisory Committee on the treatment of those detained because of suspect loyalties. National Archives, HO 283/24.

[71] Condemnation quoted in KV 2/793 (National Archives), originally being contained in correspondence since destroyed.

[72] Quoted in Griffiths, op. cit.

with a number from the far right of British politics. Amongst his closest associates were John Beckett, formerly a member of the National Socialist League, and Ben Greene, whom Tavistock described as 'a man of very upright character'. Greene was a cousin of the brothers Hugh Carleton Greene (to become head of the German service at the BBC) and novelist Graham Greene, like them being a native of Berkhamsted in Hertfordshire. Beckett and Greene had also together formed the right wing British People's Party which contested at least one by-election but otherwise made no impact. Other far right associates of Russell included Captain Gordon-Canning and the BUF's Director of Policy, Raven Thomson.

Taking a firmly anti-Polish stance during the crisis that led to Britain's entry into the war, the Marquess described the German position as 'extremely reasonable,' but Britain's declaration of war upon Germany shattered all but the last remnants of fascism in the UK. Some took cover in genuine pacifist organisations such as the Peace Pledge Union, whilst others joined rather more shadowy bodies. One such was the British Council for Christian Settlement in Europe (BCCSE), to which Russell, Greene, Gordon-Canning and Beckett gravitated in 1939. The BCCSE was regarded by MI5 as 'undoubtedly a subversive organisation whose purpose it is to undermine public opinion in the interests of Germany' and its leaders – including Russell – held their meetings at Greene's Berkhamsted home.

It was under the auspices of the BCCSE that Tavistock put out peace feelers towards German officials in the early stages of the war. It ought to be noted, however, that he was not acting entirely independently of the government: Chamberlain's Foreign Secretary, Lord Halifax (an unrepentant appeaser), authorised Russell's visit to neutral Eire to approach personal contacts that he had in the German Legation in Dublin, although Halifax made it expressly clear that permission to travel was the extent of the authorisation. Widely publicised at the time (Beckett ensured this), nothing came of the approach to the Germans.[73] Furthermore, genuine peace campaigners such as Dr Maude Royden and Dr Donald Soper disassociated themselves from the peace proposals when they realised the strong fascist element that was contained within it.

---

[73] Trent, Christopher. *The Russells* (Frederick Muller, 1966).

When Beckett, Greene and Gordon-Canning were interned together with up to one thousand others in 1940, the BCCSE disintegrated, although Hastings Russell remained as its nominal chairman. His position was kept under constant review but successive Home Secretaries, John Anderson and Herbert Morrison, decided that he should remain at liberty (there was a difference of opinion on this within the security services). As one of MI5's secret reports put it:

> We have not recommended any action against Lord Tavistock as he does not appear to us at present to be a potential danger. We regard him as a comparatively harmless crank who was being used as a figurehead by men who were much more astute and unscrupulous than himself.[74]

Whilst the propaganda teams fought their war from his estate, the 12th Duke of Bedford fought his. Attempts by the Ministry of Food's local War Agricultural Committee to turn the wide open spaces of his parkland for food production, and to cull the deer population for meat, were firmly resisted. He stood his ground to refuse to supply grazing for 150 cattle and 400 sheep, even when the Ministry tried to prick his patriotic conscience by pointing out that in World War One his father had agreed to take 200 cattle and 500 sheep.[75] Bedfordshire's War Agricultural Committee preferred to tread carefully, partly because the Duke's respected agent, W. B. Higgs, was clearly sympathetic with the Ministry's aims, offering to try to persuade the Duke to be more co-operative.

There was another reason, however, for not rushing into a confrontation with the Duke through the issuing of a ministerial decree. It was acknowledged by the Bedfordshire War Agricultural Committee that '"getting across" the Duke reacts in so many ways in the country's agricultural life'. One member of the Committee who did 'get across' the Duke was Henry Hobbs, also farm bailiff on the Duke's Ampthill Estate, and who was abruptly dismissed in April 1943 for allegedly being 'a bad master, a bad servant and a bad farmer'. A petition was swiftly raised in response, providing testimony to Hobbs' competence and the regard in which he was held, but the Duke remained unmoved. Hobbs therefore sued for libel (as did later Higgs), winning £500 in 1946.

[74] B7 report dated 17.8.1940. KV 2/793.
[75] National Archives, MAF/48/415.

For a pacifist, Hastings Russell appeared to show precious little tolerance or sensitivity. Upon becoming Duke one of his first duties was to oversee the redundancy of a number of estate workers. One such worker received a terse note thanking him for past services but the bulk of the letter then went on to outline the Duke's condemnation of the war. The consolation was completed by the inclusion with the letter of nine separate leaflets in which the Duke set out his views on monetary reform. There were few amongst the estate's staff with much time for the 12th Duke, one former employee being one of the security services' more detailed and vitriolic informants.

Hastings Russell further alienated himself from mainstream British opinion by resisting the removal of the iron railings from his Bloomsbury estates in London during the great scrap metal collecting drive early in the war. In October 1941, the statue of the 5th Duke of Bedford in Russell Square (itself surrounded by some of the railings that the 12th Duke wanted to preserve) was vandalised. One morning, the statue was discovered wearing an upturned paint pot and its base adorned with the following daub: 'Grandfather of a Quisling/Down with traitor/1941, and his railings/Down with the Duke.'[76] Two years later, in Leighton Buzzard, Hastings Russell's name was formally erased from an inscription on the foundation stone of the local Conservative Club. The Duke continued to speak at Peace Pledge Union rallies (at which he was heckled) and contributed to *Peace News*. In all his utterances, the Duke of Bedford consistently blamed the British Government for the war, placed no condemnation upon Nazi policy or practise and claimed that Britain's best hope for survival lay in a negotiated peace. He spent his time alternating between a house in Woburn village, and his Kirkcudbrightshire estate in Scotland.

By the autumn of 1941, security service attitudes had hardened towards the Duke of Bedford. The internment of his former confederates hadn't shut him up. Anonymous leaflets were being circulated carrying such titles as *Have Britons Brains?*, *What A Game*, *The Eighth Deadly Sin* and *These Spitfire Funds*. There was little doubt as to the authorship and the message within them remained consistent: Hitler was a reasonable man

---

[76] *Evening Standard* 27.10.1941. A 'Quisling' was a traitor and fifth columnist, the name being taken from Vidkun Quisling, pro-Nazi leader of the puppet government in Norway.

who should be approached with 'wise, practical, genuine friendliness', Germany would conquer Russia, all British resistance was futile, and defeat was inevitable unless she sued for peace. In other words, the Duke was moving from a stance of pro-German pacifism to one of pro-German defeatism. *These Spitfire Funds* covered the Duke's obsessions, both old and new, declaring that the mass savings schemes 'provides an excellent example of the ignorance and gullibility of the British public in regards to questions of monetary policy'. Complaints were coming from Regional Security Officers in Bristol, Manchester, Newcastle and Cardiff, as well as from the commanders at the barracks at Aldershot, where copies had been intercepted on their way for distribution amongst soldiers. There was little doubt that the Duke of Bedford was not only the author of these pamphlets but also the financier of their publication and circulation.

The concern remained that the Duke's utterances would still carry some influence, not so much in Britain (although that might alter in the event of German landings), but it was feared that it might persuade those in enemy and neutral countries that there was a significant 'Peace Party' in the UK. This would serve to dishearten the resistance efforts in occupied Europe (where the leaflets were found to have been distributed) and discourage American support for Britain at a time when the British Government was doing all it could to counter powerful isolationist sentiment in that country. Worse still, in the event of successful invasion it was feared that the Duke 'would be likely to be set up as a *gauleiter* or the head of a puppet British government'.[77]

Initially, it was felt that an official warning would be sufficient. Roger Fulford, one of the most uncompromising of his critics within MI5, described the Duke as 'a chicken hearted creature. It is obvious from his letters that he is very scared of the authorities'. There were those who advocated searching the Duke's premises 'in order to button up our evidence with regard to the authorship of the documents of which we complain. It seems improbable that he will deny authorship and it may be that the search would reveal further material... the Duke, like a lot of cranks, is somewhat of a coward'. The Home Secretary ruled this out because, on balance, there remained a desire to keep the Duke's activities

---

[77] Opinion expressed by security officer E. B. Stamp, KV 2/793, National Archives.

above ground whilst simultaneously giving him as little opportunity for publicity as possible.

Nonetheless, there was a growing sense that the Duke was, as one informant put it, 'dangerous rather than eccentric' and his association with the Strickland Press, run by anarchist Guy Aldred, further damned him. The Strickland Press published the radical journal *The Word*, to which Hastings Russell contributed as a writer and probable financier. Within MI5, security officer E. B. Stamp steadily amassed his evidence, both corroborated and uncorroborated, and underpinned by a fear of the Fifth Column, which he submitted in early December 1941. Although never interned, on 7 December 1941, the 'troublesome' 12th Duke of Bedford was added to the list of those to be immediately detained in the event of invasion. On the same day, the Japanese attack upon the American Pacific Fleet at Pear Harbour was to lead to the entry of the United States into World War Two, whilst a few hours earlier the Siberian divisions of Marshal Zhukov smashed into the German armies at the gates of Moscow and drove them back two hundred miles. These simultaneous events ensured that the prospects of German invasion would permanently recede. Although continuing to use his privileged position in order to campaign on behalf of Britain's fascist detainees, the Duke similarly receded from public consciousness until his mysterious death in 1953.

Part II

Psychological Warfare

Life in the 'Country'

Once established in the vicinity of Woburn Abbey, the propaganda teams spread steadily through the Russell's domain. Maryland had formerly served as a model hospital for the estate workers, and it was here that the Political Intelligence Department (P.I.D.) printing unit was eventually based (having been initially housed in the redundant aeroplane hanger of the late 'Flying Duchess'.[78] Seven bedrooms were prepared for Bruce Lockhart (he got another small one) and others, together with a dining room and a drawing room that were fitted into what had once been the hospital's main ward. The charming George Martelli, who apparently caused the heart to flutter in at least one of the female domestics, was accommodated downstairs before his later move to a farm at Eversholt. Partitions were erected along the length of the Riding School with a corridor down the centre: 'above the tops of the modest partitions one looked towards a remote roof' noted Campbell Stuart.

The Riding School, Woburn Abbey, photographed during World War One, when it was being used as a military convalescent home (*Luton and Bedfordshire Archives*).

[78] The 'Flying Duchess' was the former Duchess of Bedford who acquired a love of flying, piloting her own Gypsy Moth. Denis Dolton recalled that estate staff (including him) had to help keep the tail down as it taxied across the park prior to take-off. The Duchess disappeared on a flight on 23 March 1937 and although wreckage was washed up on the east coast of England, her body was never found.

Approximately 120 staff moved into Woburn during this first phase, sharing the Riding School with the overflow of the Abbey's collection of paintings: 'every inch of wall space was taken up by immense canvases in massive frames. Some of them were quite good, others were not so good ... the one feature which they all shared in common was size'.[79] As staff poured in, domestic fittings were still being installed 'so that the propagandists had to spend their first few days in a state of grandeur and misery' reminisced Stuart.

An aerial view of Woburn Abbey, probably taken before World War Two, showing the stable block and Riding School in the foreground (*Luton and Bedfordshire Archives*).

The Riding School/Stable Block lay to the immediate east of Woburn Abbey but was physically separated from it. This was mutually convenient, allowing the propaganda team ample space and a relaxed atmosphere, whereas for the immensely shy Herbrand, Duke of Bedford it permitted the opportunity to put part of his home at the disposal of the war effort, without enduring physical proximity. Presently, with conversion of the stable block into accommodation complete, the old

[79] Stuart op. cit.

Duke was persuaded to take a tour of inspection. Arriving in the pouring rain the tour party

> *passed on to the sleeping quarters, which unexpectedly provided the chief success of the morning. Stopping in front of the chauffeurs' quarters he had such a fit of laughing as might have carried him off. "Four men in one loose-box" he wheezed; "four men in one loose-box", and set off home through the puddles still chuckling on what he had seen.* [80]

Having established its 'Secret Country Headquarters' in the form of what Stuart described as a 'little settlement' around which 'stretched Woburn Park, studded with lakes and woods and splendid rhododendron groves', a sense of amateurism continued to persist. In general terms, it was perhaps understandable that there should be certain fluidity as different departments groped towards a coherent response in the fields of propaganda and intelligence. 'We did our best with no story to tell,' observed Stuart, of the winter of 1939 and the spring of 1940. In fact, Bruce Lockhart summarised the whole first part of the war thus:

> *Indeed the first two years of the war may be described as an experimental period of trial by error, and we were fortunate in being able to improve our technique at a time when our propaganda was not only inefficient but could, in fact, have little effect on a seemingly victorious enemy.* [81]

There is also a strong impression that, in the early stages, British anti-German propaganda was falling back on the techniques deployed in World War One, the effectiveness of which had probably been exaggerated in hindsight. The preponderance of leaflet production over broadcasting effort has been attributed to the simple fact that Campbell Stuart was working with what he knew. *Radio Italia*, which went on air for the first time on 17 November 1940, was a case in point. It endeavoured to appeal to the Italian working class, frequently making unfavourable contrasts with their supposed German allies when compared with the British. It wasn't until the following year, however, that John Barry, of the Woburn planning team, discovered that only 4%

---

[80] Stuart op. cit.

[81] Ibid. p.143. Harold Keeble noted 'That period before May 1940, must be written off with all the other mistakes of the phoney war.' Keeble, Harold. *Alphabet and Image* (Shenval Press, 1947). See also FO/898/28 National Archives.

of Italian workers possessed sets that were capable of picking up the broadcasts of *Radio Italia*.[82]

In addition, there were already signs of the sort of organisational problems that were to punctuate Britain's attempts at conducting a structured propaganda and psychological campaign. 'One of the most distasteful jobs I had to do,' recorded Thomas Barman of early co-ordination meetings with corresponding departments. Frank Pick, Duff Cooper's recently appointed Director General at the Ministry of Information, was, according to Barman, invariably 'most offensive' in meetings, even though his voice rarely rose above a whisper. His 'barbed rudeness' was usually directed at the BBC and especially its struggling Director General, Prof. F. W. Ogilvie.[83] Nonetheless, the confusion and inter-departmental in-fighting also reflected a degree of poor organisation, something that was manifested in the loose working hours and liquid lunches. Remembering the occasion when Campbell Stuart good naturedly asked the window cleaner whether he was happy in his work, Barman observed that 'Stuart made a great point of cultivating the best possible relations with his staff. He was on nodding terms with everybody ... (he) never interfered with our work. So long as you had his confidence, he left you alone.'[84] Another staff member, Robert Walmsley, recalled:

Work was apt to go on until the early hours of the morning. This was not quite so arduous as it sounds, since the Lyons canteen was supplemented by an excellent small bar in which you could have five sherries or a reasonable bottle of French claret for half a crown: I was told that one tenth of the salary bill of the whole Department passed through this bar. There were also the days in which gallon jars of sherry and bottles of gin enlivened the evening working hours of secretaries and others, somewhat to the surprise of regular civil servants who visited us from time to time.

---

[82] Garnett, op. cit. Radio Italia had Captain Ivor Bulmer-Thomas as its responsible officer. Bulmer-Thomas (1905-1993), a former journalist who had been seconded from the Norfolk Regiment, served until an unspecified breach of security led to his abrupt removal. Bulmer-Thomas later became a Conservative MP and sharp critic of PWE. John Barry was in favour of something specific, such as a service aimed at the Italian navy.

[83] Barman op. cit. Pick was the man responsible for the distinctive corporate design associated with London Underground and London Transport. Duff Cooper's successor, Brendan Bracken, was to force out Ogilvie and replace him with his own nomination.

[84] Ibid.

> *It was not unusual, also, for people to take two or three hours off in the afternoon, encouraged in this by Valentine Williams himself. There was wonderful skating on the lakes and the Duke of Bedford's beautiful park was full of interest to the zoologically minded (Vernon Bartlett used to allege that he had been butted by a llama and bitten by a rhea).*[85]

A Recreation Committee ensured that a cinema, two billiards tables and a dance floor were installed in the stable block for the use of staff. Swiftly, Woburn Abbey closed in upon itself, providing a mood that was distinctly odd. David Garnett noted that the secrecy, segregation and 'continual preoccupation with enemy conditions which combined to create a rather unreal mental atmosphere … one of the strangest that the writer has ever experienced. There was more than a touch of madness about it'.[86] The visiting civil servants from London found that there was nowhere for them to particularly go and felt that they were unwelcome.

Already there were snide references being made in Whitehall to 'Leeper's Sleepers', or 'resting at Hogsnorton' and, notwithstanding the occasional flurry of activity, the dispatch boxes going to and fro between Bedfordshire and London, the police guards at the entrance to Leeper's house at Eversholt Old Rectory, and the precaution of not maintaining the usual habit of a guest book, there still seems to be a measure of justification in a perception of laxity. There appeared to be various people hanging around that didn't possess a clearly defined function, almost as if Bedfordshire was a nice alternative to wartime London. One such visitor was Maurice Peterson, nicknamed 'Uncle Beastly' by the Woburn staff. Displaced from his ambassadorial position in Spain in order to find a job for the old appeaser, Samuel Hoare, once Churchill came to power, Peterson had 'sulked ever since', clearly preferring to feel sorry for himself in the peace and quiet of the country.[87]

Spouses were permitted to join the staff and a combination of the estate's food supply and the black market ensured that the basics of wartime rations could be supplemented more than adequately. Daimler provided chauffeurs, two of whom were accommodated in converted bed-sits

---

[85] Garnett, op. cit.

[86] Ibid.

[87] Barman op. cit.

Eversholt Rectory, the Leeper's home between 1941-43, and the scene of countless meetings and official visits (*Luton and Bedfordshire Archives*).

above the garages to the rear of the Old Rectory, an arrangement that was apparently convenient both for the Leepers and their house guests, as well as for the enthusiastic love life pursued by one of the drivers. The Leepers moved much of their personal furniture to Eversholt, as well as their ankle nipping dachshund, Mitzi, and the presence of so many important (and relatively affluent) persons provided additional income for the domestic staff. Col. Chambers, the elderly head of security at Woburn, was one of a number there who tipped £1 a month in respect of valeting services carried out by domestic staff whose weekly wage was just 30s. (£1.50).[88] 'Rex thinks we shall win this war by (1) sea-power and (2) propaganda. God help us if the sea-power is as mishandled as the propaganda,' Lockhart sourly noted.[89]

This relaxed atmosphere of a surreal country house weekend was abruptly broken in the spring of 1940 with the sudden defeat of the allies in Norway, France and Belgium. The first of these disasters spelt the end of

---

[88] Mary Neal op.cit. Col. Chambers died suddenly, whilst at Eversholt Old Rectory.

[89] Young op. cit. 25 September 1939. Of a meeting at the Old Rectory in December 1941, Lockhart exclaimed 'Oh gosh, how many plans and how much waste paper.'

Neville Chamberlain's lacklustre government, whose appeasement had placed Britain so poorly prepared to meet the coming menace, leaving it to his successor, Winston Churchill, to revitalise Britain's response and resolve. In so doing Churchill drew in personnel that had been hitherto excluded from Chamberlain's hapless administration. Many of these figures had shared Churchill's hostility to appeasement; some of them were brilliant; a number were difficult characters: a few were all three.[90] One such person was the influential Socialist Dr Hugh Dalton, described by historian, Peter Clarke as 'vulnerable, even at his most cynical ... (a) social subversive, political schemer and romantic patriot'.[91] Churchill personally disliked Dalton (he was hardly alone in this), but recognised his abilities and perhaps also the need to find the right hole for this particular square peg. Dalton was made Minister for Economic Warfare in 1940, taking oversight of all aspects of the work of the Special Operations Executive. Its brief was to 'coordinate all action by way of subversion and sabotage against the enemy overseas': in short, Dalton was told to 'set Europe ablaze' in Churchill's famous phrase. Dalton's former civil servant at the Foreign Office, Gladwyn Jebb, was placed in charge of SOE.

Dalton changed the atmosphere at Woburn, more often known as CHQ (Country Head Quarters) or simply 'the country'. Up until that time, a combination of defeat, uncertainty and poor leadership had left it in what Anthony Howard described as 'something of a twilight era'.[92]

Hugh Dalton (*Imperial War Museum, H8191*).

---

[90] Upon arrival at Woburn Bruce Lockhart was immediately struck by the fact that there were none of the old appeasers there. Leeper was not the only one opposed to the miserable Munich agreement: as Lockhart put it, 'there were no "guilty men" at "Foxgrove" ...'

[91] Clarke, Peter. *A Question of Leadership* (Penguin, 1982).

[92] Howard, Anthony. *Crossman. The Pursuit of Power* (Jonathan Cape, 1990).

The men in London who were associated with the old appeasing order, such as Laurence Grand (the Head of Section D) and Campbell Stuart were held in ill-concealed contempt by 'Dr Dynamo' and barged aside. Stuart assisted in his own demise; ten days after the fall of France, with the Germans seemingly poised at the Channel ports to invade England, the man in charge of Propaganda to Enemy Countries volunteered to scuttle off to his native Canada in order to spend two months personally negotiating the purchase of a short-wave radio station on behalf of the BBC, even though they had expressed no firm interest in using it. One wonders whether, at any stage, Stuart pondered why Dalton had been such an enthusiastic supporter of the trip but, when he eventually returned, his resignation almost immediately followed.[93]

The clear-out was under way, Dalton aggressively sweeping down upon 'Leeper's Sleepers' at Woburn (a description which the Minister generally thought 'undeserved') like a whirlwind. Heads rolled there too, including Leeper's Deputy, Valentine Williams, who eventually left in July 1941 (to represent SOE in New York), and was replaced by David Bowes-Lyon, King George VI's brother-in-law, and one who was able to maintain Woburn's tradition of heavy imbibing. The new use to which the Abbey was being put certainly appealed to the socialist in Dalton when he went down there in July 1940 to meet 'my blokes': 'I went into the country and there met an intelligent group of persons in the Harness Room of an Aristocratic Establishment, now fallen down to the level of practical use as part of our national war effort.'[94] Dalton noted this in his diary, a legacy that has been described elsewhere as 'a devastating exposure of human frailty and folly, not least his own'. In it, however, he provides an insight to his methods of control that he sought to exert over affairs at Woburn.[95]

Dalton liked to surround himself with *protégés*, one such being the future Chancellor and Labour leader, Hugh Gaitskell. With his characteristically cheerful lack of sensitivity Dalton blatantly used Gaitskell as his eyes and ears at Woburn, installing him at 6 Leighton

---

[93] 'Duff (Cooper) is to perform the task of getting rid of Campbell Stuart,' noted Bruce Lockhart in his diary on 12.7.1940.

[94] Pimlott, Ben. *The Second World War Diary of Hugh Dalton 1940-45* (Jonathan Cape, 1986).

[95] Peter Clarke, op. cit.

Hugh Gaitskell (*Luton Museum Service/Luton News*).

Street, Woburn, one of the Department's expanding number of houses in the district. Gaitskell's wife, Dora, and his daughter, Julia, also moved to Woburn but rarely saw much of Gaitskell, such were Dalton's demands, even though Dora rose at 6.30 every day to prepare his breakfast. Although Gaitskell was briefed to help build up SO1 (secret propaganda, taking over from Department EH and actually Leeper's responsibility), SO2 (which dealt with sabotage) and SO3 (the administrative unit – an utter failure), the senior staff at the Abbey knew full well as to Gaitskell's true function. Thomas Barman was probably not alone in suspecting that Gaitskell was aiming to force Leeper out altogether and 'get his job'.[96]

The senior Woburn officials probably resented the imposition as much as they resented Dalton's habit of undermining their authority by communication directly with their subordinates. Barman, described him thus:

> *He was a great booming bully; and even at breakfast time his manner was horribly hearty. He used to dress himself up in a sort of heavy white jersey, as worn by the best goalkeepers, and called for volunteers to go for a walk with him of a Sunday morning. Walkers became hard to find after a while; people tended to go to earth when they heard his voice and that could be heard almost everywhere.'*[97]

---

[96] Young, op. cit. 28.1.1941.

[97] Barman, op. cit. M. R. D. Foot suggested that although Dalton's behaviour appalled civil servants (he used Christopher Mayhew and Robin Brook in similar fashion), it was also a demonstration of the degree of freedom that had been bestowed upon SOE and upon him personally.

In fact, the man with 'a laugh that rattled the windows in a way church organs often do' was swiftly making decisions about the Woburn operation. 'They were a mixed lot,' Dalton noted, 'with much talent and much temperament ... Most of them were continually active, and some were sleepless prima donnas. I found the atmosphere highly charged with personal rivalries ...nor was the little garrison quite solid in its loyalties.'[98] He operated via his placemen, where necessary using them to front discussions with the officials. On one occasion he recorded that at 'a certain stage of the conversation I allow Gaitskell to make the running and myself to remain silent,' but was little more considerate towards his personal entourage. The walks so dreaded by Barman and others, had another purpose: a way of emphasising who was top dog. 'Some responded better than others' noted Dalton of his Woburn walks, or 'jogs' as he called them. Recording a visit to his home by Gladwyn Jebb, Dalton gleefully recorded: 'I take him for a quick walk through the village ... delighting myself with walking briskly up the hill until he asks me not to walk so fast. This is a favourite trick of mine to play on those younger than myself.'[99]

Having asserted himself he then received reports. The day after playing his 'trick' on Jebb, Dalton repeated the technique upon Gaitskell and another personal assistant:

> I make Gaitskell ask me not to walk so fast and then suggest to him that we should run instead but he does not like this idea either. They have both been down to the Country House for the weekend and report that progress is slowly, but only slowly, being made.[100]

Another of Dalton's favourite ploys was to invite a subordinate over for drinks on the rooftop of his Mayfair club. When the air raid warning sounded Dalton would refuse to go to the shelter, obliging his squirming junior to sit there also as Dalton's voice 'boomed away' above the sound of falling bombs. 'He was not particularly scrupulous in his methods,' recalled Barman with considerable understatement. He thought nothing of sitting the Woburn staff in a semi-circle and then proceed to lecture them:

---

[98] Dalton, Hugh. *The Fateful Years. Memoirs 1931-45* (Frederick Muller, 1957).

[99] Pimlott, op. cit. 15 September 1940. That is not to say that Dalton did not appreciate the Bedfordshire countryside. In mid December 1940, he noted that 'the pine woods are pretty good to walk in'.

[100] Ibid. 16 September 1940.

More than once I detected a look of embarrassment, and even shame, flash across Gaitskell's face as Dalton indulged himself in one of his habitual tactlessness. Even Crossman was not too happy … "Jesus!" was the only comment that Valentine Williams was capable of when the séance ended.[101]

Richard Crossman. His future cabinet colleague, Denis Healey, observed that he 'had a heavyweight intellect with a lightweight judgement' *(Hulton Getty).*

The 'Crossman' referred to by Barman was another future Labour cabinet minister, Richard Crossman, appointed by Dalton as the head of the important German section at Woburn and who was already working on programmes in that language at the BBC, in collaboration with Hugh Carleton Greene (appointed BBC German editor in October 1940). Troublesome and argumentative, 'he seems to prefer a good argument to almost anything else in the world' noted Thomas Barman. This was an assessment echoed by Bruce Lockhart, who found the turbulent Socialist '…certainly brilliant in many ways … but also unreliable in judgement and untrustworthy in performance. His ego was unblushing and cocksure. He knew everything much better than the experts'.[102] He must have driven his line managers to distraction: 'An order or a reprimand would automatically become the occasion for a great debate that Crossman would inevitably win on points. When his superiors had an order to give they used to call him on the telephone, give the order, put the receiver down and hope for the best.'[103]

---

[101] Barman, op. cit.

[102] Young op. cit. 6 August 1955.

[103] Barman, op. cit.

Significantly, Lockhart added that 'I saved him twice when he would have been sacked. I did it because we were short of good men.'

Crossman's attributes were immediately recognised by Dalton ('he is loyal to his own career but only incidentally to anything or anyone else') who, upon his appointment, pointedly remarked 'I am confident that you will now show, not only your habitual virtues of intelligence, energy and courage, but also those more difficult gifts of conciliation, tact and discretion.' Needless to say, Dalton exploited the latter deficiency, easily drawing Crossman into indiscretions over dinner: 'A most amusing picture, supplementing Gaitskell's, of events at C.H.Q. The new Section Heads have a complete contempt for all the officials.'[104] The feelings were reciprocated. 'One curious feature of this Woburn organisation,' noted Bruce Lockhart in his diary, '(which includes many freaks, some genuine antiques, several fakes and a few geniuses) is the almost universal contempt for the professional politician, including the ministers. Yet the ministers preen themselves, pout and patronise as if they were making a tremendous impression on everyone.'[105]

Enter Delmer

As personnel became established, the nature of propaganda also became clarified. Both PWE at Woburn Abbey and the BBC, which jealously guarded its nominal independence from government, broadcast 'white' propaganda. Campbell Stuart had repeatedly struggled (and failed) to get the BBC to conform to requirements of Department EH, and was obliged to develop his own broadcasts in May 1940, using a German right wing political dissident who had fallen foul of his former allies. Unfortunately, the German drive towards the English Channel made 'Herr Spieker', or 'Mr Turner' as he was also known, feel so nervous that he fled to the USA by the end of the year.[106]

---

[104] Pimlott, op. cit. 17 September 1941. Dalton was able to discover that Bowes-Lyon was unhappy with Minister of Information, Brendan Bracken, and critical that he rarely went to Woburn. He was soon to find out why.

[105] Young, op. cit.

[106] Garnett, op. cit. Spieker was apparently a former member of the Freikorps, and an associate of the Strasser brothers, who had become alienated from Hitler in the early 1930s, Gregor Strasser being murdered in the 'Night of the Long Knives' in June 1934.

PWE was to have no better luck in monitoring the Corporations' news gathering service because it was updated so frequently that it was almost impossible to follow. Furthermore, the BBC's broadcasters – notably Hugh Carleton Greene – resisted all attempts to broadcast anything of doubtful origin or content, aspiring towards the highest tone in their output. There were nonetheless some differences between the various foreign language sections of the BBC, especially between the German output and the rest. Leonard Miall, producer of talks at the latter, emphasised that the German Service was 'where we do the dirty work, where our colleagues try and raise their listeners' morale, we try and lower it'.[107]

Overall, however, whatever the nature of a BBC programmes' content, the origin of the broadcast was made clear: it was coming from the British perspective. With hindsight it is universally acknowledged that although some foreign language services made a superb contribution – the French Service is the outstanding example – white propaganda to Germany, trying to encourage ordinary Germans to act against Nazism, was far less effective. As Asa Briggs put it, in his history of British broadcasting, 'in general there was a lack of punch in the content and style of the programmes which cannot have made them appealing to any sizeable audience'.

At the time there were already those that doubted the effectiveness of the whiter than white approach to broadcasting, believing there was absolutely no purpose in making vague appeals to the sensibilities of the 'Good German'. Chief amongst these was Dennis Sefton Delmer, a British journalist from Lord Beaverbrook's *Daily Express*. Unlike Dalton, who apparently 'had an emotional dislike of all things German', Delmer, known as 'Tom' to his friends, possessed a strong affinity with the country. He had been born in Berlin, and was capable of speaking like a native Prussian, being apparently able to speak in a number of different German accents. As a foreign correspondent in Berlin during the inter-war period Delmer had closely followed Hitler's campaign as the Nazis manoeuvred towards power. His entry into Nazi circles was via an initial introduction to Ernst Röhm, the scar-faced leader of the Stormtroopers of the Nazi movement, the S.A. (*Sturm Abteilung*),

---

[107] Briggs, op. cit.

or the 'Brownshirts' as they were popularly known. He attended Brownshirt rallies, even sat on their platforms, a vantage point that gave him the opportunity to study these Stormtroopers close up, for the first time appreciating the appeal of Nazism to men, many of whom were drawn from the ranks of the unemployed.

Although, in his vivid, highly impressionistic autobiography, Delmer admitted that the first Stormtrooper rally that he attended was 'wonderful fun,' he was immediately aware of the menacing side.[108] In the dying days of the Weimar Republic, Röhm offered to take Delmer out on the town in Berlin, introducing him to some of its racier nightclubs. Given Röhm's well deserved reputation as an indiscreet and promiscuous homosexual, Delmer accepted Röhm's invitation with some trepidation ('there was one little discomfort I was not prepared to undergo for Lord Beaverbrook'), an unease that was heightened when, at the notorious *Eldorado*

Ernst Röhm *(Hulton Getty)*.

nightclub, Röhm introduced Delmer to a strapping 'Stormtrooper' in full frock and wig. Via Röhm, Delmer got to know all the other leading Nazis, including Dr Josef Goebbels (cackling, sadistic, dapper – 'a venomous dwarf'); Hermann Göring (Delmer's parrot 'Popitzshka' defecated on the laughing Göring's shoulder at one dinner party), Rudolf Hess and Heinrich Himmler (the first contact with whom was when the bespectacled head of the SS confiscated and searched Delmer's case during a train journey to a Nazi rally).

---

[108] Delmer, Sefton. *Trail Sinister* (Secker and Warburg, 1961). Upon being introduced to the brutal Edmund Heines, Delmer recalled saying to himself "'Tom, my lad, you are shaking hands with a killer". And so I was'. Both Röhm and Heines were to be killed during Hitler's 'Night of the Long Knives' purge of the SA in 1934.

Sefton Delmer was, therefore, one of the first Englishmen to get to know Adolf Hitler, being also the first to visit him at his Munich headquarters, the 'Brown House' in April 1931. Delmer was initially unimpressed, later recalling his host as 'rather gauche ... the poor man, he did have a definite, rather proletarian, lower middle class, class complex ... dreadful, you know'.[109] There was something else there, however:

The truth is that the very first impression he made on me was that of a rather ordinary fellow ... He reminded me of the many ex-soldier travelling salesmen I had met in railway carriages on my journeys across Germany. He talked like one too ... But I will say this. None of the railway carriage politicians ever talked with the passion, the volubility and the concentration of Hitler.[110]

A snapshot by Sefton Delmer depicting Adolf Hitler, meeting and greeting, during his 1932 election campaign (*courtesy of Felix Delmer*).

Delmer suspected that it wasn't merely the Party connections but his fluency in German that secured his place as the only foreign correspondent within Hitler's entourage as the firmly mono-lingual leader of the Nazis built up his power base in 1931-32. 'Hitler was prepared to have me around because I spoke German like a German and there was no need for an interpreter,' he modestly recalled. During the 1932 Presidential elections, the *Daily Express* man flew with Hitler in his private aeroplane, all the time noting the character of the man and the inter-relationship with those who orbited around him, vying for his attention. At dinner, the vegetarian, teetotal leader had showed a marked preference for cakes and sweetened coffee: 'He had no small talk. And he did not like others to have any either ... Argument was

[109] An extract of a 1960s interview with Sefton Delmer was featured in the 1987 Anglia TV documentary *Woburn at War*.

[110] Delmer, op. cit.

taboo. Only questions were welcome ... What he liked talking about most was war, war of the future and war of the past.'

The extent to which Hitler precisely intended events to lead to war in 1939, and the degree to which responsibility lies upon his shoulders, remains one of the great historical controversies. As far as Delmer was concerned, from the moment of his very first visit to the 'Brown House' eight years earlier when he observed regular *Reichswehr* officers collaborating with SA leaders in a strategic exercise directed towards Poland, he was convinced that the Nazi Party – and Germany – was gearing for war. What was also striking was the contrast between the public and the private figures of Hitler, and Delmer was an intimate witness to the manner in which Hitler's carefully contrived public posture evoked a willing response in Germans of all types. He observed how the magnetism was turned on and off, and how Hitler disliked making awkward decisions. Delmer was intrigued to hear how many referred to him as 'Führer' on the election tour of 1932; he noted the acquiescence of local officials throughout Germany, especially the police (who turned a blind eye to the extreme violence perpetrated by Hitler's SS bodyguard), and the judiciary (who so lightly punished it).

Adolf Hitler and Joseph Goebbels photographed by Sefton Delmer in Hitler's plane during his 1932 election campaign *(courtesy of Felix Delmer)*.

This unique insight led Delmer to conclude that there was no chance of a popular uprising against Hitler, that there was no likelihood of the German people being prompted into overthrowing the Nazis through exhortations from Britain. A different approach was needed. Under Delmer, propaganda was to darken, acquiring a 'black' or 'grey' characteristic.

Grey propaganda gives no clue to its origin, leaving the recipient to guess, whilst black blatantly pretends to come from somewhere else. In other words, broadcasts and printed matter issued to Germany, in

German, ostensibly pro-German (fiercely so, in fact), but carrying a deft subtext that carried a defeatist message. In Bedfordshire, and under Delmer's leadership, British black propaganda was to acquire a distinctive characteristic: entertaining, subversive, dishonest, crude, even pornographic (although this was far more limited than has recently been suggested in popular media circles). It would operate in a similar vein to a modern sensationalist tabloid newspaper that provides censorial detail about acts of vice and corruption in order to secure an even higher circulation amongst a public eager to read about it. Delmer believed that propaganda should appeal to baser instincts. 'For talks, one of the best subjects is corruption of leaders,' he argued. 'We should serve up inside dope which is new and true. Talks should strike a rough note frequently, be rude and robustly offensive.'[111]

In fact, Hugh Dalton had already spotted that black propaganda was among the many areas of the Woburn operation that left something to be desired, noting in his diary on 19 July 1941 that 'a good deal of improvement is possible here, and it would be best to have one man ...'. It wasn't Dalton that first approached Delmer in September 1940, however, but Leonard Ingrams, a former banker who was now employed at the Department of Economic Warfare, and who had been appointed as the liaison officer between that ministry and Department EH. An acquaintance of Delmer from their Berlin days, Ingrams possessed what Delmer thought were the perfect qualities to play 'the part of the mysterious Mr X to perfection ... his eyes and mouth had just the right expression of drawling, sardonic pity...'[112] Ingrams wanted an alternative to what he perceived to be the left wing inclinations of 'this racket of broadcasting' that emanated from Woburn under Crossman (Brendan Bracken, the Minister of Information from 1941, shared Ingram's judgement). Like Delmer, he had no faith in the possibility of a 'Good German' coup against Hitler, believing that existing 'white' propaganda to Germany would prove to be fruitless, but still believed that broadcasting could assist the work of SO2.

Once the Nazis achieved power in 1933, Delmer steadily distanced himself from his erstwhile dining partners. He was relieved to be

---

[111] Letter to Leonard Ingrams, 31 August 1940, quoted in Garnett, op. cit.

[112] Delmer, op. cit.

temporarily posted to Paris and later covered the Spanish Civil War from 1936. Delmer was in Poland as the Panzers crashed through in September 1939, feeling shame at his flight with other foreign correspondents. He had a second narrow escape the following year as he got away from France during its collapse in 1940, fortunately securing a berth aboard the P&O Liner *Madura* as it left Bordeaux, with his wife Isabel and other fleeing (and extremely lucky) ex-patriots, by which time he had already seen the effect of Nazi propaganda on disintegrating French morale.

The result of these experiences made Delmer determined to undertake work 'more directly connected with the conduct of the war than writing about it,' but, at 'the age of thirty-six and with a weight of seventeen and a half stone to drag around, I did not feel that I would be much use as a soldier.' There were many skills that Delmer had to offer but his Berlin background, and specifically the association with Adolf Hitler, prejudiced official opinion against him. Bewildered and just a little hurt that this attitude repeatedly blocked his requests to play a fuller role, Delmer was 'exhilarated' to presently receive a personal invitation from

Sefton Delmer broadcasting for the BBC, November 1941 *(Hulton Getty).*

Duff Cooper, the Minister of Information, to sharpen up the BBC's German output by delivering some talks over the radio. There, he met Richard Crossman and made an immediate impact. In the wake of the defeat of France, it was Delmer who famously rebutted Hitler's appeal to 'common sense', made at a triumphal Reichstag rally on 19 July 1940. Delmer listened to the Führer, in a fit of hubris, boasting that 'Providence' had selected him to destroy 'a great empire' unless the British saw 'reason' and sued for peace. Within an hour and without any reference to anyone except the BBC, but with the authority of one whom Hitler had consulted in the past as to the mood of the British people, Delmer delivered his response in personal terms – and on behalf of 'we here in Britain'. The language was not, as Delmer later confessed, 'diplomatic ... or very elegant', but Hitler would have got the message when informed that 'we hurl it right back at you, right in your evil smelling teeth ...' A distinctive style of broadcasting, that Delmer was to later make his own once in Bedfordshire, was also born in that transmission.

In his failure to refer to any Foreign Office personnel (though the Germans certainly took the broadcast to be an official response), Delmer opened himself up to criticism from the officious minded, as well as from a residue of pacifists and appeasers. Delmer escaped higher sanction, however, as he had clearly articulated the response of most in Britain, and it was with some pride that he later found that he had earned himself the position of number thirty three on the Gestapo hit list of those to be apprehended in the event of Germany's successful occupation of Britain. It evidently endeared Delmer to Ingrams who extended his initial invitation and arranged a meeting with Valentine Williams. Unfortunately, Delmer's spontaneous riposte to Hitler had still not convinced everyone in the security services as to his patriotic integrity and, to his surprise, Williams' notification that a vetting process was about to be undertaken was not to lead to his appointment but to yet another rejection.

To judge from his own account, the next few weeks were spent footling around the margins of British counter-intelligence (working on behalf of S.I.S.), whilst continuing to write for the *Daily Express*. He assisted in unmasking a Nazi agent, who was masquerading as an American reporter and travelled to Lisbon serving in both journalistic and intelligence capacities. There, he made renewed associations with Germans who were fleeing Nazism so, whilst not yet fully deploying his talents, Delmer was making contacts with individuals (including the Hitler family's Jewish doctor who had bounced young Adolf on his knee), that would prove to be invaluable when he did so. It was whilst in Lisbon that the security services evidently had a change of heart and Ingrams promptly sent a telegram to Delmer, urging his return. Thus, in the early part of 1941, Sefton Delmer began the work that would entail a lengthy leave of absence from the *Express* and take him into Bedfordshire.

On the occasion of his first visit to CHQ, Delmer remembered that he was driven out of London in a 'vast Daimler'. He was not alone but had for company 'a German-Jewish economist from the Bank of England; a goatee-bearded, Harrow schoolmaster who was the expert on Spain; a portrait painter in RAF uniform; and a couple of girl typists'.[113] Carrying an appointment to meet Richard Crossman at an unspecified location, 'at last we drove into the little village of Woburn, turned right, and a few minutes later I found myself at the gates of Woburn Abbey'. This was the guard house and Delmer got no further until he signed the Official Secrets Act.

Delmer was at first accommodated at 'Larchfield', a substantial house in the nearby village of Aspley Guise and known by the coded prefix 'LF'. At Woburn he joined a small team that included Leeper, Walmsley, Ritchie Calder and Richard Crossman, whose task was to oversee the development of propaganda against the Germans. Whereas Crossman was responsible for 'white-ish' propaganda to Germany (that is to say his left wing inclined station appealed to 'Good Germans' to see the futility of following Nazism), the arrangement evolved whereby Delmer became the master of the darker side of things: 'never lie by accident, only deliberately' became their motto. A letter that he sent to Ingrams on 8 June 1941 emphasised the difference between the approaches:

> *The objective of LF is subversive… We are making no attempt to build up a political following in Germany. We are not catering for idealists… Our politics are a stunt. The purpose of this is to provide ourselves with a platform from which to put over our stuff…Our listeners are intended*

---

[113] Delmer, op. cit. p.34.

to feel that they are eavesdropping on the private wireless of a secret organisation; that Wehrmacht soldiers, the best element in the Volk, are being bumped off… whilst the SS party police are being given cushy jobs at home. And masses of stuff proving the corruption of the machine, the selfishness of its leaders. We concentrate our attacks on the lesser known political leaders.

He integrated intelligence gathering, as well as the output of broadcast and written propaganda and, in so doing, he and Ingrams recruited a formidable team, described by Asa Briggs as 'a brilliant, supremely loyal, motley band of writers and broadcasters'.[114] A number were drawn from Fleet Street, such as Karl Robson of the *News Chronicle*, who was already seconded to the War Office.

This 'motley band' also included Ellic Howe, a brilliant forger, whose encyclopaedic knowledge of printing styles had been somewhat under-employed up until that time. Entirely commensurate with the nature of what was dubbed the 'Phoney War' or 'Sitzkrieg', Ellic Howe had spent the early part of the conflict as a Lance-Corporal 'leading a distinctly al fresco existence' in charge of a Territorial Army anti-aircraft unit located in a field at Cardington, just outside Bedford. According to John Taylor, Howe was also given the assistance of another forger, this one of the illegitimate variety, who was released from prison in order to serve his country for the duration.[115] Also recruited into this side of the team (which was principally based in London) were two young illustrators, Marion Whitehorn and Liz Friedlander. In her early twenties, Marion Whitehorn had recently married Lt. Commander Colin McFadyen of Naval Intelligence, but was German by birth, having escaped from the country in September 1937. Although rejected by a succession of uniformed services, she was determined to make a more dedicated strike at a regime that she hated than merely working for the *Britain in Pictures* series published by Collins. This eventually led her to an interview with Sefton Delmer and some pretty intimidating staff officers who made a point of reminding the delicate young woman before them that should she ever talk about her work she would face 'twenty years with hard labour'.

---

[114] Briggs, op. cit.
[115] Howe, op. cit. p.13. Taylor, op. cit., p.73.

500 g Weizenmehl — Führergeschenk

Lebensmittelkarte

3 766068 ✳

FÜHRERGESCHENK

für Fronturlauber

500 g Marmelade — Führergeschenk

500 g Zucker — Führergeschenk

500 g Butter oder Margarine — Führergeschenk

500 g Nährmittel oder Hülsenfrüchte — Führergeschenk

An example of the output from Ellic Howe's forgers, packed at the Leagrave Press and dropped over German cities by the USAAF. This ration card – the Führer's Gift – was produced by Marion Whitehorn and Liz Friedlander. It allowed German soldiers on leave an allocation of basic foodstuffs. By the latter stages of the war these items were in very short supply and to be suspected of being involved in forgery ran the risk of incurring severe penalties (*Courtesy of Heather Woods*).

At the beginning of the war, proposals by Vernon Bartlett to drop forged ration cards had been vetoed by Neville Chamberlain as too underhand. Now, under Delmer's direction, the output of black printed matter was to increase significantly and Howe's contribution was to include all manner of tricks, some of which worked and some which didn't. They included a revival of the fake ration cards scheme, designed to disrupt and discredit the German food distribution system, and much of this sort of material was printed in great secrecy at Waterlows in Dunstable, Gibbs, Bamforth (the owners of the *Luton News*), as well as specialist printing firms in London.

* * *

A low power 7½ KW short wave transmitting station was established first at Gawcott, then at Potsgrove (a tiny hamlet close to Woburn), the two transmitters here being nicknamed 'Poppy' and 'Pansy'.[116] Broadcasts, however, were still not made live. They were recorded on to disc at improvised recording studios, initially at Whaddon Hall then later chiefly at Wavendon Towers (known as 'Simpsons' after the name of the nearest village, just over the Bedfordshire border), before being then taken by courier for transmission. This was a tricky technical operation and obviously diminished the 'live' feeling that Delmer was seeking to achieve, especially if the arm jumped whilst playing the disc. An early example of programming produced this way was *Wehrmachtsender Nord*, a bogus radio station ostensibly based in occupied Norway until February 1943. German intelligence apparently worked out that it was a British radio station but came to the erroneous deduction that this meant that the British were planning to invade Norway.[117]

'Aspidistra' the huge 600KW medium wave transmitter built at Crowborough, Sussex, transformed the capabilities of the broadcast teams, and its use from the autumn of 1942 coincided with the almost simultaneous move to purpose built studios at Milton Bryan (MB). Again, Harold Robin and Richard Gambier Parry, together with Ralph Murray, were the driving forces behind the establishment of these studios contained within their own secure compound. Now programmes could be produced live, transmitted via landline to Crowborough and broadcast to all parts of Germany via a transmitter so powerful that it could

The former black propaganda studios at Milton Bryan, photographed in 2006 *(Amy Rich)*.

---

[116] These were used, for example, to throw propaganda into North Africa directed at Rommel's Afrika Corps. Good information on the broadcasting techniques, mostly based within Buckinghamshire, is contained within chapter 3 of Taylor, op. cit.

[117] For some of the best details on the process of recording and broadcasting, as well as the sites involved see www.clutch.open.ac.uk/schools/emerson00/home

swamp or replicate the frequency of domestic German stations. Broadcast propaganda was transformed.

Although 'Simpsons' was still used for recording programmes broadcasting on the short wave frequency, the hub of creativity gravitated to Milton Bryan with numerous huts being added to the austere, brick built station designed by another member of the black propaganda team, Edward Halliday, a trained architect who was serving in the RAF. Each of the broadcasting and propaganda teams were known as Research Units or RUs. In addition to anti-German propaganda, by the end of 1941 RUs had been established that were directing their effort at Norwegians, French, Slovenes, Italians, Bulgarians, Serbs, Croats, Poles, Belgians, Dutch, Romanians, Hungarians, Danes, Czechs, and Slovaks. By October 1943 there were twenty four RUs, but black propaganda employed as many as forty eight different RUs at various points during the war.

The RUs worked under three broad headings. There were the 'Freedom Stations' that blatantly broadcast against Germany and her collaborators. Second, there were the Co-operative Stations that endeavoured to work closely with local resistance organisations. Then there were the 'black' stations that pretended to be something that they were not. Some were very subtle, quite focused in their target audience. For example, *Blauwvoet* was an RU focused upon demoralising Belgian collaborators. *The Marshal's Order* aimed at the Romanian middle and upper classes, 'the audience being considered basically anti-German but still more anti-Russian'. The Hungarian *Magyar Nemzet* was targeted at 'opposition factions and middle class intellectuals with the object of diminishing all aid to Germany'. *Nova Evropa* pretended to broadcast from inside occupied Czech 'Protectorate'. *Danish Freedom* illustrated the difference that Delmer was bringing about: it took 'a strong line on personalities, the King, sabotage, and other subjects in a way which was not possible for the BBC'.[118] 'On the use of refugees, Delmer always had the greatest contempt for BBC staff,' observed Robert Walmsley, 'but maintained that there were excellent refugees to be used if you knew where to find them.'[119]

---

[118] FO 898/51. RU Papers: General Correspondence. National Archives.

[119] Garnett, op. cit.

There is little doubt that some of these broadcasts were very effective but this could prove to be a double-edged sword. In his memoirs, Hugh Dalton recalled his amusement at hearing of a 'house to house search carried out by German troops in heavy boots' in Bucharest endeavouring to locate a Romanian 'Freedom Station' that was, in fact, broadcasting from Bedfordshire.[120] A coup for the propagandists, perhaps, but Dalton was aware as anyone else that this was rather less enjoyable for those who were on the receiving end of the Nazi's 'heavy boots'. They even had a station that had to pretend to be a Bulgarian collaborators' station run by Germans that would be conducted so badly that it would discredit the German cause in that country. They needed, therefore, two people from amongst the refugees who could speak fluent Bulgarian with a German accent. Delmer found them.

One can picture the highly charged atmosphere within the facility at Milton Bryan as Sefton Delmer describes the eclectic mix that greeted the representatives of the various allied intelligence services when visiting this picturesque corner of Bedfordshire:

> A more weirdly assorted group it would have been hard to find in Britain at that time. German refugees, German prisoners, Balkan beauties, Italians, Hungarians, Rumanians, Bulgarians, British girl secretaries, British and American editors and executives, all jostled each other in the passages of MB talking their different languages and their assorted varieties of English. Each of them dressed as the fancy took him or her.

The last sentence is a reference to a recurring feature of the propaganda operations in Bedfordshire and neighbouring counties. Paraphrasing the military historian John Keegan ('inside every army is a crowd struggling to get out'), David Reynolds observed 'that one might add, inside every soldier is a civilian trying to escape'. The propaganda operations in Bedfordshire gave the uniformed civilian a length of leash not normally allowed others in the services.[121] Phil Luck recalled that the transmitting stations at Gawcott and Potsgrove were run on civilian lines, despite the

---

[120] Dalton, op. cit.

[121] Reynolds, David. *Rich Relations. The American Occupation of Britain 1942-1945* (Phoenix Press, 2000), p. 61.

fact that many of the workers were put in Observer Corps uniform. The Warrant Officer in charge of the former was simply known as 'Mr Pryke' whilst others even called him by his Christian name, Tommy.

There was also an informality derived from expediency as there wasn't time to train people – the war effort was recruiting people with existing expertise built up in other spheres and, in a sense, were donning a uniform just for the duration. Delmer himself was extremely casually attired, in stark contrast to the usually published photographs that show him clean shaven, or even wearing the uniform that he was to later sport whilst serving as part of the allied occupation forces in Germany. Delmer wore a beard, which he had trimmed in the basement barber at Bush House on his weekly visits to the capital. In fact, dressed in open neck shirt and old suede jacket that had seen service when covering the Spanish Civil War, he even looked quite scruffy to the recollection of one of his drivers.[122]

At Milton Bryan, furthermore, there was a strong sense that Delmer revelled in the potential of this intensely creative, combustible and polyglot environment.

> Into new barracks hastily erected in the compound of MB marched Intelligence teams, editorial writers, speakers and secretaries from Italy, Hungary, Bulgaria and even Rumania. Our canteen became a tower of Babel, as dark-eyed gypsy beauties from the Balkans flirted with my fair-haired German prisoners over toad in the hole, powdered egg omelettes, spam fritters, soya bean sausages, and other irresistible delicacies from the repertory of war-time cooks.[123]

Delmer was clearly delighted with the experience of one young German POW, Major Wolfgang von Virchow, who had been persuaded to work for the British, under the direction of Molly Fitzpatrick.[124] An artilleryman, and a member of an old Prussian family, he first became friends with Dennis Clarke, a former journalist who as a soldier lost an

---

[122] Interview with Denis Dolton, 26 August 2005.

[123] Delmer, op. cit. p.103.

[124] A cartoon of whom Delmer described as 'a witty young German speaking Irishwoman' is reproduced on p.53 of Taylor, op. cit.

arm in the same battle in which Virchow had been captured, and then became engaged to Marianne, one of the Balkan secretaries – and a Jew.

The broadcasters, swollen by expatriates of all nationalities who had escaped from Europe as well as an increasing number of German POWs, were accommodated in requisitioned homes in the Woburn area. As the numbers increased, more and more houses were taken over to the extent that Aspley Guise (often known by its abbreviation AG) and the purpose built studio at Milton Bryan 'resembled German enclaves in the Bedfordshire countryside', in Howe's words. From the end of 1941 the numbers of foreigners steadily rose as the foreign language output increased and following the successful Normandy landings in 1944, further houses had to be requisitioned to accommodate the additional Germans who already had seven houses around Aspley Guise and Woburn Sands.

Some RUs shared individual houses in Aspley Guise, others shared a 'housemaster' or 'housemistress'. The Slovak RU shared a housemaster with the Czechs and both seemed to share a house with the Poles (given the abbreviated designation THA). Additionally, the Slovak RU comprised two permanent scriptwriters and speakers, one part-time scriptwriter and speaker and one female Slovakian secretary and speaker. From September 1943, they were producing four programmes a week.[125]

* * *

Although broadcasts were made in numerous European languages, by far the most important were those made in German, as efforts worked towards the fulfilment of Ingrams' and Delmer's dream of producing a 'genuine' German forces radio station. One of these Germans was

---

[125] Ibid. Other RUs were housed in the following: LF (Central and Eastern Europe – probably Leys Farm); NL – the Grange, Newton Longville (Italy and South Eastern Europe); BH (Free French – possibly Braystone House); NHH (Low Countries); TM (German – The Mount); RAG – Rookery (German); DE – Dawn Edge (German); GLM (Scandinavian); WPF (Scandinavian – possibly either Wavendon or Woburn Park Farm); THA (Polish & Czech – possibly The Holt); MAH (French – possibly The Mount, Aspley Heath). The Italians were additionally at QC and 43 Aspley Hill. Delmer's empire also had Netherhill House, Broughton Rectory and 'The Shrubbery' in Aspley Guise, plus the Rectories at Holcot, Woburn and Tingrith – another French post. The initials were designated as part of a wider security procedure to limit knowledge of the RU locations.

Corporal Peter Secklemann, otherwise known as 'Paul Sanders'. Born in Berlin, he had left Germany in 1937 and, like many expatriates who volunteered to serve, was placed in the Pioneer Corps. It was under Delmer, however, that his talent for mimicking the upper class Prussian Junker drawl was to find its full fruition. Sanders became 'Der Chef' – The Chief or 'The Boss' (an echo of what Hitler himself had been called by his subordinates). Sanders' radio character appeared in the broadcast Gustav Siegfried Eins (GS1) and impersonated a type easily recognisable to Germans – a nationalist reactionary officer of the old school. A 'tough Prussian patriot', in his broadcasts 'Der Chef' railed against the British (the King was described as 'a stuttering fool') but also 'the corruption and depravity prevailing in ... Nazi regime.' This especially targeted Himmler and his SS but was careful to exclude Hitler. The Nazis were portrayed as incompetent self-serving idlers that were bent on betraying the army and under whom Germany was 'going to the dogs'.126 The idea was 'not to win Germans to our side but to turn Germans against Germans and thereby weaken the German war machine'.

Preparations for the first broadcast of *Gustav Siegfried Eins*, on 23 May 1941 coincided with Rudolf Hess' abortive peace mission to Britain. From the outset *GS1* introduced techniques that were to become Delmer's trademark, spicing up carefully researched material drawn from a variety of intelligence sources, with a bit of inspired guesswork. As with all subsequent programmes produced by his black propaganda teams, the first broadcast of *GS1* implied that it was a well established programme that the German listener had just happened to stumble upon. Taking advantage of their good fortune provided by Hess' brainstorm, Sanders quickly hit his stride:

> *Now at last I can answer questions sent in after our last broadcast when I warned listeners that Hess was about to do something stupid... First of all let's get this straight: this fellow is by no means the worst of the lot. He was a good comrade of ours in the days of the Freikorps, but like all the rest of this clique of cranks, megalomaniacs, string pullers and parlour Bolsheviks who call themselves our leaders, he simply has no nerves for*

---

126 National Archives, FO 898/60. Papers released January 2007 thanks to the perseverance of Lee Richards and the Freedom of Information Act. When 'Der Chef' acquired an 'adjutant', it was in the form of another political dissident, Johannes Reinholz who also wrote the scripts. GS1 ran between May 1941 and November 1943.

a crisis. As soon as he learns the darker side of the developments that lie ahead, what happens? He loses his head completely, packs himself a satchel of hormone pills and a white flag, and flies off to throw himself - and us - on the mercy of that flat-footed bastard of a drunken old Jew, Churchill. And he overlooks completely that he is the bearer of the Reich's most precious secrets, all of which the f*****g British will suck out of him as easily if he were a bottle of Berliner Weisse.[127]

The line 'the darker side of the developments that lie ahead' was an example of the inspired guesswork that punctuated the work of Delmer's teams. It was also a lucky one because, just four weeks later, Germany invaded the Soviet Union. Ironically enough, this was something which Hess was assuring his British captors was not imminent, but for listeners in Germany it indicated that here was a credible renegade station with access to classified information at the very highest level.

There was plenty more where this came from. With every broadcast proceeded by the announcement '*Es Spricht der Chef!*' ('The Chief is Speaking!'), Sanders railed against the passive *Luftwaffe* (Göring's fiefdom), for failing to take adequate revenge for the RAF's bombing of German cities. He denounced 'shirkers' with Nazi Party connections who stayed at home whilst the wives of serving soldiers were forced into factories. He detailed the cover up of the case of a named SS *Oberführer* who requisitioned an empty hospital ward in order to bed 'his minion' and then resisted attempts by doctors and nurses to bring in wounded soldiers, firing his pistol at them. Although the Reich's snoopers quickly worked out that this was a British station, nimble adjustments of the wavelengths on GS1's frequent repeats avoid the Nazis' attempts to jam its output. If SOE's Stockholm office was correct the bulk of the German public, on the other hand, seemed to have genuinely believed that they had stumbled upon an authentic voice whose 'sender is run and financed by army circles'.[128] According to the Swedish source, GS1 was 'the most listened to in the Third Reich'. Interrogation of German POWs seemed to confirm this, with one man telling his captors that it was common knowledge that GS1 was broadcast from the Hamburg area.

---

[127] Translated extract broadcast on BBC Radio 4, *The Radio War*, 1993. The *Freikorps* was a quasi-military right wing organisation, formed in the chaos of Germany after World War One. *Berliner Weisse* is a low alcohol wheat beer, usually sweetened with syrup.

[128] National Archives, FO 898/60.

The language of 'Der Chef' may have been full of 'barrack room adjectives', but its authenticity was also good enough to fool the US Embassy in Berlin.[129]

It also ran Delmer into trouble at cabinet level. In June 1942, Sir Stafford Cripps, a puritanical Labour member of the coalition War Cabinet, wrote to Delmer's ultimate boss, Foreign Secretary Anthony Eden, bristling with indignation.[130] 'My Dear Anthony ... As you read this letter you will see why I could not dictate it to my young lady typist' began Cripps. He then went on to explain that he had happened to listen in to GS1 and was at first astonished to hear Paul Sanders in full flow (vividly recounting the details of a supposed orgy involving a German Admiral, his mistress, four sailors and an army helmet), and then outraged to find that this was actually a British station. As far as Cripps' was concerned, GS1 contained 'the worst foul and filthy pornography of which I am sure you cannot be aware'. Having recently returned as British Ambassador to Moscow, Cripps pointed out that such pornography could only serve to undermine the integrity of Britain's standing with their Russian allies, to say nothing of the sensitivity of the poor Germans: 'the decent minded liberals, socialists, Catholics, protestants ... will be disgusted'.

Eden passed Cripps' protest down to Delmer, via Leeper and Bruce Lockhart. Delmer made his case, explaining the method that lay behind GS1. He reiterated that the crudity was to attract the listeners, to make them susceptible to the hidden propaganda and, in any case, Cripps' repugnance was misplaced: 'There is a sadism in the German nature quite alien to the British nature and German listeners are very far from being revolted by the sadistic content of some of these broadcasts.'

The natural instinct on the part of Leeper and Lockhart to defend their 'rare artist' was made easier by the fact that both could smell a rat. In his letter Cripps had acknowledged that he had asked 'someone who could understand to listen in'. Furthermore, enquiries established that the broadcast dated from the previous autumn – when Sir Stafford was still

---

[129] When America joined the war it fell to SOE's Washington representative, David Bowes-Lyon, to explain to President Roosevelt that one of their key sources of German information came from Bedfordshire.

[130] National Archives. FO 898/60.

serving in Moscow. Leeper and Lockhart saw right through Cripps' synthetic outrage, perceiving that some individuals who had been 'edged out' at Woburn had been 'getting at' the Labour minister, tapping his moral indignation to pursue their own ends. As Bruce Lockhart put it, 'there is obviously a cabal working in London against the Country'.[131] This made Leeper's job of briefing Eden much easier. The Foreign Secretary should turn down flat any offer of a meeting with Cripps and even if, on this occasion, Delmer had gone 'too far' he wouldn't want to apply any 'hampering restrictions'. Furthermore, 'If in the Secret Service we were to be too squeamish, the Secret Service could not operate ... this is war with the gloves off.' Who cared what nice Germans might think? For that matter, the same sentiment applied to Britain's eastern ally: 'Have you ever met an Englishman who could shock a Russian?' noted Leeper in a postscript.

* * *

The brothers Max and Heinrich Braun arrived in August 1941. They helped provide the welter of data that were to give the German broadcasts such a high degree of authenticity. Max initiated a vast card index drawing upon the details of interrogation of captured German servicemen as well as an extensive cull of German newspapers (including the family announcements). This index, providing the minutiae of the lives of German citizens – their dwellings, their occupations, their families, their tastes, even their slang – was the source material that made the broadcasts so realistic.

Two other key appointments were Clifton Child and C. E. Stevens. Child had originally been a Foreign Office PID appointment to Woburn but stayed on to work with Delmer at his invitation once the PID function at the Abbey had been wound up. Child was placed in charge of the Intelligence Section, applying his first class mind to drawing together and making sense of the myriad evidence that was being collected, and which could be used for propaganda purposes. Of similar calibre was C. E. Stevens, recommended by Ingrams and seconded from the Ministry of Economic Warfare. Widely read and knowledgeable,

---

[131] Ibid. In his reply Eden noted 'I fear that the Woburn establishment has two very bitter opponents in Mr Voigt (Right-Wing) and Mr Thomas (Left-Wing) ... both harbour bitter resentment.'

Stevens possessed the rare gift of a virtually photographic memory. He perfectly complimented Child, and Delmer was willing to draw upon the judgement of both men in dealing with some of the more dubious of human sources.

Sefton Delmer scanning for sources. In the words of Hugh Dalton, Delmer brought 'a crude and earthy ingenuity all his own' to Britain's black propaganda (*Hulton Getty*).

Delmer's genius lay in part due to his ability to appreciate not only the need for propaganda efforts to be co-ordinated, but to dovetail these with intelligence gathering in order that they could all be applied to immediate strategic requirements. Notwithstanding the constant sniping and jockeying for position between the various propaganda and psychological warfare sections, Delmer was able to both draw, and most crucially collate for optimum effect, information from a wide range of sources. Data was gathered from Bletchley Park, SIS, the Foreign Office, the BBC, POW interrogation and forces' intelligence sections. This included SHAEF, the inter-allied organisation under Eisenhower that was co-ordinating the assault upon German occupied Europe. For example, Delmer's staff would take the broad details of an air raid over

Germany and then, using the meticulous detail contained in the card indexes, utilise these combined sources to provide the basis of an immediate broadcast which would contain an authentically local resonance for German audiences. By contrast, Robert Walmsley's specialist function at Woburn was to analyse the output of German news propaganda, a methodology that became so sophisticated as to be able to anticipate Nazi strategic intentions. He had noted that Goebbels had a tendency not to boast of any achievement unless it was a near certainty (the use of V bombs were an example of this). This analysis Walmsley passed on to Delmer and Crossman for use in their respective wings of propaganda.

Leonard Ingrams was certainly feeding much additional information (as well as German refugees) from MEW but a key source of information lay at the Admiralty, the Royal Navy being conspicuous amongst the services for being especially co-operative. This in part led to the effort concentrated upon U-boat crews by *Atlantiksender*, the black propaganda programme created specifically for German submariners (at this stage the Navy being engaged in a life or death struggle with German submarines in the Atlantic). Simultaneously a desperate cat and mouse code breaking game was being played out between Bletchley Park and its German rivals. The Naval Intelligence Division that had so successfully operated in World War One was resurrected under Admiral J. H. Godfrey, 'a steely irascible taskmaster whose high-handedness antagonizes many, but who manifestly got things done'.[132]

Godfrey, regarded in some quarters as pro-German in many of his views, was also described as someone with 'a wonderful talent' for recruiting the right people (a process that he had the foresight to start before the war). Two of these key appointments were Lieut. Donald McLachlan and Godfrey's Personal Assistant, Lieut. Ian Fleming, the future creator of 'James Bond'. Each were responsible for vital sections and both enthusiastically assisted Sefton Delmer, even after Godfrey's departure in 1942, making every effort to ensure that there was integration between operational policy and propaganda. Donald McLachlan also established a Bedfordshire base, taking the tenancy of 'Woodcote', yet another

---

[132] Lycett, Andrew. *Ian Fleming* (Weidenfeld and Nicolson, 1995). Godfrey is one of the leading candidates as the model for the character of 'M' in Fleming's 'James Bond' novels.

Woburn Estate cottage. In his crisply written (but also guarded) memoirs, he underlined the depth of the collaboration between intelligence and propaganda, and, in a deft sideswipe at other sectors of the British war effort, McLachlan observed, 'Fighting commanders, technical experts and political leaders are liable to ignore, under-rate or even despise intelligence. Obsession and bias often begin at the top.'[133] Not so the Navy whose experience of the Norwegian defeat in 1940 underlined the vital importance of local intelligence – and the more localised that it was the shorter the time span for its collection and subsequent use.[134]

Naval Intelligence worked closely with the personnel based at the POW interrogation centres at Latimer and Beaconsfield, feeding all relevant information on to both the PWE and BBC, (the latter in turn fed the information gleaned by its own Monitoring Service on to PWE). In respect of the latter, it is worth noting that Naval Intelligence didn't discriminate just in favour of 'black propaganda', feeding information for equivalent programmes provided by 'white'. When later serving as Director General of the BBC, Hugh Carleton Greene paid this (slightly cryptic) tribute in correspondence with McLachlan:

> *I can honestly say without hesitation that the material provided by your section in the Admiralty to the German Service programme for the German Navy was extremely good. I remember wishing at the time that we could get such good stories out of the War Office and the Air Ministry. You were not a nuisance at all.*[135]

A key source lay in neutral countries such as Sweden, where the Naval Attaché, Captain H. M. Denham, fought his own private war with the *Abwehr* under the leadership of Col. Hans Wagner. With many Swedish senior commanders harbouring pro German sentiments, Denham found

---

[133] McLachlan, Donald. *Room 39. Naval Intelligence in Action 1939-45* (Weidenfeld & Nicolson, 1968). McLachlan was careful to keep all cryptographic details out of the book. Correspondence between Godfrey and McLachlan emphasised how the latter's book was being published with the full approval of the Royal Navy, and that 'the security aspect is being taken care of'. McLachlan papers in Churchill College, Cambridge, MLBE 6/3.

[134] Ibid.

[135] Letter from Hugh Greene to Donald McLachlan, 14 April 1966. MLBE 6/3, Churchill College, Cambridge.

himself under surveillance from the Swedish police (reacting to pressure from Germany) whilst the British legation had to improve its own physical security with steel grids and shutters fitted onto a strong room. Under this pressure Denham endeavoured to obtain any information that he could from his cautious hosts amongst whom 'reticence was bought to a fine art in the conversation of every Swedish officer or Foreign Office official'.[136]

Any such knowledge that British naval intelligence gatherers could obtain, such as the location of German merchant shipping or *Kriegsmarine* movements against Britain's own vital convoys, was fed back to the NID. In turn, McLachlan ensured that the propaganda teams in Bedfordshire were fully informed in order that they could assist in every way possible. For example, one of Ellic Howe's tasks as printer and forger was to produce a bogus horoscope. This was to take advantage of the curious belief system of the Nazis (Hitler was reckoned to be an assiduous follower of astrology) which sought to replace Christianity with a mish-mash of Führer cult, folk religion, Nordic mythology and astrology. It also sought to take advantage of the endemic superstition amongst the U-Boat crews. *Der Zenit*, as it was called, sought to advise of auspicious and inauspicious times to put to sea (needless to say there were few good days). It was reinforced by broadcast horoscopes on *Atlantiksender* as well as advice provided by a 'medium'. This role was played by another German refugee, Margit Maas, with some difficulty as she kept giggling at the complete nonsense that she was supposed to be reading. McLachlan noted the frequency that British interrogators of POWs reported how landlocked Bedfordshire's *Atlantiksender* carried a double effectiveness because prior suspicion that they had been listening to a British black propaganda station all along did not necessarily diminish its impact. On the contrary, the U-Boat crews were impressed (and a little demoralised) at the extent of supposed British knowledge about their activities that was evident in their propaganda broadcasts.

Recruited into Naval Intelligence over a good lunch with Admiral Godfrey at the Carlton Grill, Ian Fleming rose under his mentor's patronage to the rank of Commander, being seated in Room 39 adjacent to Godfrey's office next door. Nicknamed the 'chocolate sailor', Fleming

---

[136] Ibid. 1/9.

was, according to McLachlan, an inveterate name dropper but he provided such indispensable service that he soon reached the point where he 'had a finger in virtually everything'. More than just a secretary and gatekeeper, Fleming was constantly encouraging Godfrey (his boss observing that Fleming 'was familiar with all NID secrets during World War Two'), and continually coming up with new schemes, most of which were consigned to the waste bin.[137]

'The Chocolate Sailor': Ian Fleming during his time in Naval Intelligence (*Provenance unknown*).

Delmer and Fleming were already familiar with one another having forged a friendship in the spring of 1939 over an 'indigestible breakfast' of caviar, cream and Russian pancakes (they washed them down with vodka) whilst in a Pullman car that was travelling through the Soviet Union towards Moscow. Delmer was there in his capacity as foreign correspondent of the *Daily Express*, Fleming ostensibly fulfilling a similar role for *The Times*, although Delmer suspected that he was on some sort of espionage work. Six months later, when Delmer visited Fleming in his 'vast barn' of an office, the latter took him next door and introduced Delmer to Godfrey and presently to McLachlan in the Naval Propaganda section.

Fleming had already broadcast for the BBC on their German service but black propaganda was something else altogether. In the opinion of one of Fleming's biographers, Andrew Lycett, 'Delmer's extravagant untruths appealed to the fantasist and prankster in Ian.. Fleming's future wife, Ann, put another perspective upon their relationship when she first was introduced to Delmer: 'He is a clever, interesting man and rouses all Ian's brain mania, plus his sublimated homosexuality. Still, despite Ian's possessiveness, it was an amusing evening.'[138] Fleming paid visits to

---

[137] Pearson, op. cit. Rosenberg, Bruce A. & Stewart, Ann Harleman *Ian Fleming* (Twayne, 1989).

[138] Lycett, op. cit. On one occasion Fleming dined with the Delmers at their Lincoln's Inn apartment together with a house party that included Leonard and Victoria Ingrams, Prince Bernhard of the Netherlands and Martha Huysmans (the daughter of the Belgian Prime Minister). The dinner party was drawing to a close when a bomb exploded nearby and blew the 200 year old staircase out into the street. Retaining impeccable manners and a commendable sang-froid, Bernhard picked himself up, dusted himself down and, after thanking the Delmers for 'a most enjoyable evening' lowered himself twenty feet down to the next surviving remnant of staircase and left. After a short period (and a couple more drinks), Fleming duly followed.

Delmer at Aspley Guise, and was part of Sefton and Isabel's party that holidayed to North Cornwall. Always ready to come up with an original idea Fleming even tried his own form of interrogation by taking captured German naval officers (including those from the *Bismarck*) out to lunch in order to lure them into loquacious indiscretions. The plan unfortunately backfired as Fleming, a bit of a lightweight in the drinking stakes, got hopelessly drunk first and into trouble with Godfrey.

German personnel using a military version of the Hellschreiber (*provenance unknown*).

A key tool for Delmer was a *Hellschreiber* news teleprinter which was installed in the newsroom at MB situated next to his office. This was a mechanism by which Dr Goebbels sought to communicate simultaneously with all German news agencies via his centralised DNB (*Deutsches Nachrichtenburo*), yet another means by which his Department of Propaganda and Enlightenment sought to control and co-ordinate all information. One DNB *Hellschreiber* was inadvertently left behind upon the hurried departure of German correspondents in 1939 – and Delmer got his hands on it. This meant that he was able to obtain information from the heart of the Nazi propaganda and news machine as quickly as any German news agency. Unlike them, however, Delmer was not so inhibited as to wait from guidance from Berlin. It was thus possible for German civilians or servicemen to receive their news first from a Milton Bryan German broadcast – all with Delmer's ingenious slant, of course.

This method can be contrasted with PID's efforts, initially relying upon German newspapers flown in from neutral Sweden, Spain and Portugal by the RAF. Because this could be done no more than once a week, much of the information was too out of date to be of any more than the most general use. This became refined, with a Press Reading Bureau being established in Stockholm that served to trawl though European newspapers before telegraphing back extracts. These were reproduced by Walmsley's section in a daily 'News Digest' that would run to as many as fifty eight pages.

Delmer was eventually housed at 'the Rookery' in Aspley Guise (to be known as RAG), his previous home at 'Larchfield' being close to Crossman at 'Dawn Edge' (although Denis Dolton, one of his drivers, recalled also having to collect Delmer from the main hotel in the heart of the village). Their physical proximity notwithstanding, there were still security considerations imposed upon both households which meant that although Delmer and Crossman could visit each other, their wives could not, even though Zita Crossman had helped prepare 'Larchfield' for the arrivals of the Delmers. A plainly irritated Crossman (it didn't usually take much) sent a memo to Leeper: 'The Delmers and the Crossmans live the life of English émigrés in little Germanys. The little Germanys of DE and LF are adjacent. May not the wives as well as the husbands be permitted to cross the English corridor …?'[139] Crossman was more of an isolated Englishman than he thought as Delmer's household (at various times) included Rene Halke, Frank Lynder (the Sergeant'), Dr Leslie Beck, Otto John, Ernst Albrecht (Dr Ernst Adam), Alexander and Margit Maas. Ernst Albrecht and Alexander Maas were two early recruits, having first met Delmer in his time covering the Spanish Civil War, at a time when Maas was serving as a Captain in the International Brigade.[140]

Locals could hardly have missed the presence of so many foreign voices in their midst, nor the location of the Milton Bryan compound, but in this respect Bedfordshire and the Secret War coexisted rather than mixed. Standing Orders issued in July 1941 laid down the rules. All members of an RU household had to be approved by PWE's Col. Chambers, in his capacity as Security Officer, and they were not to discuss their work with the members of other RUs: 'As a general rule, members of one RU should not be informed of the existence of the other RUs.'

Access was generally restricted and controlled, with even the identity of each national RU being denoted by no more than a simple letter prefix, (the Italians got 'W' for 'Wop'). The door of each RU house had to be answered by an appointed servant or other British resident, telegraphing and phone calls were supervised, private ones being prohibited except in

---

[139] FO 898/51. National Archives.

[140] Garnett, op. cit.

an emergency. The non-British wives of RU members were not permitted to live in the RU house unless employed there. The members of the RUs were not encouraged to mix with the locals and forbidden to use the local public houses, including Woburn's *Bedford Arms*. The 'housekeeper' or 'housemaster' (who might be a local), was also sworn to silence under the terms of the Official Secrets Act and even Robert Walmsley, who ran the Analysis Department with a team of seven secretaries, was deliberately only given limited information about the RUs. Even the domestic staff assigned to each RU, normally able to access privileged information in any sort of establishment, acquired very little inside knowledge. Mary Neal, for example, worked as cook and housekeeper for a RU based at Broughton Old Rectory for six weeks. Overcoming an initial trepidation at having to share a house with eight foreign men that caused her to lock her bedroom door at night, Mary came to appreciate their company and was touched by a present that they gave her when she was transferred to new duties. It was not merely her deficiency in languages that meant that she never got to know their nationality because neither did she ever find out their names, nor even that of the house master.[141]

Milton Bryan's five acre compound was protected by a small company of special constables who, accommodated in a guard house at the entrance, were armed and were accompanied by Alsatian dogs. This feature was immediately noticed by Otto John, one of a handful of survivors of the savage backlash to the failed 1944 attempt to assassinate Hitler. After a series of adventures he made his way to Britain and was eventually recruited into the Delmer team via 'C' (the Head of MI6), and Bruce Lockhart. In his memoirs he clearly blurred Woburn and Milton Bryan, something that could be attributed in part to failing

Otto John *(Hulton Getty)*.

---

[141] Mary Neal, op. cit.

memory but perhaps also to a circuitous journey through blacked-out Britain. His recollection of his first nervous meeting with Delmer provides further testimony to the level of security that surrounded Bedfordshire's nest of dark arts practitioners.

> *We drove out of London on the Great North Road, stopping for tea in a small town, and in the evening arrived at the great gates of a park full of ancient tall trees. A blonde girl in a uniform was at the gate and she directed our driver through the blackness of the park. Finally the car stopped before an iron grille behind which was a door leading into a guard room. Through the half open door I could see men in uniform and sub-machine guns with their barrels glistening against the wall.*

> *A policeman came up to the car, took a careful look at our guide to identify her, opened the grille and let us through. A short distance farther on the car stopped once more in front of a hermetically blacked-out building. The girl in uniform asked me to get out, the captain and driver to wait in the car. I felt uneasy. The girl led me along a brilliantly lit corridor to a door above which was a red light...*

Otto John was then greeted by Sefton Delmer.[142] To his surprise and disappointment, his anti-Nazi credentials did not give him a free hand. Taken under the wing of Clifton Child, John was questioned (talking openly proved to be a novel and curiously difficult experience for him) but, as Delmer later confirmed, higher authorities had ordered that he should never be allowed to be broadcast and had to work within very strict parameters.

Already working amongst Delmer's small personal team by the time that Otto John arrived was the future novelist, Muriel Spark. Escaping the claustrophobic bigotry of the white community in southern Africa, and a disastrous marriage, Spark had arrived in England in the spring of 1944 looking for some way to contribute to the war effort. At an interview in the secretarial division of an employment bureau, she fell into conversation concerning literature with the Recruiting Administrator. The latter then pushed aside the index of secretarial jobs that were on her desk and reached for another card in her desk drawer. This led to an

---

[142] John, Otto. *Twice Through the Lines* (Futura, 1972). John was given the name Oskar Jurgens.

Muriel Spark (*The National Library of Scotland*).

appointment in a room at the top of Bush House, 'a kind of eyrie overlooking London'. 'The immensely large and fat man,' (Delmer) who interviewed her in the company of his secretary (Betty Colbourne) 'looked too big for the room.' Following the successful outcome of the meeting, in which she was told her duties but not the precise nature of her work, Spark had to wait a further three weeks whilst her security credentials were cleared by the security services. Should anyone be so indiscrete as to ask about the work that she did, Spark was advised to simply reply that she worked for the Foreign Office.[143]

* * *

Hugh Dalton's ministry was one of three departments that made up the Political Wartime Executive, an attempt to co-ordinate propaganda, intelligence, information and covert operations. The other departments represented by the Foreign Office and the Ministry of Information, and whose ministers were (for the most part of the war) Anthony Eden and Brendan Bracken (a confidant of Churchill and succeeding Duff Cooper) respectively. So, instead of one minister, PWE had three. It functioned as a standing Ministerial Committee, meeting from September 1941, with day-to-day running entrusted to Robert Bruce Lockhart (the Foreign Office appointee), Reginald Leeper and Brigadier Dallas Brooks, head of the military wing. Dalton described Brooks as 'another key man at Woburn … He had a very smooth manner and keen powers of observation', but things were less smooth at the top where every impression is of a very uncomfortable senior triumvirate. Bracken was

---

[143] Spark, Muriel. *Curriculum Vitae. Autobiography* (Constable, 1992).

Dalton's equal in abrasiveness and intellect and, whilst he didn't have the standing in the Conservative Party that Dalton had amongst Labour (a card that the latter was quite willing to play in disputes), Bracken did have the Prime Minister's ear and was defter in the art of political manoeuvring.

Brendan Bracken and Vernon Bartlett, July 1941 *(Hulton Getty)*.

Taking over from a succession of short lived Ministers of Information, Bracken was determined to make good the ground that Dalton had bullied from his predecessors, pursuing what was described as 'a vendetta' against the Minister for Economic Warfare even to the extent of refusing to let his staff talk to SOE.[144] One has to feel a measure of sympathy for Eden in such difficult company (whose refined manners did not inhibit Bracken from picking a quarrel with him also), and gatherings were punctuated by 'futile, infuriating and time wasting rows'.[145] Since Bracken was to add to Woburn's company of heavy-duty drinkers, one has to feel a little pity for the domestic staff as well: precious half day's holidays that commenced with the clearing of luncheon were

---

[144] Boyle, Andrew. *Poor Dear, Brendan. The Quest For Brendan Bracken* (Hutchinson, 1974).

[145] Dalton, op. cit.

interminably delayed once the Minister of Information got his hands on the after-dinner whiskey bottle.[146] Bruce Lockhart's diary entry for 26 November 1940 encapsulates the bitterness, the tension and the personal effect of the pressure upon these individuals:

> There is a huge battle going on about control of propaganda in the field. SO2 want this. Rex is opposed but is likely to lose the fight. The whole organisation is at sixes and sevens. Rex and Jebb are fighting. Whole thing is disgusting. Hours, days, weeks are wasted on the personal questions, and no work is done. Drank too much.[147]

The creation of PWE had served to intensify rather than harmonise the infighting in Whitehall, the BBC and at Woburn. Harman Grisewood (a BBC official who was appointed to assist Ivonne Kirkpatrick, a senior Foreign Office mandarin who had been imposed upon the Corporation to act as an 'advisor' in February 1941), described the whole cast of colourful characters in London and Bedfordshire as being like something out of 'a long Tolstoyan novel'.[148] According to Grisewood:

> The main structure of the 'novel' was the tension between the PWE people, with the headquarters at the ducal mansion Woburn Abbey, and the BBC people at Bush House. The tension was basically a power struggle in which the men at Woburn wanted to dominate and direct BBC's service in detail.

Although there were those at the BBC who resented Kirkpatrick's imposition, according to Grisewood he defended the BBC against attempts to control from Woburn. Another of Gaitskell's biographers summarised the whole propaganda mess thus:

> It was troubled by a series of distinct but overlapping conflicts. There were differences about the content of propaganda between Left and Right; personal rivalries amongst the propagandists, among the bureaucrats and between the two groups; and clashes between the staff and the Minister. There was departmental friction between Whitehall ministries and new

---

[146] Mary Neal, op. cit.

[147] Young, op. cit. 26 November 1940.

[148] Grisewood, Harman. *One Thing At A Time. An Autobiography* (Hutchinson, 1968).

> Whitehall outfits; between the Foreign Office which was "slow to realise the importance of broadcasting" and the Woburn enthusiasts with their "tendency to try to make foreign policy by means of propaganda", and above all between MEW and the Ministry of Information, which had been left in charge of "open propaganda".[149]

Grisewood was pointing out the tensions inherent within the wartime political coalition, where personal and departmental enmities were given extra spice by the presence of party rivalry. The Conservative-Labour schism at PWE between Bracken and Dalton found its Bedfordshire dimension where 'Leeper's Sleepers' were being challenged by a Socialist element led by Gaitskell, Crossman and Martelli. Bruce Lockhart, who did not possess a high regard for Leeper, supported Dalton's reforms in principle but 'the methods chosen are wrong …This is no way to run a show'.[150] Churchill eventually imposed a ceasefire in February 1942 by promoting Dalton to the post of President of the Board of Trade, although the two remaining ministers of the committee continued to meet. Dalton's successor as the head of SOE, R. C. Palmer (3rd Earl Selbourne), although a friend of Churchill, lacked Dalton's presence or desire to control, neither was he given oversight of propaganda. These factors were to have profound implications for the operations at Woburn.

* * *

PWE had evolved during the summer of 1941 to the point that, by August, there was 438 staff working at Woburn Abbey, like 'a little village' in its own right according to the recollection of Mary Neal. The death of the 11th Duke in 1940 permitted expansion into the Abbey proper, to the occasional consternation of Abbey staff who, on one occasion, found the Italian team lighting a primus stove that was placed upon one of the antique carpets. There were so many windows that, during winter, black out operations had to begin around 14.30, (and when the teams of Bletchley Park WRENS were billeted there the black out curtains became doubly important lest they provide a bathtime show that was visible from a number of vantage points outside the Abbey).

---

[149] Williams, Philip M. *Hugh Gaitskell* (OUP, 1982).

[150] Young, op. cit. 7.2.1941.

The Abbey figure of 438 personnel, however, represented a peak as the 'white' part of the Woburn work was ultimately to lose its fight against central control. Dalton had immediately spotted that Leeper and the other officials were keen to evade ministerial oversight and went further in asserting that he only ever visited Woburn out of a sense of ministerial duty in order to provide the required 'control and stimulus' so as to shake things up. In a meeting with Bruce Lockhart and Bracken he made his views clear: 'I had no doubt that my frequent visits to, and detailed interest in CHQ, had been essential in order to get things moving and properly staffed. It had been necessary to take strong action in order to remove certain people, e.g. Valentine Williams'.[151]

In fact, Bruce Lockhart also swiftly came to the view that the Bedfordshire operations were too remote for adequate ministerial control or for close liaison with the rest of the 'white' propaganda effort. 'Rex undoubtedly suffers and will continue to suffer from being down here' noted Lockhart of a man whose 'absence from London does and *must* handicap him – and us'. Routing intelligence material to Woburn before the staff in the capital (based at Bush House, also the home of the BBC World Service) got to see it was reckoned to be especially unsatisfactory and telephone communication frequently failed, but there were suggestions also that Leeper wanted to ensure his personal safety by putting some distance between him and the blitzed capital: in short, 'Rex was afraid of bombs'.[152]

Despite Leeper's resistance, this scepticism towards the value of Woburn Abbey was also shared by Brendan Bracken. In March 1942 the Minister was at last given a formal conducted tour of the site, although before arriving he took a little detour *en route*: 'On way to Abbey passed Brendan's old house near Dunstable or, rather, turned up little side road for a few minutes to see it. Charming Queen Anne house (1710), lovely coloured brick, but situation low and uninspiring country around. Brendan put in many improvements...'[153]

---

[151] Pimlott, op. cit. 10 September 1941.

[152] Young, op. cit. 13 January 1940 and 1 January 1948. At other times in his diaries Lockhart noted Leeper's personal failings such as his inability to delegate, his frequent despondency or his poor nerve in a crisis. Leeper's protection against bombs was a substantial air raid shelter built in the grounds of the Rectory. This was surveyed by Kevan J. Fadden on behalf of Ampthill & District Archaeological and Local History Society in 1997.

[153] Ibid. 31 March 1942.

Once at the Abbey, Bracken's party was taken round by a plainly uncomfortable Leeper and, although expressing approval of the organisation, Bracken showed much more obvious enthusiasm for the Canaletto paintings and the architectural details than he did for the work of PID. He entertained the staff by consenting to be recorded by Gambier-Parry; declaring that he was 'glad that the house of the quisling Duke of Bedford is being put to the best possible use in this war'. Bracken made clear the problems presented by the geographical distance between Bedfordshire and London, however, not least in the waste of precious petrol in trundling large, official, chauffeur driven cars between the two.

Knowledge of this profligacy was already known at Cabinet level, at least since an early Campbell Stuart *debacle* involving the leader of the Labour Party, Clement Attlee, who was to serve as Churchill's Deputy Prime Minister in the wartime coalition. Staying at a nearby cottage, Attlee was due to be given a conducted tour of the Woburn operations with an official car sent to collect him. Stuart was apparently horrified to hear that a Rolls Royce had been dispatched to collect Attlee, something which Stuart was convinced would strike the leader of British Socialism as a quite unnecessary extravagance. A 'tawdry little pool car' was sent in haste to try and overtake the first car and to return with Attlee. Unfortunately, the Rolls got to his cottage first and was already waiting outside. Undeterred by the fact that Attlee had already seen the original car, the driver of the humbler vehicle pulled up, issued Stuart's countermanding order and sent the Rolls Royce away, returning with a bemused Attlee, doubtlessly reassured that every effort was being made to control expenses.[154] This sort of nonsense had to stop and it was left to Bruce Lockhart to move the bulk of the department back to Bush House during the remaining months of 1942.

Just a skeleton service was behind in the stable block, notably the Director of Plans and Campaigns, Ritchie Calder ('a pearl without price', according to historian Kenneth Young), and the substantial library of press cuttings and files. Woburn remained in theoretical reserve, however, and the onset of the V1 and V2 rocket campaign from 1944 onward did lead to a serious contemplation of once again relocating to

---

[154] Barman, op. cit.

'the country'. This would have been a tricky logistical exercise as by this time the Abbey was host to the large numbers of WRNS that were working in shifts at Bletchley Park, and the swift overrunning of the rocket bases by allied forces in Europe meant that this plan was never implemented.

* * *

Following the move of PWE to Bush House, the RUs remained behind. They were now free from the direct oversight of a powerful minister such as Dalton or Bracken, with the fluid propaganda situation seeing Bruce Lockhart taking over the day to day running of PWE. In the opinion of Cruikshank, Bruce Lockhart was 'anything but a dynamic leader. He seems to have been more interested in finding reasons for not doing things than in taking the lead in shaping the policies of the Executive'.[155] Given the immense pressure upon Lockhart who, it should be remembered, was not a politician with attendant political clout, this is arguably an unfair assessment and Dalton (not one to throw around compliments lightly) regarded Bruce Lockhart as a 'steadying influence'.

Whatever the validity of Cruikshank's judgement there is no doubt that the same could never be said of Dennis Sefton Delmer. Provided with the official designation of Director of Special Operations Against the Enemy and Satellites (although not until June 1944), Delmer was theoretically answerable for much of the duration through a line of accountability that ran upwards through Barman, Leeper (whilst the two of them remained in post) and to Lockhart. In practise, in the emergency of the war, he did what so many did: he just got on with it. He played his hand very carefully, Walmsley recalling his behaviour at the Woburn planning sessions: '... at these meetings Delmer used to assume an attitude of innocence and modesty ... Delmer never asked to control anything until it seemed not only ripe but over ripe'.[156]

Under Delmer's direction the RUs maintained a high degree of independence from central control, but it should be noted that they were given this luxury through the political cover that was provided by

---

[155] Cruikshank, op. cit.

[156] Garnett, op. cit.

Leonard Ingrams, and doubtless by Bruce Lockhart also. He was additionally fortunate that the senior officers of the newly formed and centralising Directorate of Political Warfare Intelligence (PWI) did not realise just how independent Delmer's team had become. Its Director, Brigadier Eric Sachs was of the view that a news teleprinter and some phone lines would be sufficient to serve the remaining black propagandists. He had no idea of the extent and means by which Delmer was gathering intelligence nor, astonishingly, of the existence of 'Aspidistra'.[157]

The RUs jealously guarded their autonomy not merely from the PWE in London, but from the influence of exiled foreign governments who, it was correctly felt, might attempt to exert a degree of control over the broadcasts that were being made to their own country in their language. The French RU, for example, was based at the Old Rectory in Toddington (Howe also refers to Tingrith), with the broadcasts being recorded at 'Simpsons'. *Radio Inconnue* purported to be broadcasting from the Paris area but the deception was not just aimed at the occupying Germans, its whereabouts were kept secret from De Gaulle, the leader of the Free French. As John Taylor records, the French broadcasters contained many varying stands of political opinion that were so politically, personally and emotionally opposed to one another that they had to be kept physically apart. There was absolutely no question of the French producing joint broadcasts, and this was perhaps one of the reasons why the output of the French RUs were 'completely overshadowed' (to quote Briggs) by the BBC French Service. This effectively promoted a sense of reassurance to France that they 'had lost a battle, but she had not lost a war', and through this introduced personalities such as Charles De Gaulle and Jean Moulin.

The Norwegian government in exile also presented a tricky diplomatic challenge. They knew the location of the Norwegian RU at Aspley Guise, and made some effort to control it through the Foreign Minister, Trygve Lie. The overworked Bruce Lockhart (also responsible for liaising with the Czechoslovak government) tried to gently dissuade Trygve Lie over lunch at Crowholt (Lockhart possessed 'the perfect bed-side manner', according to a contemporary French civil servant), whilst Tom

---

[157] Ibid.

The Tempsford crews carried no braver passenger than Jean Moulin. A young prefect, he attempted suicide rather than lie to satisfy the demands of the conquering Germans, was sacked by Vichy administration for refusing to comply with their orders, and then escaped to Britain. He became, in effect, De Gaulle's ambassador to the Resistance, making efforts to co-ordinate their activity. Captured by the Gestapo, he refused to name his associates despite torture, and was murdered by Klaus Barbie, dying on a train carrying him to a concentration camp (*Hulton Getty*).

Barman by-passed him altogether and worked with Oscar Torp, the Defence Minister. Barman's point, fully accepted by a sympathetic Torp, was simple: because the RUs dovetailed with strategic operations, they had a responsibility to the Ministry of Defence (whose Minister was Winston Churchill), and could not, therefore, fall under the control of any single body, whether it be PWE, SIS or a government in exile.[158]

---

[158] FO 898/51. National Archives. Barman, op. cit. Trygve Lie became the first Secretary General of the United Nations in 1946.

The biggest problem lay with the George Martelli's Italians. Temperamentally and politically diverse, in February 1942 Martelli was forced to admit:

> It would, however, be dishonest to pretend that this RU has ever been or will ever be a very pliable instrument. Its character and constitution both tend to make it independent. Its members are all men of strong political views, who regard themselves not as agents of the British Government but as allies co-operating in the democratic cause. This gives their work authenticity but makes it difficult for us to influence ... each of the five has his own political outlook ... It can be guided to a certain extent, but cannot be constrained.[159]

Unfortunately, part of the problem lay with Martelli himself. In the opinion of Tom Barman, Martelli was 'little more than a figure head' in a RU where the dominant figure was an 'Italian subject who was until recently a Fascist journalist'. This was Ruggero Orlando, who had been based in London and broke with the regime at the outbreak of war. That didn't save him from being interned on the Isle of Man, from where Martelli subsequently recruited him. Regardless of its personnel's feelings on the matter, the Italian RU *was* broadcasting to an enemy country, it just seemed that Martelli couldn't persuade his Latin colleagues of that unpalatable fact. There was, therefore, no serious attempt to undermine Italian morale. As Barman put it, 'their purpose seems to maintain Italian friendship after the war rather than get Italy out of the war as quickly as possible by means fair or foul'.

This position contrasted with Delmer's control over the Germans, the differences further highlighted by Martelli's poor use of Intelligence, his seeming reluctance to work with the new American allies, and that he seemed to be out of touch with the altered nature of that country under Mussolini. When it came to the deployment of propaganda Barman felt that Martelli had no awareness of the mass involvement in politics 'brought about by the centralising process, for good or evil, of Fascism'. Aiming at a middle-class, liberal political elite, Martelli 'conceives of Italy in terms of his sentimental memories of a country which for all practical purposes was ground out of existence in the first decade of

---

[159] National Archives. FO/898/60.

Fascism'. 'Why should Italians listen at all' queried Barman of a section which, in short, 'pulls it punches'.

Barman, Leeper and C. E. Stevens acted promptly, breaking up the troublesome RU (although Martelli was permitted to stay on as an Intelligence Officer), and recruiting new staff to give the section 'just the backbone it lacks'. Old stations were reorganised: *Radio Italia* now drew more heavily on POWS rather than anti-Fascist refugees. It purported to be an 'anti-Fascist group with no political bias, composed of a small body of well informed people with entrée into diplomatic circles in neutral countries'. Pretending to broadcast from northern Italy, POW interrogation indicated that it had a significant following amongst Italian soldiers in Libya. New stations were also created. *Italia Risorgi* aimed directly at patriots disillusioned by Fascism. Whereas the old output had featured 'stories about the closing down of factories', the new output, mixing 80% fact and 20% fiction, covered 'the story behind the stories about closing down factories'. Tales were now told of Italian units sacrificed on the Eastern Front to permit the Germans to retreat. Rumours were spread of Fascist Party corruption, favouritism and profiteering. There were also the wedge drivers: resentment was expressed at the swaggering 'arrogance of the German in the streets of Italy' (something that was supposed to be based upon the 'arrogant feeling of racial and sexual superiority' carried by German soldiers, and concomitant Italian sense of inferiority). The output was sharper, deliberately tailored to the operational requirements of SOE in Italy. It sounded just like Sefton Delmer's.

* * *

Of the effectiveness of Sefton Delmer's RUs, Walmsley emphasised 'even so, in spite of what he may say himself, it was his training that made them what they were'.[160] As to Delmer's method of working, Walmsley offered this insight:

I myself was a regular visitor to his house. He was not only an indefatigable but an unceasing worker, and after dinner, from nine until one or two in the morning, discussions on new projects and new themes

---

[160] Garnett, op. cit.

*were only broken by listening to his own station or even to rival ones ...
The more one reflects, the more one appreciates Delmer's complete
singleness of purpose and untiring application to work. I have seen him
squatting on his vast settee at RAG reading through a paragraph of a
talk, not once or twice but literally dozens of times, muttering crossly
to himself as he did so, then sending the wretched composer off to change
a few words and repeating the same process with the same talk almost
once an hour for three or four hours on end... Stopping in the middle
of a sentence, a worried wrinkle would appear on his large brow and,
retrieving at least one of his shoes, and giving his braceless trousers a
heave, he would stump rapidly out of the room to impart a new
brilliant idea to one of his writers, probably by that time in bed.*[161]

Delmer was additionally remembered by Ellic Howe as 'a hard and
exacting taskmaster but drove himself to the limit.' Because the working
hours were long he also endeavoured to cultivate an environment that
promoted creativity. 'I recall my impression that RAG's residents
constituted a closely knit family party,' noted Howe, an impression that
would have been accentuated by the many high ranking visitors who
travelled up at the weekend. 'We all lived in a gaggle and that helped
communication,' added Ingram Murray, whose father Ralph was one of
the team of gifted individuals who comprised this 'family party'.[162] Upon
his arrival into the embrace of the Delmer household Otto John was
amused to note that the German translation of 'Rookery' was
'krahenhorst', also a colloquialism for 'den of thieves' (an irony that
doubtless was not lost upon the mischievous side of Sefton Delmer).

Crossman's house, 'Dawn Edge,' also served as a recording studio in the
early days of the war, broadcasting *Sender Der Europaischen Revolution
European Revolution Station).* Described by David Garnett as 'really the
BBC in sheep's clothing', it was also summarised by historian Anthony
Howard as 'earnest, missionary ... (but) lacked the courage of its
fraudulent convictions'. It was overshadowed by Delmer's output.[163]

---

[161] Ibid.

[162] *The Secret Wireless War* (Grindelwald Productions). Delmer recalled that Otto John was a
particularly 'stimulating' member of the 'household brigade'.

[163] Pether, John and White, Peter. 'Political Warfare in Bedfordshire' *Bedfordshire Magazine*
vol. 26, no. 208, pp. 320-325. Garnett, op. cit., Howard, op. cit.

The nature of the programme reflected the fact that, when it came to accommodation he shared 'Dawn Edge' with a number of left wing dissident German political scientists, essentially like-minded individuals under himself as 'housemaster' and Zita as 'matron'. Eventually the numbers grew to a point where it was necessary to accommodate two Germanic RUs within his house – one exclusively Austrian.

Just as with the French, it was necessary to separate the Germans from one another, as well as from other nationalities, as alienation from the Nazis was often the only thing that they had in common. These people were frequently political, even personal rivals, and to protect their identity against reprisals they were simply known by a false Christian name such as 'Kurt' or 'Hans'. The political refugees of the 1930s, for example, were different from the captured POWS – up to 40 individuals who had been 'turned' under interrogation, and who brought with them invaluable inside knowledge.

One would expect that the security restrictions that applied to other RUs would be even more rigorously applied to the German POWs but, according to Muriel Spark's account, not only were secretaries permitted to take them for walks within the perimeter of the Milton Bryan compound, but even go cycling and picnicking with them in the Bedfordshire countryside.[164] 'The villagers stare at them with contempt,' she later noted, incorporating the experience in her fictional novel *The Hothouse By The East River*, 'not knowing in the least what is going on, but knowing only that their countryside is peppered with Germans and that somehow the authorities permit it'.[165] Roy Tink, a member of the GPO's Engineering Department whose job it was to service Milton Bryan's teleprinters was also permitted to lunch in the canteen hut not far from the guard house, and mingle with the German personnel. He recalled one, by the name of Zimmerman, who was keen to practise his English on Roy (especially his swearing), and invited him into one of the studios where Roy heard him playing the violin.[166]

---

[164] Spark, op. cit.

[165] Spark, Muriel. *The Hothouse By The East River* (Macmillan, 1973).

[166] Correspondence and conversation with Roy Tink, January 2007.

Two German POWS in particular, were kept even further away from the rest. Wolfgang Von Putlitz had been a diplomat who met Delmer when he was a correspondent in Berlin. Von Putlitz wasn't kept at Aspley Guise, partly because he had been away from Berlin too long to be much use and partly because he was such a dreadful gossip. Delmer instead lodged him at Paris House, conveniently a separate building within the walls of the Abbey parkland proper, but he did allow him into the Milton Bryan unit where he 'lounged elegantly around the compound cheering up the secretaries with the happy smile which at Berlin cocktail parties in the golden twenties had earned him the highest of Berlin social accolades: "Er hat ein gutes Auftreten!' (He has good presence)."'

'Dr Nansen' (real name Zech-Nenntwich) was another matter: 'I disliked and distrusted him from the first moment …rightly so, as it was to turn out after the war.' A 'bright eyed, bouncy, rosy cheeked young cavalry man' with a 'high pitched tenor voice', he was a former member of the Waffen SS who claimed to have been the leader of a dissident cell *within* Hitler's elite organisation, and who had been smuggled out via neutral Sweden. Delmer believed much of Nansen's story on balance, but regarded him as 'an opportunist' and wouldn't let him have any contact with the German POWs or 'some of my more emotional collaborators'. He too was exiled to Paris House where Delmer preferred to visit him.[167]

'In my house, RAG,' Delmer admitted 'we lived well enough, much better, in fact, than most people in Britain.' Delmer brought the contents of his considerable wine cellar with him, free range chickens were available as were hare, rabbits and venison from the Duke's estate, Otto John recalling that immediately after informing him of the ceasefire on 5 May 1945 Delmer went into the garden to shoot rabbits. Vegetables were grown in the garden, eaten young at the insistence of Isabel Delmer whose experience of French cooking helped her make the most of these additions to wartime rations in the time that she remained with her husband. Furthermore, there were seasonal bounties that were unavailable to many others at this anxious time; mushrooms for example,

---

[167] Delmer would occasionally be accompanied by Child, Stevens, Sanders or Max Braun. After the war Zech-Nenntwich denounced his former Social Democrat colleagues at MB to Konrad Adenauer, the Christian Democrat Chancellor of West Germany.

Paris House *(Luton and Bedfordshire Archives)*.

collected by the household from a nearby field. When the cherries were ripe their presence at mealtimes allowed Delmer, from his position at the head of the large dining room table, to preside over stone spitting contests.

The anniversary of the first broadcast of GS1 was always commemorated with a party. Among the guests were the German POWs and Father Andreas, a young Austrian clergyman (simply known as 'the Priest') who gave short talks on religious matters. Needless to say, these were beacons of integrity amongst the scurrilous output that usually emanated from Delmer's team.

Nachrichten

Broadcasting remained the principal means of delivering misinformation to the Germans once the continent was over run. Leaflets aimed at the Germans in the early part of the war were largely failures. The content was vague and amateurish, demonstrations of blustering confidence in the effectiveness of Anglo-French unity being such that they could hardly have shaken even the most lukewarm of Nazi supporters, let alone the fanatics of the Panzer Divisions as they rampaged across Europe. On the contrary, the bombast contained within them indicated uncertainty, even an underlying fear.

Once the battles for France and Norway were lost, however, for European nations under occupation the leaflet drops acquired an enhanced significance. There were clear reasons for this and Harold Keeble (the 'layout genius' from the *Daily Express*) best expressed this perspective:

> *This was the reasoning at the time: with Germany on the crest of triumph, propaganda directed exclusively against the enemy was practically valueless – or, at all events, only of long range political character. The one immediate useful task was to help keep alive among the peoples of France, Holland, Belgium, Norway, the faith that, although the battle of Western Europe was lost, the war itself was not.*[168]

Then, in the summer of 1944, the success of the allied invasion of Europe changed the picture. Another barrack was constructed at Milton Bryan, and this was devoted to the production of a newsletter for the German armed forces in Europe, steadily retreating before the allied build up.

Commencing publication as the allies prepared for the Normandy landings, *Nachrichten fur die Truppe* provided essentially factual information but slanted in the inimitable style by now perfected by Delmer's team. Awards for bravery were cited, appointments were reported, girl next door types of pin-ups were included, and troop movements were noted – invariably in the direction of Berlin. Alongside news of heroism by units or individuals of the Wehrmacht might be official denials of luxuriating, or even profiteering, by leading Nazis. It utilised the same sources as did the 'Freedom Stations' and, as with the broadcasts, it was the speed and accuracy of Delmer's newsgathering capabilities that gave *Nachrichten* such a high degree of authenticity. This meant that even if the German soldier on the receiving end guessed that this 'grey' propaganda came from the allies, the credibility of the information still carried an impact.

---

[168] Keeble, op. cit. Keeble later became Features Editor of the Mirror Group of newspapers.

Maryland *(Amy Rich)*.

The content for each edition of *Nachrichten* was produced together by an Anglo-American team at the PWE offices led by the one armed Maj. Dennis Clarke (*Daily Express*), and John Elliot (*New York Herald Tribune*).[169] The layout was carried out at Maryland, under the direction of Harold Keeble. It was here that much of the printed propaganda, under the auspices of the Political Intelligence Department of the Foreign Office, was designed. By the time that the first Americans arrived, in the autumn of 1942, Keeble had already established a smoothly working operation: 'The procedure at this time was fairly simple. Writers, translators, layout artists, proof readers were all located around the composing room: (We lived and ate up above the shop – literally),' with special constables guarding the premises.[170]

The Americans and British were able to pool their respective experience and expertise into a single Joint Production Unit, covering all aspects of propaganda. For the production of *Nachrichten* the work would take a full day and it would be in the early hours of the morning (invariably around 03.00) before the final copy would be ready for Sefton Delmer's approval. Delmer himself provided a vivid description of what happened next:

---

[169] Erdman, op. cit. Erdman implies that this was produced in the Woburn estate proper.

[170] Keeble op. cit. Garnett wrote that only white printed material was produced at Maryland and that black was carried out in the capital because of the need to use the specialist print firms located there. By no stretch of the imagination could *Nachrichten* ever be described as 'white'. Giving no real clue as to its origins, it could best be described as 'grey'.

... the door of my bedroom would softly open, a hand switched on the lamp on my bedside table, and a girl's voice spoke.

'Mr Delmer' it said sweetly through my dreams, 'Major Clarke's compliments'.

Standing beside my bed, solicitously offering me a large buff envelope containing a dispatch, I saw a blonde angel, blue uniformed, breeched and high booted. From under a crash helmet peeped corn coloured curls. Her slender waist was tightly strapped in a leather corset. There she stood awaiting my command, her cheeks flushed by the icy before-dawn air, her crimson lips slightly parted – the dream vision of a James Bond fetishist. But this was no dream. She was the dispatch rider sent over to my bedside from Marylands ...

(Isabel Delmer asked for separate rooms: 'That was the beginning of the end of my first marriage' concluded Delmer.)[171]

Once Delmer had approved the copy it went back to Maryland, and was at Luton by 05.00. This was the base of Home Counties Newspapers, owned by the publishing company Gibbs, Bamforth & Co., and embracing a number of local newspaper titles as well as the publishing business, the Leagrave Press. The *Nachrichten* edition was printed up at the Manchester Street offices of the *Luton News*

A contemporary charicature of Harold White, Director of the Leagrave Press
(*Courtesy of Peter White*).

---

[171] Delmer, op. cit. p.153

The headquarters of the *Luton News* in Manchester Street, Luton
(Luton Museum Service/Luton News).

and then packed into the special containers a couple of miles away at the premises of the Leagrave Press. Although the operation was highly secretive, incongruously the children of John Gibbs, one of the company directors, assisted in packing in the *Nachrichtens*, adding a few stale buns as well, 'just for Hitler'.[172] By 14.00 the copies were ready to be collected from the loading bays by drivers from the USAF Ordnance Department. Just over twelve hours after Delmer had run his sleepy eyes over the draft copy, they were being taken to the 422 Squadron's base at Cheddington in Buckinghamshire.

An average of two million copies was churned out night after night at Home Counties Newspapers (the edition for 12 October 1944 ran to 3,611,000 copies). 'These Luton printers were as proud of *Nachrichten* as we were,' noted Delmer. 'They looked on it as their special contribution to the annihilation of Hitler and they worked smoothly and punctually without ever a hitch.' There seems to have been a few

---

[172] Information from Heather Woods, interview 22 November 2005.

hitches in fact, largely concerned with pay, conditions and unionisation but that this should be the case is unsurprising in a plant taking on extra work with what Gibbs, Bamforth acknowledged was 'very depleted staffs'. Overall, however, the operation was carried out very efficiently and Delmer was right in claiming that the *Luton News* (whose print shops apparently ran on a constant supply of tea and buns – perhaps the same that found their way into the canisters) was very proud of its achievement. Foreman Ernest Palmer described John Gibbs' enthusiasm as 'expansive and catching, and each one of us in those early days, felt we had done something'.[173]

For the American crews who were detailed with the delivery of *Nachrichten*, and other printed propaganda, this was work that required specialist training and readjustment. Mentally prepared to fight back against the enemy through bombing, they were initially resentful at what they disparagingly described as 'Bumwad' missions. Furthermore, dropping propaganda material of any kind was as specialised as dropping bombs – or secret agents. In the earlier part of the war, bundles of leaflets were just shoved through the flare chutes, a method that was slow and inaccurate (Neville Chamberlain apparently objected to leaflets being dropped in bundles that were heavy enough to kill someone – even a German – should they be inadvertently hit by one).[174] It could also be

---

[173] *The First Daily Newspaper in the World. Being an account of its production by Home Counties Newspapers Ltd., Luton and Gibbs, Bamforth & Co. (Luton) Ltd., The Leagrave Press, Luton.* (Produced privately for the staff of the companies c. 1946).

[174] Barman, op. cit. On one mission Freddie Clark recalled laughter coming from his rear gunner, F/O G. H. Ash, as he saw one package 'plummet to the ground with the string still tied around it. I trust it did no hurt to those below'. Clark F., *Agents by Moonlight. The Secret History of RAF Tempsford During World War II* (Tempus, 1999).

An example of early leaflet dropping method from a Whitley bomber
(*Imperial War Museum, C286*).

The production of *Nachrichten,* from conception to delivery by means of the Monroe
propaganda bomb, depicted in a contemporary cartoon. In the 'Cutters' wagon can be
seen Home Counties Newspapers and Leagrave Press Directors, Harold White and
John Gibbs (*Courtesy of Heather Woods*).

dangerous for crew members – such as the rear gunner – to leave their primary duties in order to post propaganda leaflets.

Arthur 'Bomber' Harris, the chief of Bomber Command, made this point to Bruce Lockhart, emphatically pointing out that a plane flying over occupied Europe, with night fighters on the prowl, could not afford to have its personnel distracted for ten seconds, let alone between five to ten minutes that it normally took.[175] Harris suggested that he might be happier if someone could come up with a mechanical dropping device but this was only part of the problem, accuracy was a far more pertinent challenge since without it even the most ingenious of propaganda stratagems had no real focus. Discovering that only 4% of leaflets were getting through to the intended target, efforts were made to develop a container that wouldn't immediately burst in the plane's slipstream, and it was at Sharnbrook, a village lying to the north of Bedford, that the problem was solved.[176]

Sharnbrook was the location of a one of the U.S. Ordnance Department's bases, the 1907 and 1908 Companies making their temporary home there. Establishing a camp to the west of the vicarage, the Americans also used the buildings of Cobb Hall. In the words of Captain James L. Monroe, the 422s Technical Liaison Officer, it was one of 'these little organisations stashed away … all over England'. The companies' function was to distribute bombs to the US airfields in the neighbourhood, and to break up wrecked aircraft, a significant number of its personnel being recuperating combat casualties. It 'wasn't really very busy' according to one recollection, so it was the ideal location to develop the 'Monroe Propaganda Bomb' (T.1), named in his honour. Around five feet long, made with laminated paper and cardboard caps, the Monroe Bomb was fitted with a fuse that was designed to release the container at different altitudes. 'It was a simple device which should have been employed much earlier,' observed Harold Keeble. The work was embraced with enthusiasm by the Sharnbrook Americans because, as Monroe put it, 'they were going to be part of the war again'. After

---

[175] Young, op. cit. 27 April 1942. Lockhart found Harris 'very tough and anti all foreigners including Americans'.

[176] Erdman, op. cit. p. 285-301. Many leaflet drops initially took place as part of the work of OTUs (Operational Training Units). One of these, flying out of Bassingbourne, crashed at Clophill.

USAAF ground crew loading Monroe Propaganda bombs (*Provenance unknown*).

successful testing over the Wash, packing operations were set up at Melchbourne (later moved to a larger scale operation near Watford).

Each bomb could carry 10,000 copies of *Nachrichten* (and many more leaflets), being set to split open as low as a thousand feet from the ground. This technological innovation permitted a shift in the focus of Bedfordshire's propaganda output. Now drops could be focused, areas or units precisely targeted aiming, as Keeble put it, at 'those 800 men in that wood'. This was no exaggeration: after the war, John Gibbs was proud to report the instance of a two day battle by Canadian units in the Falaise Gap to clear a wood of its German defenders. The morning after a *Nachrichten* drop revealed '2000 Jerries surrendering with our newspapers in their hands'.[177]

One of the most vital editions of *Nachrichten* (and the radio broadcast *Soldatensender Calais*) was the one that helpfully informed German troops that Allied troops had successfully launched the D-Day landings on 6 June 1944, thereby breaching Rommel's Atlantic Wall. Delmer's purloined *Hellschreiber* picked up official German confirmation of the invasion, and *Soldatensender* was announcing the news by 04.50, but in fact Delmer and Keeble were already aware of the plans which, frustratingly, had to be briefly postponed due to poor weather conditions in the English Channel. Delmer had been informed of Eisenhower's decision to launch the attack (thanks to critical reassurance

John Gibbs, Director of Home Counties Newspapers, publishers of the *Luton News* (*Courtesy of Heather Woods*).

---

[177] *The First Daily Newspaper in the World*, op. cit.

Nr. 187, Freitag, 20. Oktober 1944

NACHRICHTEN FÜR DIE TRUPPE

Die Russen in Ostpreussen

Die Schutzstellung überrannt, Eydtkau und Schirwindt genommen

An der ostpreussischen Ostgrenze haben die Sowjets Eydtkau und Schirwindt besetzt und stossen weiter in Richtung auf Insterburg vor.

Die „Schutzstellung Ostpreussen", an der viele Zehntausende Männer, Frauen und Kinder acht Wochen lang bauen mussten, wurde zwischen Schirwindt und Eydtkau von den Sowjetpanzern überrannt und liegt jetzt schon viele Kilometer hinter den Angriffskolonnen der Sowjets.

An der ostpreussischen Südgrenze greifen seit gestern Morgen starke Sowjetverbände aus dem Narew-

Volkssturm kämpfen, wo sie eben noch schanzen.

Nach dem Durchbruch der Sowjets durch die sogenannte „Schutzstellung Ostpreussen" sind die Schanzarbeiten jetzt Nebensache geworden. Jeder muss sich einbuddeln, wo er gerade steht.

Vom Nordabschnitt der Ostfront wird noch gemeldet:
In Kurland greifen die Sowjets südöstlich Libau und zwischen Dobein und dem Rigaer Meerbusen unablässig an. Mehrere Einbrüche wurden von den deutschen Truppen im Gegenangriff abgeriegelt.

Im hohen Norden sind die Sowjets erneut beiderseits der Eismeerstrasse zum Angriff angetreten, um nach Kirkenes durchzubrechen. Die Kämpfe sind in vollem Gange.

Flüchtlinge aus Aachen werden von den Amerikanern auf LKWs. hinter die Frontlinie in Sicherheit gebracht

Letzter Widerstand in den Ruinen von Aachen

Amerikaner landen auf Philippinen

Der Rest der deutschen Besatzung in Aachen kämpft in den letzten Widerstandsnestern in der Innenstadt. Der grösste Teil von Aachen ist jetzt in der Hand der Amerikaner.

So eng ist der Raum auf dem die deutschen Truppen zusammengedrängt sind, dass die Amerikaner ihre Luftangriffe eingestellt haben aus Angst, ihre eigenen Leute zu treffen.

Starke amerikanische Truppenverbände sind gestern an mehreren Stellen der Leyte-Insel, die in den mittleren Philippinen gelegen ist, gelandet und haben somit die Rückeroberung ihres Schutzgebiets begonnen, das 1942 von den Japanern besetzt wurde.

Amerikanische Kriegsschiffe unterstützten die Landung mit schwerem Bombardment der japanischen Küstenstellungen.

Wie das kaiserlich japanische Hauptquartier meldet, liegen in der Bucht von Leyte zahlreiche Transporte, die unter dem Schutz eines amerikanischen Flottenverbandes z.Zt. bedeutende Truppen-Kontingente und grosse Mengen Kriegsmaterial an Land setzen.

Gen. Schroth „verunglückt"

Als erstes Mitglied des vom Führer eingesetzten Ehrenhofs zur Aussonderung der Offiziere des 20. Juli ist der bisherige Befehlshaber im Wehrkreis XII, General der Infanterie Walther Schroth, der Vergeltungswelle gegen die Richter zum Friedensputschisten zum Opfer gefallen.

Amtlich wird über den Tod von General Walter Schroth lediglich mitgeteilt, dass er durch „einen tragischen Unfall" jäh aus dem Leben gerissen wurde.

Ungarnfront bleibt ohne Nachschub

·Brückenköpfca bei Serock und Rozan an, mit dem Ziel, auf Danzig durchzustossen und Ostpreussen zu umfassen.

Das ist der Stand der Umfassungsoffensive der Sowjets gegen Ostpreussen, die vor vier Tagen mit dem Angriff auf Wirballen begann.

Einige Kilometer westlich Eydtkau machen jetzt deutsche Panzer Gegenangriffe, um die Sowjets wieder aus Eydtkau heraus und über die Grenze zurückzuwerfen.

Überall in Ostpreussen werden die letzten Reserven aufgeboten.

Die Schanzarbeiter werden in Kompanien und Bataillone zusammengefasst, erhalten polnische oder sonstige Beutegewehre und müssen als

Westlich und ostwärts Debrecen stossen jetzt Sowjetpanzer nach Norden vor und drohen, die deutschen Truppen in Nordost-Ungarn einzukesseln, die sie noch nach Westen zurückziehen können.

Letzte Versuche werden noch in aller Eile unternommen, um Verstärkungen und Bresche zu werfen, die die Sowjets zwischen Debrecen und den Karpaten in die besetzte Abwehrfront geschlagen haben.

Aber nicht viel kommt bis an die Front durch. Der Eisenbahnverkehr in Ungarn ist noch immer durch den

Streik der Eisenbahner lahmgelegt.

Ein Aufruf der Szalasi-Regierung an alle Eisenbahner, bis spätestens zum 21. Oktober zur Arbeit zurückzukehren, hat bisher keine Wirkung gezeigt.

Honveds überfallen Nachschubzüge

Ungarische Partisanen und Horthy-treue Honveds über fallen die Nachschubzüge, die auf den Strecken festliegen, berauben die Munitions- und Lebensmittellager der Wehrmacht und setzen die Treibstofivorräte in Brand.

Um das Notwendigste durchzubekommen, stellt sich

die Wehrmacht immer mehr auf Pferdetransport um. Aber es ist schwer, den ungarischen Bauern die Pferde und Fuhrwerke zu beschlagnahmen, da sie alles vor den deutschen Soldaten verstecken.

In Budapest hat der Zusammenbruch des Eisenbahnverkehrs schon zu einer Hungersnot geführt. Es gibt kein Brot, und die Bauern aus der Umgebung bringen kein Getreide und Fleisch mehr in die Stadt.

Der Widerstand der Horthy-treuen Bauern wird noch verstärkt durch die Haltung der katholischen Kirche. Während die Geistlichen ihre Gläubigen zum Wider-

Ruinen von Aachen

Die schweren Regengüsse der letzten Tage haben die meisten Brände in Aachen zum Erlöschen gebracht. Nichts wie verkohlte Ruinen sind übriggeblieben.

Mit Flammenwerfern und Phosphorgranaten wurden die deutschen Truppen gestern aus einem Häuserblock nach dem anderen vertrieben. Der peitschende, kalte Regen auf der Strasse war für viele Soldaten das einzige Wasser, das sie seit Tagen gesehen haben.

5 deutsche Angriffe abgeschlagen

Fünfmal im Laufe der Nacht zum Donnerstag versuchten die deutschen Verbände, bei Würselen, ausserhalb von Aachen, den Einschliessungsring um die Stadt zu durchstossen. Nach fünf verlustreichen Angriffen war aber nur ein einziger Strassenblock erobert.

Jede Hoffnung, die restliche Besatzung aus Aachen noch herauszuziehen, muss jetzt aufgegeben werden.

Von den Kampfabschnitten in Holland wird gemeldet: Im Brückenkopf über die Maas südlich Nimwegen mussten sich die deutschen Truppen weiter in Richtung Venlo zurückziehen, nachdem der wichtige Strassenknotenpunkt Venraij am Mittwoch verloren ging.

Einen tiefen Einbruch in die deutschen Stellungen erzielten die Engländer während

(Fortsetzung Seite 3)

(Fortsetzung Seite 4)

T.187

The *Nachrichten* edition for 20 October 1944. For Germany there was precious little good news (*Courtesy of Heather Woods*).

provided by the Meteorological Office at Dunstable), the day before. Once again the critical source was provided by Donald McLachlan who, as Delmer recorded in *Black Boomerang*, on the evening of 5 June 'strode into my office at MB, flung his naval officer's cap on my desk and announced "It's on! Ike is definitely going through with it"'. The security that surrounded this operation was so great that once the *Nachrichten* edition (already prepared in anticipated advance of the landings) had been delivered to the *Luton News*, no printer was permitted to leave the premises until after the invasion had been formally announced.

*　*　*

The invasion of Europe inevitably shifted the emphasis of the radio programmes directed at Germany. For some years a well established practise had been to promote 'sibs' (false rumours, the word coming from the Latin *'sibilare'* meaning 'to whisper' or 'to hiss'), with a 'sib' committee established to this effect whose members included Delmer and Ralph Murray. Almost any means were used to spread them, not merely the obvious means of black and white broadcasting and leaflets, but subtler methods also such as briefing key representatives in neutral countries, as well as agents in occupied Europe, to let slip snippets of information which would, it was hoped, finally reach the finely tuned ears of German Intelligence. PWE even went as far as to forge inserts into the censored correspondence of German POWs and British people who were writing abroad, as well as forging letters to the families of German servicemen officially posted as 'Missing in Action', but which the British knew to be already dead. These letters, ostensibly from sons who had escaped into a neutral county, or who was now in captivity, could be used for all sorts of misinformation.

A famous early 'sib' had been promoted with the imminence of a German invasion of Britain in 1940. Genuine but limited experiments to see whether inflammable material could be ignited in the sea near to the beaches in the event of attack became, via the 'sib', a wall of fire that would engulf any attacking German force. In one of his early radio efforts, Sefton Delmer contributed to this on the BBC by broadcasting a helpful phrase guide for this new generation of German tourists: (*'Das Boot sinkt* – the boat is sinking'; *'Das Wasser ist sehr kalt* – the water is very cold'; 'Ich brenne – I burn'; 'Du brennst – you burn'; 'Der SS Sturmführer brennt auch ganz schon – The SS Captain is also burning quite nicely'). In 'Operation Periwig' PWE decided to keep to feed the Gestapo's paranoia by steadily building up the fiction of an internal German resistance movement. This culminated in four German anti-Nazis being dropped into the country to make contact with resistance cells that they honestly thought were functioning, but which their British handlers knew did not. The incredible good fortune that all evaded the Gestapo to survive their task carried an ironic bonus: two claimed to have made contact with resistance cells that PWE obviously hadn't known existed![178]

For German troops suffering increasing hardship on various fronts, 'sibs' were spread to remind them of home, especially the plight of wives and girlfriends left behind. The vast numbers of foreign workers that were being drafted in to the Reich were, it was rumoured, taking every opportunity to provide comfort for Germany's millions of lonely women. The SS were frequent targets, as every effort was made to cleave them from the experience of other Germans. Not only were foreign workers taking the place left by absent lovers but the privileged officers of the SS (always depicted as taking advantage of their position to avoid dangerous duties) were being given official sanction to impregnate German women (forcibly if needs be) in order to sow the seeds for the next generation of the Aryan race. Worse still, some (named) SS officers were apparently taking advantage of their position to prey upon young children, their activities being covered up by the Nazi state. Efforts by the SS to maintain a pure 'master race' (being genetically countermanded by the romantic inclinations of foreign workers – especially the French and Italian) was also undermined by a crisis in the army's blood transfusion service as casualties mounted on the eastern front. So bad had the situation become, it was rumoured, that the blood of executed Jews was being drained and bottled to be sent to the desperate military hospitals.

As Allied armies pushed into the Reich itself the mirror of 'black' and 'white' propaganda once again became apparent: '… it was Delmer's task to confuse, it was the BBC's task to provide reliable instructions which Germans could trust'. The BBC would provide news as to cities that

---

[178] Young, op. cit.

were bombed or to the movement of the armies. Delmer meanwhile had trained his announcers to perfectly imitate their German counterparts. With prior knowledge of designated RAF objectives, his team awaited the approach of a raid and the moment that the German transmitter in the target area would shut down. As it did, the mighty 'Aspidistra' switched on (German listeners apparently heard no more than a faint click) and Milton Bryan took over. Now, German civilians heard that Nazi officials were to be evacuated from front line areas, that they were requested to post examples of allied shrapnel in post boxes for collection and analysis, and it directly contradicted the BBC. Whereas the Corporation advised German civilians near to front line areas to stay at home for their own safety (to the fury of Churchill: he referred to the BBC as 'one of the major neutrals'), completely the opposite advice came from Bedfordshire. In an echo of what the Germans had done to France in 1940, German civilians were ordered to take to the roads, thereby hampering the desperate deployment of German reinforcements, and to muster at non-existent assembly points.

As for the beleaguered German Army, Ellic Howe's printed guide to malingering, for the benefit of the increasingly demoralised soldiers of the *Wehrmacht* units in the west, was a printed example of something that could serve as a 'sib'. Illustrated by Marion Whitehorn, these were secreted inside replicas of German Army song books and scattered by the RAF and USAAF in the vicinity of the German lines.[179] Delmer then followed this up in *Soldatensender* by emphasising that reinforcements from the German armies in the West were urgently needed to shore up the Eastern Front against the vengeful millions of the Red Army. Naturally, only the fittest, most disciplined and dedicated soldiers would be good enough to face the merciless terror of Stalin's savage mincing machine. Those who were scruffy, slipshod and lacked fighting spirit would just have to stay put…

In mid-April 1945 it was decided to abruptly halt the last of the main broadcasting stations, *Soldatensender West*, as if the position had been over run by allied troops. *Nachrichten* disappeared at roughly the same time but its passing was marked in some style. Harold Keeble threw a

---

[179] This has now been reproduced with a foreword by Lee Richards. See *Illness Saves: The British World War Two Black Propaganda Malingering Campaign* (www.psywar.org).

136

fancy dress party at Maryland to which staff from MB, with security restrictions spontaneously lifted, were also invited. Leonard Ingrams was chauffeured there by 'his pretty driver, a demure young woman called Peggy Black', whom Delmer was ultimately to marry. Ian Fleming, never one to miss a party, was also present, as was the *Luton News*' John Gibbs who 'romped' in, fetchingly attired in a suit of *Nachrichten* front pages printed on calico. The morning after the party Delmer symbolically shaved off his beard: 'There, staring at me, was the pallid, flabby mouthed face of a crook. Was this, I asked myself, what four years of "black" had done to Denis Sefton Delmer?' He then gave a speech to the assembled staff at MB, congratulated them on their efforts and reminded them to maintain the secrecy of their work in the years to come: '... mum's the word. Propaganda is something one keeps quiet about'.[180]

Detail of *Nachrichten* train. Virtually none of the characters can be identified with any certainty but the lead figure in the 'Editorial' wagon is almost certainly Sefton Delmer. If so, this is the only surviving image of him wearing his wartime beard (*Courtesy of Heather Woods*).

---

[180] Delmer op cit. p.219.

Part III

Covert Operations

Intelligence gathering

Intelligence, the knowledge of what the enemy was doing, planning – even thinking – was critical to the successful conduct of Total War. In Bedfordshire, this was devoted to information gathering via the monitoring of radio traffic and primarily worked at three levels: the IDA Unit based within the compound of Dunstable's Meteorological station, the RAF Y Station based at Chicksands Priory, and the dedicated work of private listeners who served with the Radio Security Service.

Dunstable's IDA Unit worked closely with Bletchley Park, which provided the initial training for its staff. It fed encrypted enemy weather reports to Station X and in turn received decoded information from them which it then used to develop weather forecasts for British military units. WT (Wireless Telegraphy) operators based at the station passed on the data to the unit, some of which it was able to decode itself (that from Vichy France, for example). Motorbike despatch riders delivered the material to and from Bletchley Park four times a day on regular runs between 08.00 and 22.00 and Brian Audric certainly believed that the use of the One-Time code pads protected the British forecasting and weather reports from similar penetration by the enemy.[181]

The One-Time pad had been adapted and developed by Leo Marks, the cryptographic genius who provided many SOE agents with the codes by which they could communicate with Britain and yet keep their secrets free from the Germans. Marks never worked at Bletchley Park, being described as 'the one that got away'. His true talents were first discovered in January 1942 in Bedford at the Inter-Service Special Intelligence School, an off-shoot of Bletchley Park, when he was called up to train as

---

[181] Audric, op. cit.

a cryptographer. Marks was the only one of his intake not to be recruited to Bletchley Park; instead, having in an evening cracked a code intended as a group exercise to be spread across a week, he was labelled a misfit and eventually called for an interview at Bedford to join SOE. He recalled that 'my audition took place at a large private house which tried to ramble but hadn't the vitality'. Although Marks made little further reference to Bedford in his memoirs, he generously acknowledged the quality of the initial instruction that he received there.[182]

The Inter-Service Special Intelligence School had been initially based in Ardor House, on the corner of The Broadway, Bedford and it evolved so that, by 1942 it was the specialist centre for trainee Japanese linguists. This part of the Secret War was hardly a secure unit, Ardor House incorporating the Gas Showroom and apparently being known locally as 'the Spy School'. The tutor here was Captain Oswald Tuck, a man who had learnt Japanese during the early years of the 20th century when he was based in the Far East and when the two countries were allies. Brought out of virtual retirement, Tuck was remembered by one of his former pupils, Alan Stripp, as 'a bearded, spectacled, quiet and benevolent man', but also by another as 'a natural teacher, able to instil his own enthusiasm for the Japanese language in his students'.[183]

The Japanese School had been initiated by Col. John Tiltman, one of Bletchley Park's senior cryptanalysts who was aware of a glaring shortcoming in Britain's intelligence resources. Tiltman approached the University of London's School of Oriental and African Studies with a view to establishing a training school for Japanese linguists. With characteristic academic caution SOAS informed Tiltman that such a process would normally take two years at the absolute minimum, clearly of no use in the desperate position that Britain was finding itself in the early stages of the war. So Tuck, who had gone on to serve in Naval Intelligence during World War One, was approached instead to see if he could better SOAS' guarded estimate. Tiltman wanted to produce adequate linguists in six months.

---

[182] Marks, Leo. *Between Silk and Cyanide. A Codemaker's Story 1941-45* (Harper Collins, 2000).

[183] Stripp, Alan. *Codebreaker in the Far East* (OUP, 1995); Smith, Michael *The Emperor's Codes* (Bantam Press, 2000).

Tuck apparently recalled that 'the idea sounded impossible but was worth trying', a modest understatement in the light of what was to follow in Bedford. His Japanese School was to produce a succession of graduates that learnt the language in far shorter time than had hitherto been thought possible. Stripp's tribute to Tuck was simple, eloquent and concise: 'his patient, unassuming and kindly expertise had directed some of the most successful crash courses in educational history at one of the most crucial moments in recent British history'.[184] A later tribute was equally direct, describing Tuck's achievement as a 'tremendous triumph over wrongheaded experts, red tape, neglect and almost impossible conditions'.[185]

Ardor House, the site of Oswald Tuck's initial Japanese decoding school
(Luton and Bedfordshire Archives).

[184] The papers of Captain Oswald Tuck (1876-1950) are held in the archives of Churchill College Cambridge. Hinsley, F. H. and Stripp, Alan (eds.) *Code Breakers. The Inside Story of Bletchley Park* (OUP, 1993).

[185] Letter from Frank Birch (Deputy Director of Bletchley Park Naval Section) to Tuck, 7.12.1945. Quoted in Jarvis, Sue. *Captain Oswald Tuck R. N. and the Bedford Japanese School* (The Bletchley Park Reports, Report no.19, June 2003).

The first course commenced on 2 February 1942, staying at Ardor House just a few months before another temporary move to 7 St Andrews Road on 15 June. 'So we started at this course in Bedford, above the noisiest crossroads in town,' recalled Maurice Wiles, the youngest on the first course and recruited on the recommendation of his tutor at Cambridge, 'and in walked Captain Tuck, who was a very small, very dignified man with a neat white beard and this old-world civility which seemed old-world even in those days'. From the very first moment, Tuck proved himself to be an innovative instructor promptly informing his new students that they needed to greet him correctly. To his welcome '*shokun ohayo*' ('all you princes are honourably early'), they were to reply '*ohayo gozaimasn*' ('honourably early it honourably is'). So Tuck turned, left the room and, when he came back in, their crash course in Japanese was off and running. With a shortage of writing paper and just five books (Tuck's personal property) for twenty five students, a 'spirit of desperate improvisation forced them to depend on their memories' which Tuck enlivened with his imaginative teaching style. Students didn't have time to get comfortable because each day Tuck would move them one place back, with those at the rear of the classroom moving down to the front.[186] By the time that Alan Stripp noted his first impressions upon joining the school in 1943 it had moved to 52 de Parys Avenue:

> The course was held in a large room in a detached house in De Parys Avenue, a tree-lined road not far from the town centre. There were about 35 on the course, including two girls, all of us aged about 18 or 19, and most from university classics courses. We eyed each other sheepishly.

Like Wiles, Stripp had attended Cambridge (Trinity College), a reflection of Tiltman's notion that Oxbridge classicists would provide the most suitable trainees for the Japanese School. He felt that they were best suited to problem solving and the interviews of the recruits tended to show that an interest in crosswords, chess or music was also deemed to be an advantage. As Christopher Andrew observed:

> The improbable combination of pupils chosen for their proficiency in languages utterly remote from Japanese and a 64 year old novice teacher

---

[186] Smith op. cit.

De Parys Avenue, to which Tuck's school relocated in 1943
(Luton and Bedfordshire Archives).

with no experience of higher education using untried teaching methods is striking evidence of how Bletchley Park's faith in the potential of intelligent, creative amateurs remained undiminished half-way through the war. The improbable combination worked.[187]

By contrast with his students, their self-taught tutor had left school at fifteen. Tuck fostered an informal atmosphere of learning amongst his students, but pushed them very hard. Formal classes didn't take place on Saturday afternoon or Sunday but even then students were expected to devote available spare time to refining language skills, an expectation that even applied to Christmas Day. In order to achieve speedy results the course was necessarily narrowly defined. Students worked with material drawn from military communiqués before moving on to code breaking exercises. They were also assisted to some degree by the carelessness on the part of Japanese communications, perhaps over confident that the inscrutability of their language to Western ears provided a code in its own right.

---

[187] Langhorne, Richard (ed.) *Diplomacy and Intelligence During the Second World War. Essays in Honour of F. H. Hinsley* (CUP, 1985).

One successful graduate facetiously observed that they had learnt the word for 'submarine' but not 'I' or 'you', as they didn't appear in official communiqués. This would be an unfair representation of Tuck's work since, by all surviving accounts, he endeavoured to instil within the students a wider understanding of Japanese life and culture. Nonetheless, the Bedford course was designed to confront a very real emergency and its students were able to translate a captured Japanese air force code after just five months' training. Assessments provided by both the Japanese Diplomatic Section, and SOAS turned out to be extremely favourable, so favourable in respect of the latter that SOAS began to develop their own short courses in imitation, and enquiries were also received from the parallel organisations in the USA. Of the 225 students that passed through the eleven courses at Bedford, the failure rate was just 4%, far better than the equivalent SOAS course.

Oswald Tuck (seated centre) and his class of Japanese language students (*Provenance unknown*).

By 1943 Tuck was being assisted as course tutor by one of his first students, Eric Ceadel, 'a man of logic and pattern' whose 'quick, cool, lucid and methodical' approach perfectly complimented Tuck's. Later still, the two of them were further reinforced by David Hawkes and Frank Winston. Approximately half the graduates of Tuck's Bedford school were sent to Bletchley Park (the Japanese section there eventually taking over 'F Block), the rest being deployed to a variety of locations including Admiral Godfrey's Naval Intelligence Department in the Admiralty, and to the Far East. This included Japan itself after its surrender, where there was a sudden demand for colloquial Japanese to assist in the process of interrogation. Hugh Denham was interviewed whilst at Jesus College, Cambridge, and remembered being excited at the prospect of being sent to 'that little sun-drenched intelligence unit in Malaya (Singapore had not yet fallen)'. In the end he got to Kenya and then to Ceylon (Sri Lanka). Whatever the destination, demand always outstripped supply.

Tutor and students were provided with digs around the town, Tuck being lodged with a Miss Hammond, a retired music teacher. He was able to receive visitors, including monthly visits from his daughter, Sylvia (working at the Ministry of Economic Affairs), and more occasional ones from his wife, travelling up from their home in Bromley. Alan Stripp shared with another student from a similar course devoted to Arabic being run in Albany Road, a venue that was possibly the location for other undisclosed work. For those in Bedford, the presence of the relocated BBC musicians and singers provided opportunities for relaxation. Because they were part of a service organisation, the students were entitled to free tickets: 'we had endless wonderful first-hand music,' recalled another student, Jon Cohen, whilst Alan Stripp also sang with the depleted Bedford School Choir.

* * *

Chicksands Priory, near Shefford, was acquired by the Crown in 1936 and was operational as a listening station from the beginning of the conflict. RAF Y Service personnel of 3 Squadron established their Communications Intelligence (COMINT) service in the main Priory building in the summer of 1940 with the main antennas being erected by

Chicksands Priory *(Luton and Bedfordshire Archives).*

September of the following year.[188] Chicksands was thus to become an intercept station – or Y Station – picking up German enigma traffic which was being decoded at nearby Bletchley Park, taking on the work previously carried out at Chatham. Nearby, at RAF Henlow, was the Air Force's Communications School but many of the Chicksands personnel were trained at different points around the country.

The proposed move of the service from Chatham to Chicksands drew an immediate, if lengthy (fourteen pages), response from a concerned group of Bletchley Park's senior code breakers:

> We understand that a proposal has been put forward to transfer the interception of enigma traffic from the experienced Army station at Chatham to the new and relatively inexperienced Air Force station at Chicksands. The object of this memorandum is to explain the conditions which must be fulfilled if a continuance of our recent success in breaking the code is to be possible. We are convinced that the projected transfer is extremely dangerous, and that it may well have disastrous affects on our work. We are told that the information contained within enigma decodes has been and is likely to be of value to all our services during operations, and we understand that the type of intelligence concerned is of such importance that our success or failure may affect the course of the war. With this in view we feel that a vital decision of this kind should not be left in the hands of any one service but should be taken by the supreme authority responsible for the co-ordination of the war effort ... we do feel very strongly that the risks of removing Chatham ... far outweigh any possible advantage that could accrue from the proposed transfer to Chicksands ...[189]

Although the authors were at pains to stress that 'the reason has nothing to do with the ability or enthusiasm of the other intercepting stations, about which there can be no possible question', after detailing the utmost

---

[188] Grayson, William C. Chicksands. *A Millennium of History* (Shefford Press, 1994). Chicksands today plays host to the Military Intelligence Museum, charting the history of military intelligence gathering from the 1500s.

[189] National Archives, HW14/6. The authors of the letter were Hugh Alexander, D. W. Babbage, P. S. Milner-Barry, G. I Crawford, J. R. F. Jeffreys, J. S. Colman and W. G. Welchman. See also Sebag-Montefiore, Hugh. *Enigma. The Battle for the Code* (Phoenix, 2001).

importance of accuracy of listening and recording, they then went on to demonstrate that 'ability' was precisely the nub of the matter:

We have compared the actual decoded messages taken both by Chatham and Chicksands on the same day and we find that Chicksands made in all from two to three times the number of errors made by the Chatham operators. This can be due only to the superior average standard of the Chatham operators.

The code breakers concluded by objecting to the inferior communications system between Shefford and Bletchley Park, compared with Chatham, and called for swapping of supervisors between the two listening stations in order to raise standards in Bedfordshire. The appeal fell on deaf ears. The memo itself is marked with derogatory notes in the margin and the comments from senior personnel in the War Office towards something that had 'wasted so much paper' could hardly be more dismissive: '... have these people got no 'boss' who could have signed this effort with some authority ... they are in such a rut they cannot see out of it and consequently proceed to tell their seniors how to run their own business'. Chicksands it was.

A large number of the new RAF Y Service personnel were members of the Women's Auxiliary Air Force (WAAF), many of them still in the late teens when they were posted to Bedfordshire. The radio Watch Rooms were based in the Priory's stately rooms and its kitchen contained a coal fired range from which a constant stream of hot tea was wheeled around for the benefit of the WT operators. The working conditions carried a palatial air, albeit one possessing 'neglect and faded glory' (in the recollection of one operator), as well as its own resident ghost 'Berta Rosata' (a naughty nun who was allegedly punished by being walled up in the priory). In the mid twentieth century propriety was strictly observed: the WAAFs were obliged to wear skirts at all times; the only concession to the wearing of trousers was during the chillier hours of night duty.

The living conditions for these girls were considerably more primitive. Yvonne Jones' training had involved three months at Manchester's five star Midland Hotel, so Chicksands camp represented a bit of a come down:

W/T Operator Yvonne Jones
(née Scrivener) (*Courtesy of
Yvonne Jones*).

*We were housed in draughty run
down huts constructed of metal ribbed
sheeting (corrugated?). The joins
parted if one leant against them...
The bath hut and ablutions had to be
seen to be believed. At first we had
to share the bath hut with the men!
There were 8 baths – 4 either side
with a high wooden partition made of
plywood erected down the centre,
then individually between the baths.
It did not take us long to become
aware that some of the knot holes had
been tampered with and unwittingly
we had been entertaining the troops.*

*The ablutions were a nightmare, cold,
draughty with damp duck boards to
stand on; long stone sinks with metal
bowls. Taps were fitted coming out of
a high horizontal water pipe and jutting
over each basin. When turned on, the
water shot everywhere but in the basin!
The worst thing was that we had
virtually no privacy ...*[190]

As the service at Chicksands developed accommodation sites were
developed across the compound, removing temptation by means of
erecting separate blocks for men and for women. These stood either side
of the River Flit, which ran through the camp site, with the men in the
lower camp. Inevitably nonetheless, romances blossomed with a number
leading to marriage. Corporal Katherine Cliffe and Leading
Aircraftsman Eric 'Bob' Newman met whilst working together on
intercepts. They married in 1945 and stayed that way for forty six years,
until Katherine's death in 1991.[191]

---

[190] Yvonne Jones (nee Scrivener), 'RAF Chicksands Priory 1941-45'. (Copy held at
Chicksands archives).

[191] Letter and miscellaneous photographs donated to Military Intelligence Museum, by their
daughter, Frances Smith, 2001.

Off duty RAF personnel outside their hut at Chicksands. 'Bob' Newman is standing, facing the camera on the left (MIM).

'We became almost civilised' Yvonne Jones recalled of the building of new blocks. Still, with more than 750 WT operators (the numbers increased with the influx of staff dedicated to the North African campaign), plus support staff, many personnel needed to be billeted in Shefford, Campton and in a further series of huts erected in Wrest Park, near Silsoe. The Nissen huts were icy cold in winter, causing the girls to pull the rugs off the floor and on to their beds, and also to make extemporised hot water bottles out of beer bottles with china stoppers that were then stuffed into socks. By contrast, the huts were extremely hot in summer, uncomfortable to the point that many preferred to sleep under the trees instead.

A group of WAAFS from Wrest Park camp, preparing for a swimming trip, photographed with local children, Silsoe (MIM).

Fancy dress time at Hut 134, Chicksands, as W/T Operators Vera Dunn, Yvonne Jones, Jan Webb, Betty Moore and two others show what can be done, despite wartime rationing *(Courtesy of Yvonne Jones)*.

'D' Flight Netball team (plus supporters) with Chicksands camp in the background *(MIM)*.

As elsewhere, the camp life was self-contained with various sport competitions between and within camps, as well as a great deal of camp generated entertainment (although personnel were expected to be prepared for imminent air attack at any moment). This included a sudden vogue for poetry writing, cookery classes and lectures on all sorts of topics. Some girls diversified into making travel bags and costume design: for Yvonne Jones the finished article was executed by a dressmaker in Ampthill. When the lure of the lectures began to pall, a number of the girls volunteered to join the male personnel at the adjacent Parrish Farm, helping during harvest. Weekly dances were held in a building adjacent to the cookhouse and a fancy dress ball was held.

Whilst the normal discretion was maintained in respect of not disclosing the nature of their work, however, there is an impression that Y Services personnel were not as isolated as those engaged in more overtly clandestine warfare. Many people from the camp drank and socialised at Shefford's main hostelries, *The White Hart*, *The White Swan* and *The Bridge*. Those with a little more time to spare went into Luton and Bedford. Sunbathing WAAFs also provided an entertainment for the deliberately low-flying American pilots based at nearby Thurleigh.[192]

Following light air raids in September and November 1940 (there were no major casualties), shelters were dug and blast walls installed. The new

Two WAAFs, 'Noreen' and 'Brownie', down a pint Chicksands style *(MIM)*.

Mabel Warr, Joannie 'B', 'Dunnie' and 'Burb' at a Wrest Park camp pyjama party, c.1943 *(MIM)*.

[192] Interview with Yvonne Jones, 17 January 2006.

technical buildings (constructed using labour from Italian POWs) were dispersed across the compound in order to lessen the vulnerability to further attack. In fact, despite fears that the Germans had discovered the purpose and were determined to snuff out the listening work, the 1940 raids were not repeated. During 1940-41, a greater fear was that German troops would invade the mainland, the feared *Blitzkrieg* featuring paratroopers in its vanguard. In the case of such an event, a coach was permanently parked in front of the Priory to carry key personnel to a reserve base in Scotland, and the WT operators had orders to immediately pick up their sets and run with them to the transport. This order was clearly a reflection of the early assumption that the operators would be men, as the weight of the equipment meant that it was almost impossible for women to undertake.

The work of WT operators required great accuracy and considerable powers of concentration were needed: chatting was not allowed but the intensity of the activity and the automatic nature of the work (a reflection on some excellent training) meant that the eight hour shifts seemed to pass quite quickly, although the girls often left their watch exhausted from their efforts. The WT operators helped maintain approximately 100 listening positions against the Germans (and a further ten against the Italians), at the peak of their activity. Each frequency was designated an individual code, such as that of a bird name – 'Chaffinch' was one example – and everything was copied down in duplicate or triplicate. The WT operators also became familiar with the idiosyncrasies of each individual German sender, even to the point of being able to recognise when they were on leave from their duties.

Intercepts were sent on to Bletchley via motorcycle courier until the teletype message centre was activated in 1941. It was the Y Service that doomed both of Hitler's mighty battleships. In May 1941 it intercepted the long coded message from the *Bismarck* as well as a sudden increase in *Luftwaffe* radio traffic from their bases on the French coast. This led to the correct deduction that the *Bismarck* was making a dash for the safety of the French ports (up until that point the Admiralty had no real idea of her location or planned route). This information sealed the battleship's doom: the Royal Navy tracked her down and sunk her. On another occasion a Chicksands operator suddenly called out, being quickly surrounded by senior staff offering the somewhat superfluous advice to ensure that he copied everything down absolutely accurately. Although he wasn't fully aware of the exact nature of the operation, this operator had swiftly realised that he was following messages from the sister of the *Bismarck*, the *Tirpitz*. Located whilst hiding in a Norwegian fjord, the *Tirpitz* was repeatedly attacked by midget submarines and carrier based aircraft before being bludgeoned under the waves by the 'tallboy' bombs of the Lancasters of numbers 9 and 617 (Dambusters) squadrons.

The episode of the *Tirpitz* illustrates that, despite the importance of their work, individual WT operators did not usually appreciate the wider significance of their individual activities. There were occasions when an informed guess could be made (the surge in German radio traffic was an early indication of the D-Day landings) but Chicksands provides another example of Phil Luck's 'egg box' principle, something which was doubtless universal (and certainly applied to Bletchley Park). 'We were more scared of the Official Secrets Act than the bombing' observed Joyce Davies, one of Chicksands' WT operators.[193]

BILLY BATS IT OUT

"Billy Bats it out": a cartoon of WT operator 'Billy Bunt' by one of her contemporaries, 'Val', from the album of Joyce King (MIM).

Chicksands was also used for sending as well as listening. The BBC's 'London Calling' broadcasts to occupied Europe were, in fact, frequently broadcast from the Corporations' Bedford bases. These would be sent to the continent via Chicksands, GPO telephone cables providing the link between the two Bedfordshire sites. PWE traffic was also transmitted from Chicksands, including the warning messages to the French Resistance immediately prior to D-Day. These messages, of course, contained their own code that held a meaning to the Resistance, but meant nothing to any other listener. Some of these were even

---

[193] See the *People's War* section on the BBC's History website (id. A4410497).

RAF Chicksands, probably taken at some time during the 1940s. The priory can be seen to the left, with the extension to the camp (mainly for men) at the bottom *(MIM)*.

hidden in the music of Glenn Miller, also broadcasting from Bedford.[194] Whilst Milton Bryan was broadcasting misleading information to the German Army in North Africa, Chicksands transmitted the more helpful variety for the Allied armies as they landed Casablanca, Oran and Algiers at beginning of the 'Operation Torch' campaign.

---

[194] Grayson, op. cit.

The Y Stations, however, couldn't pick up all radio traffic, especially in dealing with the fear that German agents based in Britain or fifth columnists that could transmit information to the enemy. It was the work of the Radio Security Service that represents perhaps the most striking testimony to the degree to which British people were able to keep the secrets of the war. Across the country, hundreds of amateur radio enthusiasts (known colloquially as 'hams') were recruited (initially by MI5) to work as monitors and interceptors for British Intelligence. They provided a role that paralleled and complimented that which was carried out by the military's Y Service, passing on what they had heard to Arkley View, near Barnet (who then sent data on to Bletchley Park).

Two such 'hams' were Freddy Halstead and Arthur Roach. Both were Luton hat manufacturers and it was Halstead who recruited Roach into a group under the leadership of Cyril Page, the Headmaster of the town's Surrey Street School. In the case of Arthur Roach, apart from the group members only his wife knew anything about the work that he did.[195] As with the Y Service interceptors, the work required immense concentration and a bit of luck. Arthur Roach worked at his hat factory from 08.00 until 11.00 and then returned home to his suburban semi in Carlton Crescent. There Arthur sat in his lounge, at his desk, often working until late in the evening. It required considerable effort 'concentrating on a tiny pip-squeak signal, often under a loud automatic and usually the ether was crammed with other signals plus atmospherics'.[196] His log of signals was sent daily to Barnet, occasionally requiring a walk to the main Post Office a mile and a half away in the town centre if the watch was so late that Arthur missed the post. A request to the Postmaster to allow one of his collection vans to take a detour round to Carlton Crescent was politely declined.

One of the local RSS group, Stan Folland (a GPO engineer), erected a 40 foot aerial in the back garden (utilising scaffolding poles) plus a further eight foot mast with two aerials on his chimney. Together with all the assorted guy wires and leads this naturally caused considerable amount of comment over the garden fence. As for Arthur, he also served

---

[195] Roach, Arthur *They Also Serve* (self published, 1987).

[196] Roach, Arthur 'The Hush-Hush War Radio Man'. Typescript notes (1991) held by Luton Museum.

as an ARP warden, covering one night duty to every six day shifts. He was also a member of a local First Aid team. These obligations permitting, Monday was Arthur's day off (where he relaxed by attending shows at the Palace Theatre), and on Sundays he closed down at 17.00. Such was the conduct of Total War in a free country.

Clandestine Warfare: Nobby's War

More than one government unit was responsible for production of weapons, MD1 being an example of one organisation that developed weaponry or other materials for military application. It was responsible, therefore, for providing an assortment of gadgetry for the regular armed forces as well as the embryonic Auxiliary Units and for SOE. It was a maverick department that attracted like-minded individuals. Officially part of the War Office, where it was first entitled Military Intelligence (Research), its tendency 'to short circuit the usual channels and go straight to the PM' may have endeared it to Churchill but it made it many enemies in the corridors of Whitehall. The bulk of MD1's work was undertaken in sites scattered around South East England, especially the Home Counties, but a number of its early creations emanated from the heart of Bedford.[197]

The man in charge of MD1 for the duration of the conflict was Colonel (later Major General) Millis Jefferis. One contemporary described the no-nonsense Jefferis as possessing 'a very brilliant brain which he prefers to use entirely for evolving new ideas and getting them to the stage when they can be developed. He does not want to be worried with administrative work'.[198] Jefferis' second in command was Captain (later Colonel) Stuart Macrae. In the summer of 1939, Jefferis had given Macrae the freedom to find whatever means he could to try to bridge the considerable gap between the effectiveness of German military hardware and its inferior British counterparts. Amongst his various allotted tasks at the beginning of the conflict, Macrae was seeking to develop a magnetic explosive device for sabotage use. Macrae recalled travelling to Bedford after seeing an article in *Caravan and Trailer* around 1937. The

---

[197] Macrae, R. Stuart. *Winston Churchill's Toyshop* (Roundwood Press, 1971).

[198] Letter to C. V. Clarke, 14 December 1941. Private collection.

article was devoted to a vast caravan that had been developed by LoLode (Low Loading Trailer Company Ltd.) of 173-175 Tavistock Street (Clarke's home and experimental workshop) and Dean Street, Bedford. At the former, Macrae had met LoLode's owner and Technical Director, Cecil Vandepeer ('Nobby') Clarke.

In his early forties, Clarke had served as a junior officer throughout World War One, moving to Bedford in 1926, where he established his business. Macrae remembered his first impression of Nobby Clarke: 'He was a very large man with rather hesitant speech who at first struck me as being amiable but not outstandingly bright. The second part of the impression did not last long.' With time of the essence and remembering Clarke's inventiveness, Macrae now turned to Nobby to help him with his magnetic device. Both men were 'brilliant at lateral thinking', in the opinion of one of Clarke's sons, John, and immediately struck up a rapport.[199]

Macrae later recalled that Clarke:

> was operating from his private house which he had converted in some remarkable way into a works. Sweeping a number of children out of the living room which also had to serve as an office, he filled me up with bread and jam and some awful buns and then we got down to business.

The next day 'Nobby created an experimental department by sweeping a load of rubbish and more children off a bench'. Thus, during eight weeks of the summer of 1939, began the evolution of what was to become known as the 'limpet mine', a device that was to have special application in the underwater sabotage of enemy shipping by sticking to their steel hulls. The two of them bought some tin bowls from the Bedford branch of *Woolworths* that were then fashioned into the required shapes by a local tinsmith. Back at Clarke's house they used 'all the porridge in the house' in lieu of explosives and proceeded to experiment with weight, buoyancy and magnetic strength, flooding the bathroom 'on several occasions' in the process. Field trials were conducted in Bedford's public baths (then closed to the public) with Mrs Clarke's griddle plate requisitioned from the family kitchen where it was used to simulate a

---

[199] Testimony contributed to BBC *People's War* website by John Vandepeer Clarke. Article id. A4376153, collected by Bedford Museum, contributed 6 July 2005. Interview with John Vandepeer Clarke, 8.11.06.

Major C. V. Clarke, M.C. 'Nobby never did stand on ceremony,' recalled his collaborator, Stuart Macrae *(Courtesy of John Clarke)*.

ship's hull. In these trials Nobby did the necessary swimming, 'looking as if he were suffering from advanced pregnancy', according to his collaborator.

If it is to *Caravan and Trailer* that the development of the limpet mine can be indirectly attributed, it is Roger, the youngest of Clarke's children, who can take similar credit for inadvertently solving the mine's major technical difficulty. The device was triggered by a spring loaded striker that would then hit a cap to set off a detonator that in turn would explode a primer to blast the main charge. This was a simple enough sequence for men of Macrae and Clarke's abilities, but required a small water soluble pellet to delay the charge for sufficient time to allow the person who had placed it to get away. Therein lay the problem as no suitable pellet could be found until the two weapons' developers accidentally spilt some aniseed balls that belonged to Roger. As Macrae popped one of the fallen aniseed balls into his mouth, the potential of this layered sweet immediately struck both men whereupon they proceeded to experiment (buying up every aniseed ball in Bedford in the process, according to Macrae) before approaching the manufacturers, Barrett.[200] As John Clarke later recalled:

> The aniseed balls were drilled and little detonator capsules put inside and my father had these ranged around the house and setting off at different times depending on the amount of aniseed ball that was used on each detonator. He would rush into the room in the house where, on the mantelpiece, one of these charges would be put in a big glass Woolworth's tumbler and he would say, "Right, that's 35 minutes." It didn't matter that probably the glass had fractured and all the water had gone - he had got something that worked and they were quickly able to establish how much of an aniseed ball was needed to give the varying times of delay that the operators would require.

The subsequent challenge was to protect the aniseed ball timing device from damp until the last moment, when the limpet mine was placed on

[200] The process of reducing aniseed balls to different sizes required the recruitment of personnel beyond Macrae and Clarke's immediate family. Nobby's secretary at LoLode, Greta Maycock (the daughter of Ampthill's chemist) also played her part. Later she observed that she had an answer for those who asked her what she did in the war – 'I sucked aniseed balls'.

the target. As Macrae put it, 'what we needed was a closed rubber sleeve of some sort which could be pushed over the tube to seal it and be easily whipped off by the diver when the time came'. The solution was again found amongst Bedford's retailers, this time the chemists. Clarke and Macrae bought up all the condoms they could find, thus ensuring that not only aniseed ball lovers experienced a frustrating weekend, whilst simultaneously 'earning ourselves an undeserved reputation for being sexual athletes' (as Macrae put it).

With the prototype nearing completion, testing now switched to a small motor boat on Bedford's River Great Ouse. John Clarke, who was around ten years of age at the time, remembered being allowed to accompany his father on trials. These indicated that Nobby's invention could cling on to a vessel travelling up to 10-15 knots.

Nobby Clarke models the prototype of the limpet mine at his Bedford home
(*Courtesy of John Clarke*).

It was thus from homespun ingenuity located in Bedford that 'the first few hundreds' of nearly half a million limpet mines were manufactured. Subsequent perfection of the limpet mine's design took place at SOE's

Hertfordshire workshops at Station IX (Welwyn) and Station XII (Aston House, near Stevenage), and the resultant weapon was one that could on average carry approximately 9lb (4 kg) of explosive and blow a hole in the steel hull of a ship a yard wide. One of its most celebrated application was in *Operation Franklin* (later eulogised in the film and book *Cockleshell Heroes*), in December 1942. This involved a British submarine surfacing off the coast of France and despatching six canoes, each with a two man crew. Their target was shipping in Bordeaux harbour, seventy miles upstream from the estuary of the Gironde River. Only two canoes made the arduous journey but the limpet mines that they attached succeeded in inflicting severe damage to five ships.

It was not just against shipping that the limpet could be applied. In *Operation Josephine* an Anglo-French team of saboteurs this time focused on the U-Boat pens at Bordeaux. They succeeded in gaining access to the guarded compound housing the power station at nearby Pessac, and attached eight limpets to the transformers. Six detonated, destroying the electricity supply not only to the U-Boat pens, but also to the railway line and surrounding factories.

* * *

This was not the end of Nobby's war, however, and with production of the limpet mine under way, he went back to the drawing board in his Tavistock Street workshop. Recalling his experience of the Western Front between 1915-17 (in which he acquired first hand experience of the methods of tunnelling used to undermine enemy defensives), and noting the apparent repeated stalemate that existed in the same sector during the autumn 1939, he devised a high speed trench forming machine. Planned to weigh around 140 tons, these were designed to drive through the earth in the direction of the German defences at a speed of 2000 yards in a night and able to withstand direct hits from most shells. Targeting the foundations of the fortified block houses on the vaunted 'Siegfried Line', the trench formed in its wake would be wide enough to carry tanks.

Nobby's detailed specifications were sent first to the Royal Engineer and Signals Board at the Ministry of Supply, with a specific request that all communication be passed through Brig. Jefferis in the research department at the War Office. Intrigued, but with a similar scheme being developed in one of its departments, the Ministry turned down Nobby's proposals with the standard 'Should we decide to pursue the matter at a later date, we ... will inform you accordingly.'

After considering the matter further for a few weeks, Nobby tried again. This time he sent the proposal to Winston Churchill, not yet Prime Minister but still First Lord of the Admiralty. The ingenuity evident in Nobby's design brought him to the attention of Churchill's chief scientific advisor, Prof. Frederick Lindemann who requested an immediate interview with Nobby. Following this, on 25 April 1940, Churchill wrote to Clarke:

My *dear sir*

I was glad to have your letter of April 11th, and have read it with interest.

As Professor Lindemann told you in the strictest confidence, experiments are in hand on somewhat similar lines and as soon as results are available, so that we can tell whether your ideas can be applied, you will be informed ...

The first rough experiments will tell us whether this line of development is promising, but until they have been carried out, it is difficult for us to go any further. I am hoping that it will not be a very long time before we are able to communicate with you again.

Yours etc.

Winston S. Churchill

Nobby's approach to Churchill secured him an Assistant Director's post in the Naval Land Section at the Ministry of Supply, at the considerable salary of £1000 per annum. A few weeks later, however, Hitler's 'blitzkrieg' attack upon France and the Low Countries rendered trench forming machines, and the whole concept of warfare that they embraced, as completely redundant. Seeing the drift of the conflict, five weeks after his appointment the former Capt. Clarke resolved to cease to be a Civil Servant.

Rejoining the army, Nobby became a serving officer in the Intelligence Corps, rising to the rank of Major. His specialist area was engineering and weapons development, much of which was to have particular application in the Secret War. LoLode continued to function, even though Nobby was no longer able to oversee its day-to-day running, leaving this to his wife (as Company Secretary), Richard Marks, the Sales Director and Nobby's own secretary, Greta Maycock. His work took him to centres in Hertfordshire and Buckinghamshire (and occasionally further, to work with diverse branches of the services such as the Eighth Army in North Africa, and Coastal Command over the Bay of Biscay).

As an Intelligence Corps Officer on Special Duty, Nobby Clarke was first appointed to work at SOE's new Special Training School (number XII), based at Aston House, near Stevenage. This was a Technical Research and Development Station and there Nobby got down to working on various incendiary and explosive devices, producing an SOE manual ('Blue Book') on their application for sabotage. One weapon with specific application for the sabotage units of SOE and the French Resistance was the spigot mortar, a missile launcher small enough to be fired by a lone operator, invented by a couple of MD1's staff, Norman Angier and Lt. Col. Stewart Blacker – two more original thinkers. Nobby worked on one in particular, the plate spigot (the plate giving the firer a measure of protection as it was fired horizontally), as well as developing a derivation of his own, the tree spigot. This was one of a series of ambush explosive devices that were developed by Nobby and his colleagues. The tree spigot was of particular use in the sort of surprise attacks favoured by the French Resistance, as the mortar was attached to a tree and operated by a wire – permitting the firer to be hidden a short distance away. A further mortar invention of his was a three inch mortar round that cruelly bounced once before detonating just above its target.

At the end of 1940 Nobby Clarke was then given command of his own centre, STS XVII, based at Brickendonbury Manor, near Hertford, specialising in sabotage training for allied agents due to be sent abroad. 'This was just Nobby's cup of tea and enabled him to become a bigger menace than ever,' noted Macrae, adding that there were no guards on the gate, trip wires and (blank) rounds from tree spigots usually serving to halt visiting vehicles.[201] A maverick as well as a lateral thinker, Nobby apparently decided that his trainees needed some hands on experience. He therefore organised a raid on the Luton Electricity Station.

Having first falsified a pass for himself on official War Office paper, Nobby took his group to Luton. Under cover of darkness the Franco-Polish saboteurs gained access to the building using scaling ladders. Once inside the station, they planted dummy explosives on the transformers and escaped again without alerting the guard. Nobby now moved to the front of the building and, presenting his official pass, announced to the officer of the guard that he was there to conduct a routine inspection of the building. To the horror of the 'poor subaltern who was in charge of the guard … knock-kneed with what he'd let happen', the inspection revealed the work of 'saboteurs'. Acting swiftly, Clarke called in his team of experts (this time by the front door), who removed the incendiaries. Taking pity on the hapless officer, Nobby kindly suggested that, in the circumstances, neither needed to say any more about it.[202]

With this expedition safely concluded, Nobby became more ambitious. This time he organised a daylight assault on the BBC transmitter at Brookmans Park in Hertfordshire. Unfortunately, although his trainees got over the fence they were apprehended by the sentries. Taking a wider perspective of matters, and since nobody got shot, Brigadier Colin Gubbins (Director of Operations and Training at SOE), wasn't too hard on Nobby.

Gubbins' wider perspective was doubtless due to an awareness of the very serious purpose behind Major Clarke's cavalier disregard for protocol. Between 20 October and 8 November 1941, towards the end of Clarke's tenure in charge (he handed over to Maj. G. T. Rheam), Jan Kubiš and Jozef Gabčík arrived in Hertfordshire for training in handling explosives under his tutelage. Kubiš and Gabčík were Warrant Officers from the

---

[201] Macrae, op.

[202] Testimony and interview with John V. Clarke. The War Office 'pass' is in JVC's private papers.

remnants of the Czechoslovak Army that had made its way to Britain in 1940 and were at STS XVII as part of a series of courses that were preparing them for a specific task: the assassination of Reinhard Heydrich. Second only to Himmler within the SS hierarchy, Heydrich was the epitome of the ruthless savagery of the Nazi's new order. A few weeks later, in January 1942, Heydrich would chair the infamous Wannsee Conference that would prepare the Final Solution to the Jewish problem – their extermination. Simultaneously, he had been appointed to take charge of Bohemia and Moravia, a 'protectorate' within Hitler's empire.

Nobby Clarke played a decisive role in the commandos' training. Two days were spent at STS XVII but the rest of the period seemed to be largely based at nearby STS XII, Aston House, with Nobby working alongside its station commander, Col. L. J. C. Wood.[203] A key weapon in the arsenal that Kubiš and Gabčík were to carry to their homeland was a modified No. 73 Anti-Tank Grenade. One of the vital adaptations contributed by Clarke was to fit this grenade with an extremely sensitive detonator, before he and Col. Wood trained the two commandos in its use.

In December 1941 SOE's Czechoslovak agents were flown out of the UK, departing from Tangmere, Sussex in a Halifax piloted by S/Ldr R. C. Hockey of 138 Squadron, being parachuted into the native country with some difficulty. It was 27 May 1942 before Kubiš and Gabčík finally caught up with the man nicknamed 'Hangman', stepping out in front of Heydrich's open top Mercedes as it turned a corner in a Prague street. Gabčík's sten gun jammed and Heydrich apparently ordered his driver to slow up in order that he could stand and fire back at the Gabčík. At this Kubiš stepped forward and threw his specially adapted bomb. Although Kubiš' throw missed Heydrich, it exploded on impact with the side of the car, fragments from the Mercedes' panelling and upholstery penetrating Heydrich's body, fatally wounding him.

---

[203] Turner, Des. *Aston House. SOE Station XII. SOE's Secret Centre* (Sutton, 2006). Turner draws upon the testimony of Col. Wood. According to some accounts, Clarke had been barred from STS XII by Wood's predecessor for sidestepping security procedure on a previous visit there. Burian, Michal; Křížek, Ales; Rajlich, Jiří; Stehlík, Eduard. *Assassination. Operation Anthropoid 1941-42* (Prague, 2002). This places their training at STS XVII specifically under Capt. Pritchard. HS4/39, National Archives.

After escaping in the confusion, Kubiš and Gabčík, together with a small number of fellow resistance fighters, were betrayed and cornered in Czechoslovak Orthodox Church in the centre of Prague. At the end of a ferocious battle with German soldiers, most chose suicide. The brutal German reprisal for Heydrich's assassination (including the complete destruction of the village of Lidice), inclined the Allies towards making 'the Butcher of Prague' to be the only senior Nazi to be attacked in an SOE operation.

The culmination of Nobby Clarke's military career came with his appointment to Jefferis' MD1 testing base at 'The Firs', Whitchurch. This Whitchurch posting was not just to prevent Nobby launching any other pre-emptive strikes on public installations in the Home Counties, but also partly a consequence of inter-department squabbling and re-organisation. MD1, always a square peg in a round hole, had been shifted from the War Office to another uncomfortable berth at the Ministry of Supply. This meant that experts such as Clarke were in separate departments to those such as Stuart Macrae with whom he had enjoyed such a productive working relationship.

Nobby had his own ideas as to where they should be based, writing to the recently appointed Hugh Dalton in his Department of Economic Warfare to advocate closer co-operation. The replies – from Gaitskell, in his capacity as Dalton's Private Secretary – indicated that such changes were already under way and the two of them would be in closer contact in the near future: 'It may interest you to know – and I should prefer you to treat this as strictly confidential and keep it entirely to yourself – that the Minister is already in close touch with Colonel Gubbins, and that the association may be a much closer one in the near future.'[204] Nobby was certainly in favour of not just setting Europe ablaze. The following spring, his proposal to lead 'an irregular detachment' of commandos to the Near East was turned down by SOE.

---

[204] Letters from Hugh Gaitskell to C. V. Clarke, 5 November 1940 and 13 November 1940. Only Gaitskell's replies survive, but they hint at wider criticism from Clarke at the conduct of the war in some quarters. Referring to his own boss, Gaitskell wrote: 'You will not be surprised to hear that the Minister is, generally speaking, in close agreement with the points you make... You will, however, appreciate that he is only one member of an All Party Government, the unity of which, it is generally agreed, is essential if victory is to be won.'

Nobby's desire for reorganisation was, not surprisingly, shared by those within MD1. Writing confidentially to Clarke a year after his correspondence with Gaitskell, an official at MD1 emphasised that:

> There is no question that our proper home is with your people, because, like you, we have always been irregular and always will be. Our job is … to design special weapons and special devices for use by irregular troops, raiding parties, agents and so forth. Is some of these weapons eventually prove of value to the regular services, all the better, but our primary object is not to design them as Service weapons.

In the end it was Major Clarke that moved, Gubbins agreeing to his request to transfer from SOE to MD1 in Buckinghamshire. The demands of this work required Nobby to frequently stay overnight with only occasional visits back home to Bedford which he made by bicycle (he reckoned that he averaged fifteen miles to the pint). Nobby's eldest son John, however, was permitted to visit the Whitchurch base, observing the testing of weapons, including Macrae trying out his personal invention, the Sticky Bomb, on a tank, and John's father firing a Projectile Infantry Anti Tank gun, or PIAT for short.

The PIAT was originally devised by Millis Jefferis and Stewart Blacker. When compared with the later breed of German panzers, allied tanks were under gunned and lightly protected: there could be little more discouraging sight for a tank commander than to see his shell bounce off the armour of one of the German leviathans as they slowly brought their huge guns round to bear upon his own vehicle. In the circumstances, the development of alternative means of knocking out a panzer – such as the PIAT – was of vital importance.

For the production of the PIAT, Major Clarke was appointed Liaison Officer with ICI. This put the focus upon Henry Mond, Lord Melchett of Colworth House, Sharnbrook. Winston Churchill, Prof. Lindemann (Lord Cherwell), together with senior MD1 personnel, were regular visitors to Melchett's Bedfordshire home, as well as to meetings in London, as key figures grappled with the task of taking MD1's prototype weaponry to a stage by which it could take the war to Germany. During

---

[205] Letter to C. V. Clarke, 14 December 1941.

the 1930s Henry and Gwen Mond had made extensive changes to Colworth, remodelling it and filling it with works of art, some specifically commissioned. It wasn't Melchett's furnishing and adornment that drew Macrae's attention, however: 'What impressed me most about his mansion was that the lavatories, in addition to being close carpeted, were equipped with pedestals having plush covered seats instead of the usual plastic or wooden ones.'[206]

Melchett was responsible for establishing eight large ordnance factories around the country, one of which was situated to the south of Bedford. In order to get the PIAT available in sufficient quantities, Melchett turned to his American contacts, travelling to the United States (meeting President Roosevelt at the White House), despite ill-health in order to arrange further production capacity. In addition to the millions that were produced for the regular forces, 1200 were parachuted into occupied France for the Maquis, although this was nowhere near the number that they desired.[207]

Whilst in charge of STS XVII, Nobby had pondered the possible means by which German aircraft could be sabotaged whilst on the ground. This ultimately evolved into the altimeter switch. Planted in the tail inspection port of German aircraft by deft operatives in the various sabotage forces, this was set to explode once the plane reached a given altitude (usually 10,000 feet).

Nobby was not the only person thinking along these lines and once at Whitchurch he worked as part of a team, where he could bring to bear his experience of working with the explosive training of SOE's saboteurs. Stuart Macrae later described Major Clarke's role:

Nobby's contribution was to insist that it should have a flexible sausage of explosive... In this instance he had worked out that such a weapon as this could not be conveniently concealed in the pocket but could without comment be carried in the trousers. He was wrong about the

---

[206] Macrae, op. cit.

[207] Jones, Michael op. cit.

'without comment' and there was always considerable ribaldry when he demonstrated this method. But actually it was sound common sense...[208]

The development of the flexible, sausage shaped explosive indicates that the Bedford workshop was still being used for weapons development. Roger Clarke who, unlike his older brother never went to Whitchurch, noted 'I retain in my mind's eye this sausage shaped explosive device'.[209]

Nobby Clarke's last contribution was the extraordinary 'Great Eastern'. This was a rocket operated self-propelled bridge that could be thrown over a gap (such as a river) or obstacle from a Churchill tank. The bridge would be sufficiently robust to carry the weight of a tank travelling over it. Some hair-raising trials took place at Whitchurch in the early part of 1945, with Lord Melchett accompanying Jefferis (the rockets were manufactured by ICI). The 'Great Eastern' was just about ready for use when, to the chagrin of its inventor, the surrender of the German Army in Europe halted its further deployment.[210]

The army and weapons development career of Cecil Vandepeer Clarke by no means reflects the true character of the man. The harrowing experience of World War One, added to a growing alarm at the spread of totalitarianism during the inter-war period led this intensely patriotic individual to a growing religious conviction. He was profoundly moved by witnessing the death of an Austrian soldier in the last few days of World War One, later writing down this memory in an unpublished document entitled 'Experience. The Induction of Value From the Conditions of Living'. He self published a volume entitled *Suggestions. For All Men, Including Englishmen* (dedicated to the dissident German pastor, Martin Niemoller), in 1939 outlining his philosophical views. After World War Two he wrote a play in which a group of men, drawn together by their placement at an SOE training school, discuss various questions facing humanity.

---

[208] Macrae, op. cit.

[209] Letter to Mark Seaman, Imperial War Museum, by Rev. Roger Clarke MBE, 1.2.1992. Private collection.

[210] Nine reels of cine film, some taken by Nobby, depicting the testing of the 'Great Eastern' and assorted sabotage weaponry, were subsequently donated to the Imperial War Museum by C. V. Clarke's sons.

Self-deprecating, with a great sense of the ridiculous, Nobby was described by his eldest son as 'very questing' and deeply interested in what other people thought. In the 1950s he began to campaign against the further proliferation of weapons, joining CND, becoming the leader of the Bedford branch and helping to organise the famous Aldermaston March of 1958. He collaborated with Bertrand Russell and the newly formed Committee of 100 in developing strategies of non-violent resistance. Although Nobby Clarke soon broke with the Committee (believing there to be a disproportionately Communist influence), he joined them in putting these tactics into practise during one of CND's 1961 rallies in London, where the campaigners all lay down in simulation of the effects of a nuclear holocaust. With Nobby now weighing in at over eighteen stone, it took four laughing members of the Metropolitan Police to lift (and good naturedly arrest) this serenely happy protestor.

Clandestine Warfare: Resistance and the Special Operations Executive

Neighbouring Buckinghamshire had became a base for Czechoslovakia's exiled government and armed forces from 1940 and, in August 1942, the wireless service operated by the Czechoslovak Military Intelligence was moved by SOE (who were training their WT operators) from Woldingham in Surrey to a farm just outside Hockliffe in South West Bedfordshire. This placed it nearer to other Czechoslovak departments as well as facilities at Whaddon Hall that supplied its equipment. From here contact was maintained with other elements of the Czechoslovak diaspora, particularly those in those legations situated in the capitals of neutral Europe (Lisbon, Berne, Stockholm and Istanbul) that the Nazis had not been able to close down and which the Czech Military Intelligence Service had the foresight to establish after their escape to Britain in March 1939.[211] There was also contact with the resistance groups in the homeland that had not yet been broken by the Nazi occupiers.[212] Teleprinter connections with SIS and

---

[211] Hawker, Pat. 'Czech Clandestine Radio From the UK. Part 1 – Flight to the UK and Agent A-54' *Radio Bygones* (No. 103, October/November 2006).

[212] Rees, Neil. *The Czech Connection. The Czechoslovak Government in Exile in London and Buckinghamshire* (Neil Rees, 2005). Modrak, V. *Radio Transmitters Between the Home and Foreign Fields During World War Two. Memoirs of the Radio Operator at the Military Radio Station.*

SOE were established, with close contact between its training centres at Chicheley Hall (STS 46) and Audley End (STS 43).

The Czechoslovaks presented a mixed blessing to their hosts. At one level, Britain was glad to receive all the help that it could get in the early stages of the war, and Czechoslovak personnel, notably the heroic fighter pilots, made an invaluable contribution. Generally speaking, relations on both sides were very good. There were difficulties, however, in integrating foreign forces with understandably different priorities into the British war effort, and these could easily lead to the ruffling of diplomatic feathers. For example, there was concern expressed in official quarters about the level (or lack) of security covering the radio traffic being sent out from Hockliffe, especially to areas controlled by the Germans. One irritated British official condescendingly noted that there was an urgent need to control 'these Private Army' signals, and it was suggested that there should be a 'sudden check' of the station and its log books.[213]

Prior to its flight to Britain, Czechoslovak Military Intelligence, under the command of Col. František Moravec, had established excellent networks of information. One key source was Paul Thuemmel, a rising officer in the *Abwehr*, and otherwise known as A-54. Intelligence was shared with their British hosts and connections were maintained with clandestine forces in their homeland. Steadily, however, this latter link was eroded as the Germans broke ciphers, penetrated underground cells, turned agents and, with the help of collaborators, rounded up operatives (including A-54). The savage reprisals for the assassination of Heydrich, accounting for at least 5000 lives, inhibited the capacity and resolve to mount further active resistance. This had never been easy due to Czechoslovakia's geographical location, which could only be physically accessed after flights of nine or ten hours and which involved flying over Germany. The failure of operations *Iridium*, *Mercury* and *Bronze* illustrate this point. All were mounted by the 138/161 Squadrons based at RAF Tempsford and resulted in a heavy loss of life amongst agents and crews. Furthermore, from 1943 onwards, the focus began to shift to Western Europe, especially France, in anticipation of an Allied seaborne invasion from that direction.[214]

---

[213] HW 34/25. 'RSS War Records: Czech Transmitters in this Country.' National Archives.

[214] Hawker, Pat. 'Czech Clandestine Radio From the UK. Part 2 – Assassination and its Aftermath' *Radio Bygones* (No. 104, Christmas 2006).

Eventually Hockliffe had a permanent complement of ten radio operators, four mechanics, a cook and a foreman, under the command of Capt. Zdeněk Gold. Kitting out of Hockliffe was still taking place in 1943, suggesting that the Czechoslovaks were perhaps relying a little on equipment hand-me-downs, although adequate radio sets for clandestine operations were in short supply for all branches of SOE.[215] There was a constant stream of requests from the Czechoslovaks for more equipment, which British officials had to concede it would be 'positively niggardly to refuse'. As the tide of war turned this the British became more appreciative that the Czechoslovaks were trying to build up a stockpile of equipment towards the eventual re-occupation of their country.

The Czechoslovaks didn't need to wait for their hosts to supply transmitters and receivers, being capable of producing their own. These had a greater range than those generally available to SOE, being specifically designed for conditions within Czechoslovakia. One of personnel based at Hockliffe, Sgt. Antonín Šimandl, designed the Marjánka receiver and a transmitter that carried his own name. The Šimandl transmitter was designed for use by agents in the field, with up to fifteen being produced.[216] One of these transmitters was lost in *Operation Bronze* when S/Ldr Gibson's Halifax crashed near Munich, killing all on board. Perhaps it was the Hockliffe design that exasperated British communications officers were referring to when, on more than one occasion, they complained about Czechoslovak operatives going out 'laden like camels'. If so, this was a failure on the British part to appreciate that the Czechoslovaks not only possessed an independent degree of technical sophistication, but also had a superior understanding of the 'special conditions then existing in our occupied country'.[217]

There were difficulties with the station's buildings also. Accommodated in a pair of Nissen huts, facilities for the Czechoslovaks were extremely Spartan, with inadequate hot water (personnel were 'lucky if they get one bath a week') and sewage disposal. The cess pits overflowed, leading

---

[215] Correspondence from Pat Hawker, 6.1.2007.

[216] Meulstee, Louis and Staritz, Rudolf F. *Wireless for the Warrior. Vol. 4, Clandestine Radio* (A Radio Bygones publication, 2004).

[217] Correspondence from Jiří Louda, 7.1.2007. Mr Louda did not personally experience any difficulties in obtaining equipment: 'Our technicians were supplied with the required material without any problems.'

Three members of the Czechoslovak personnel, Václav Retich, Capt. Václav Knotek, and Jan Štursa, photographed at the Hockliffe Radio Station in the winter of 1944 (*courtesy of the family of Jaroslav Bublík*).

to complaints from the farmers (Bunker Brothers), and a sharply critical inspection by an SCU officer on 24 August 1943 to this 'leaky' and 'dusty' installation was one that was feared might cause a minor diplomatic incident. Captain Ford's inspection was also critical of the lack of barbed wire protection that was supposed to stop encroachment by the Bunkers' cattle, who could collapse the masts should they blunder into them.[218] Perhaps Ford was being a little too officious: the horrified response of Col. Russell (whose job it was to liaise with the Czechoslovaks), to this 'Ford ebullience' was 'goodness knows the situation is difficult enough without adding complications to it'. Other British officers seem to have taken a more relaxed view of circumstances. Jiří Louda, who served at Hockliffe for three and a half years, recalled that the station 'was regularly visited by British officers and they always stayed for lunch in friendly conversation'. Nonetheless, the conditions on the Bunkers' farm meant that it was perhaps with some understandable relief that, when off duty, the Hockliffe personnel took advantage of free time to take trips to the cinema in Dunstable. For Jiří Louda, a special pleasure was to travel on to London, via Luton, to visit the Royal College of Arms or the British Library.[219]

* * *

RAF Henlow on the eastern side of the county fulfilled a wide number of functions. It contained a hospital and also hosted the Special Parachute

---

[218] HW 34/25.

[219] Jiří Louda, op cit.

Section (leaflet balloons were tested at Cardington). Part of the Special Parachute Section's brief was to develop containers that could be dropped in support of SOE and OSS operations in occupied Europe. The increase in clandestine activity in the months leading up to D-Day placed pressure on the capabilities of domestic parachute production. In order to overcome this shortfall American made parachutes were introduced but the tests, carried out at Henlow in May/June 1944 produced some alarming results when seven out of thirteen failed to open satisfactorily – one containing incendiaries exploding into flames upon hitting the ground.

The Americans, taking offence at a perceived slight to their technological capabilities, offered to conduct their own tests adding, with mischievous confidence, that they would drop theirs onto the courtyard of SOE's Howbury Hall, the ancestral home of the Polhill family on the outskirts of Bedford. The American failure rate of just one out of twelve led to some head scratching before it was discovered that modifications would need to be made to the static line in British planes before they could drop containers with American parachutes. The Air Ministry decided that the trouble of making such modifications was not worth the return.[220] The SOE containers were also often tested at RAF Tempsford (from which they would also be conveyed), from 1943 onwards. Henlow's grass runways were also used for landing and take off practise for the pilots who were to operate out of Tempsford, a key part of their training given the very specific contribution that it was to make to the Secret War.

* * *

RAF Tempsford was one of several air bases that specialised in the delivery and collection of SOE agents and support material for resistance groups in occupied Europe.[221] Located near Sandy, nine miles from Bedford, it was built upon marshy land leased from the Pym and Astell families, having been first identified as a potential airfield in 1936.[222] In

---

[220] Boyce, Frederic and Everett, Douglas. SOE. The Scientific Secrets (Sutton, 2005).

[221] Clark, Freddie. Agents By Moonlight (Tempus 1999). An immensely detailed labour of love, as comprehensive a record of operations as can be established, and a tribute to old comrades from one of the heroes of 138 Squadron.

[222] Seebohm, Caroline. The Country House. A Wartime History 1939-45 (Weidenfeld and Nicholson, 1989). O'Connor, Bernard Tempsford Airfield. Now The Story Can Be Told (published by the author, 1999). This is a thorough, authoritative and highly recommended work. See also Bernard O'Connor's contributions to the Everton-cum-Tetworth history website (www.members.aol.com/fqurk202/index.html). Information also supplied by Colin Burbidge.

that year landowners were informed by the Commandant of the Observer Corps that the Sandy area was regarded as a critical link in the air defences of the UK, and that this would require the installation of observer posts. Simultaneously, the Air Ministry indicated that they were planning to construct an aerodrome in the area. Contrary pressure was brought to bear (the heir, Leslie Pym, was MP for Monmouthshire) and the scheme was abandoned, not to be revived until the darker days of 1941, when there was now no chance of reprieve. 'A row of magnificent elms was felled to create visibility for the runways,' although the marshy land upon which Tempsford laid out ensured that it retained a boggy aspect, afflicting aircraft and personnel (upwards of two thousand individuals) alike. The area included three farms (Gibraltar, Port Mahon and Waterloo), and also utilised the Pym's house, Hasells Hall, as well as other country homes scattered around its vicinity on the borders of Bedfordshire, Cambridgeshire and Huntingdonshire (Tempsford Hall, Woodbury Hall, Old Woodbury, Howbury Hall and Gaynes Hall) that played host at different times to a number of different units, including agents of the Special Operations Executive. One can readily understand how, in some quarters, SOE was said to stand for 'Stately 'omes of England' and even now the precise functions that of each of these houses served is not precisely known. Needless to say, local gossip did its best to fill in the gaps.

Tempsford accommodated a number of facilities and fulfilled a number of functions. As with other airfields, it included its own RAF meteorological branch department, receiving reports from the Air Ministry and which in turn would have been served by the Meteorological Office that was based at Dunstable (airfield reports were sent back to Dunstable via Group HQ and the RAF's Central Forecasting Office). The Operations Room, where critical briefings were given by Intelligence Officers (only pilots and navigators amongst the crews were informed as to the destination), was based in Gibraltar Farm (the access to which was very restricted), and it was the nearby barn that was frequently used for the last minute briefing and kitting out of an agent.

The pilots were based at Port Mahon, although some crew stayed at Everton, Potton and Sandy. Additionally there was a radio training school that Bernard O'Connor believes was most likely to have been at Old Woodbury. As the site developed it acquired the usual panoply of buildings associated with air bases: accommodation, mess halls, storage depots, a sick bay, garages and hangers. Recollections often focused upon the drab, damp and muddy appearance of the place – 'a dump' often was the expression that was used. The runways, narrower than normal and appearing to be gouged out of the farm land, contributed to the makeshift atmosphere. Arriving to join his squadron, pilot Hugh Verity concluded that Tempsford was 'not much of an RAF station, I thought ... It was a rush job quickly built in war time like hundreds of others... there was a lot of mud'.[223]

Nature always seemed ready to reclaim RAF Tempsford. Ten years after the war ended, author Jerrard Tickell produced this abbreviated, but evocative description of the now derelict station in his book, *Moon Squadron*:

> We drove around the perimeter crossing the end of the main runway -
> a muddy track led to dilapidated house-slates gone from the roof -
> blind windows draped with sacking, rickety door not much left now...
> Outbuilding mildewed, cobwebbed remnants, original walls and
> mouldering thatch - buildings within buildings; sound sturdy rooms had
> been constructed. Shelves ran along the sides, electric cables still
> looped over the rafters. Parachutes stored on shelves...
> Changing rooms and rooms where men and women submitted to
> final search, final check turning out of pockets, scrutiny of documents,
> before they were driven out to the aircraft that waited in the rising moon.
> Broken rack held weapons - an alcove for continental clothes, shoes
> and hats etc. Forged papers; here radio transmitting sets - here
> lethal tablets.[224]

The geographical location may well have contributed to this dank atmosphere but if RAF Tempsford resembled Cold Comfort Farm this wasn't entirely accidental, as Tickell's description indicates. Many of these structures were given cladding in order that they resembled farm buildings (even from the ground they were said to resemble these), or

[223] Verity, Hugh. *We Landed By Moonlight. Secret Landings in France, 1940-44* (Crecy Publishing, 1998). Tibbutt, H. G. 'The Cloak and Dagger Squadrons of RAF Tempsford in World War Two' *Bedfordshire Magazine* vol. XII, pp. 269-73.

[224] Tickell, Jerrard. *Moon Squadron* (Allan Wingate, 1956). The redundant buildings were sold off in an auction on 12 April 1961, and the site returned to farmland.

Farm buildings at RAF Tempsford.('By day: the appearance of the unhurried life of farming- only by moonlight had things moved, had aircraft slid out of hangars, taken shadowy anonymous men and women on board to cast them out into the hostile skies' (*Jerrard Tickell, Moon Squadron*).

were camouflaged in order to blend in with the landscape. A few remnants of farm life (tractors, ducks, even the occasional grazing cattle), were also utilised to confuse reconnaissance and throughout the region the allies used dummy airfields. There was one such decoy airfield situated between Bedford and Great Barford, officially secret but known to the locals.[225] Publicly, the work of the aircraft was said to be devoted to mine laying operations and it was well protected. Incorporating Tempsford into a fictional novel (in which the main character is loosely based on his own), SOE agent Peter Churchill recalled 'it was one thing to reach Tempsford but quite another to gain admission to the hush-hush grounds. The sentries were sceptical and not inclined to be impressed by his rank or his appearance at face value'.[226]

For all this ingenuity and formal security, however, it must be said that Tempsford, relied as much upon discretion as it did on orders to keep its secrets. For those camp personnel who disregarded the obligations that they had attested to in the signing of the Official Secrets Act, official retribution could be sudden and fierce. Even casual, unguarded talk that might be overheard in a Sandy public house would be met with

---

[225] Information from George How in his contribution to the BBC's *People's War* website. Interviewed by Jenny Ford, id. 6097368.

[226] Churchill, Peter. *By Moonlight* (Brown, Watson Ltd.).

permanent removal from the base, as the precursor to even heavier sanctions. When first informed of his imminent posting to Tempsford, Squadron Leader Frank Griffiths found that people were a little vague as to what went on there 'but some knew that Tempsford was a bit odd … The only people who really knew what went on at Tempsford were the Germans and the Resistance units in the occupied countries of Europe! This speaks well of our own sense of security in the RAF!'[227]

The Tempsford personnel were not as segregated as the Woburn propagandists, however, mixing with villagers for occasional sports, in local pubs, or at the forces canteen in Everton Village Hall.[228] They also mixed with other allied servicemen at social functions throughout the district. Popular local establishments included the *Red Lion*, *Queen's Head*, *Lord Nelson* and the *Lord Roberts*. In Everton there was a choice of the *Thornton Arms* or 'Dirty Jimmy's', a cottage with pails of beer and to which one brought one's own mug. At Tempsford, personnel used The *Wheatsheaf*, *The Black Lion* and *The White Hart*. Two Bedfordshire schoolboys at the time, Gerald How and John Crawley, remembered the dances that were held in their native Cardington to which the airmen from Tempsford and the other bases would 'cycle miles' (bikes were available to personnel at the airfields and many others bought their own). The former schoolboys (who used to let down the tyres of the Americans' bikes as a prelude to extracting chewing gum as a reward for repairing the reported 'puncture'), added that 'every village had a dance once a week in the Village Hall, however small the village was'.[229] When added to the proximity of Bedford (with Luton and Cambridge just further afield), this meant that, duties permitting, some of Tempsford's personnel could go out dancing four or five nights a week if so inclined – and many did.

RAF Tempsford briefly hosted the Wellington bombers of 11 OTU and 109 Squadrons, but the two units that were most closely associated with the place were 138 and 161 Squadrons, falling under No. 3 Group. 161 arrived in February 1942, with 138 (a reformed squadron, merging with

---

[227] Griffiths, Frank. *Winged Hours* (William Kimber, 1981). A thrilling account, this is mainly devoted to operational matters rather than providing details of life at the base.

[228] O'Connor, op. cit.

[229] BBC *People's War* contribution recorded by Jenny Ford. Id. 6097304.

1419 Special Duties Flight) being relocated from nearby Newmarket the following month. The essential difference between the two was that 138 Squadron concentrated upon drops, whilst 161 Squadron specialised in pick ups, latterly flying Lockheed Hudsons (faster, quieter and with more carrying capacity than the Westland Lysander but whose heavy wheel loading made them prone to get bogged down in muddy fields). Denied front line aircraft due in no small part to the disregard of clandestine warfare by the head of Bomber Command, Arthur Harris (no chance of his beloved Lancasters ever being made available in significant numbers), 138/161 worked initially with Handley Page Halifaxes and Armstrong Whitworth Whitleys, as well as the Lysanders. The latter two were already being rendered obsolete from their initial roles of medium range bomber and reconnaissance aircraft respectively, and the Tempsford aircrews suspected that they got these two models 'because they weren't any good at any other operational task'.

A Lockheed Hudson landing at Tempsford (*Imperial War Museum, HU60549*).

The Whitley seems to have been a particularly unsatisfactory aeroplane: 'while its pre-war green leather upholstery and genuine ivory faced throttle control handles were impressive, those attributes did not make up for its poor performance,' noted one pilot. Freddie Clark remembered it as 'a docile enough aircraft to fly, providing the Merlin X's, developing

1145 hp, kept going… It would lumber off the ground at 95mph and climb away at 115mph'. Unreliable engines on what pilots called 'the flying barn door' were not the only shortcoming, the design of the wing structure effectively cutting off the crew piloting the aircraft from those seated in the rear fuselage.

Westland Lysander *(Imperial War Museum, HU59359).*

By contrast, the little Lysander (the Mark III and Mark IIIa) was to perform superbly in its new role (the first arrived at Tempsford in February 1942). The lack of speed provided by its 870 hp Bristol Mercury engines (not too much beyond 200mph), a feature that made it so vulnerable to the *Luftwaffe* in the disastrous French campaign of 1940, later proved to be an asset. Its wing design further assisted it in landing or taking off on short, unprepared strips of ground, making it ideally suited for delivering and collecting SOE agents in France – where the bulk of the operatives were sent. Designed to carry one pilot plus one passenger, the Lysanders were adapted to cram in two more (four was apparently the record), a ladder fitted to the side being an indication of how vital was speed of despatch and loading. The planes were painted matt black underneath. The Lysanders would often fly from the forward base at Tangmere, Sussex, thus shortening the range (although an additional fuel tank was also fitted) and, because the work was secret, necessary adaptations were not carried out by Westland but by highly

A group of 161 Squadron mechanics, including Leading Aircraftsman Scales, photographed in front of a Halifax. Doug Scales also worked on Lysanders and Hudsons (*Courtesy of Pamela Emms*).

skilled mechanics and fitters at its base. The ground crew were as specialists in their own right, although would be required to work on a number of the varied types of plane that flew from Tempsford. All aircraft had to be signed off once they had received their pre-flight inspection and, on occasions the engineers would be required to go out on test flights.

The introduction of the Halifax extended Tempsford's range. Able to carry more fuel than the Whitley, it could reach Warsaw, thus aiding the development of SOE's work in Poland. A much bigger plane, it was able to carry more containers and personnel (in relatively greater comfort) within its fuselage, and its more modern Merlin XX engines were far more reliable than those of the Whitley. Agent Peter Churchill later recalled that the Halifax took off in the 'manner ... of a goods train', wondering 'how the devil such a flying machine could ever leave the ground'.[230] He remembered his alarm at how the plane got perilously close to the end of its runway before lifting clear.

By 1944 the lumbering Halifax had been joined by the Short Stirling, which effectively superseded the Whitley. The Stirling, a not altogether successful product of 1930s design compromises, was being withdrawn from front line bombing duties by 1943 and becoming available for other duties. One of the original design features was a ventral, or belly, gun mounting turret. It was supposed to be retractable but repeated failure of this attribute meant that it was more trouble than use (the turret thus became the first part of the plane to hit the ground upon landing).

---

[230] Churchill, op. cit.

Removal of the ventral turret, however, offered a handy dropping point for parachuting agents. The Stirlings were stored in Woburn Park prior to their delivery to Tempsford, a procedure that required considerable skill on behalf of the lone delivery pilots (a number of whom were women), as apparently many of Tempsford's skilled crew found the plane difficult to land, even on normal runways. Other planes that were used included Albermarles, B 24 Liberators and Havocs.

Short Stirling *(Imperial War Museum, CH3145).*

The bald statistics are these: approximately 1000 agents, 29,000 containers and 10,000 packages were delivered into occupied Europe by 138 Squadron alone (and countless numbers collected) at a cost of some seventy aircraft and their crew. Statistics, however, are not enough. It is impossible to adequately detail or pay tribute to the efforts and to the sacrifice of these men and women in this account. Secrecy and the absence of comprehensive records combine to muddy the waters but so do the fact that, whilst the aeroplanes may have taken off from Tempsford, the agents were often collected en route from its forward airfield at Tangmere, Sussex (Andree Borrel and Lise de Baissac are two examples of that). Once operations to Norway commenced, around the beginning of 1942, the range was shortened by utilising bases in the north of Scotland at Wick, Kinloss or Lossiemouth. This made strategic sense given that most of the training centres for Norwegian agents and commandos were based in the Scottish Highlands, but it seems that occasionally a combination was used, with planes taking off from Bedfordshire and landing in Scotland upon return, or *vice-versa*.

It is worth adding that Tempsford operations were often as dependent upon the weather and the seasons as they were upon available aircraft technology. The introduction of the four engine Halifax may have brought more distant targets within flight range, but the cover of longer winter nights were still necessary to reach locations such as those in Norway and Poland. Furthermore, because the SOE missions were conducted by moonlight, on moonless nights the Tempsford crews also conducted air/sea rescue missions, additionally also providing leaflet drops and regular bombing raids. There was no let up.

Information is further obscured by the fact that some agents (always known simply as 'Joes') remained anonymous. Even Freddie Clark (who knew more than most), was forced to concede that 'there were many more, regrettably, unidentified': Frank Griffiths noted one of his female passengers as simply being 'nearer to 65 than 60'. She always took half a bottle of good cognac in order to give her courage for the jump, on one occasion her bicycle being parachuted with her. Others achieved fame, albeit in the most harrowing of circumstances.

One of the most celebrated of agents was Edward 'Tommy' Yeo-Thomas, a man with a blunt, forceful personality and for whom Leo Marks had great affection. One of the toughest of characters, Yeo-Thomas played a key role in organising the resistance groups in France, first flying out with Free French Intelligence chief Col. Passy (André Dewavrin) in February 1943. Two months later Yeo-Thomas and Passy were brought home by a Lysander sortie flown by Pilot Officer Peter Vaughan-Fowler and F/Lt. J. A. McCairns of 161 Squadron. Brought back with them were Pierre Brossolette, one of the principle architects of co-ordinated resistance in France, and a downed American officer who was seeking to evade capture. On Yeo-Thomas' third mission, to Paris in March 1944, he was captured and dreadfully tortured by the Gestapo. Refusing to talk, despite his treatment, he was sent to a concentration camp, where he set

182

Edward Yeo-Thomas *(Hulton Getty)*.

about organising resistance within the camp. He eventually escaped but was recaptured when almost to the safety of the American lines. Undeterred, Yeo-Thomas made a second daring escape (leading ten French POWs), just before he was due to be executed.[231]

Another celebrated Tempsford passenger who fell foul of the Gestapo but who also miraculously lived to tell the tale was Peter Churchill. His capture was in large part due to the counter espionage work of *Abwehr's* Hugo Bleicher and his survival was in no small part to the cool, quick thinking of the heroic Odette Sansom. Despite the fact they were both tortured (although not by Bleicher) they survived in large measure because Odette – who had her toenails ripped out – was able to convince their interrogators that she was Peter Churchill's wife, and that he was the nephew of the Prime Minister. Neither was true but they were briefly married after the war (incredibly, a house guest included Bleicher!). Less fortunate were France Antelme, Lionel Lee and Madeleine Damerment. At the end of January 1944 they were parachuted into France, virtually straight into the arms of waiting Germans. All three were executed, Antelme more than a year later. Similarly unlucky was Muriel Byck: after spending six weeks in the field in France she died suddenly of meningitis, an illness from which she had suffered before but had kept secret in case it prejudiced her application to SOE.

Many losses can be attributed to the sort of misfortune suffered by Byck, or by Jan Molenaar, who, in March 1943, fatally fractured his skull on a concrete water trough in his parachute jump. His fellow agent had to administer the cyanide suicide pill (all agents knowing their chances of

---

[231] Marshall, Bruce. *The White Rabbit* (Evan Bros., 1966).

Peter Churchill and Odette Sansom *(Hulton Getty)*.

survival were no more than fifty-fifty, carried the rubber coated suicide pill), leaving the body to be found by German Field Police the next day. Others, however, have to be ascribed to the sort of amateurism that at times seemed to punctuate the Secret War. Because of the intense effort made by German Intelligence (and the corresponding leaky nature of local Resistance groups), security measures were carefully put in place, essentially a second set of phoney codes that, unbeknown to the Germans, would warn home in the event of an agent's capture. These were duly deployed in a number of cases, but, incredibly, in a number of instances were actually ignored by SOE's receivers in Britain.

The disaster that befell Antelme, Damerment and Lee was an individual example of this but, on a much wider scale so too was the tragedy of the entire operation in Holland where the Germans were able to effectively destroy SOE /Resistance activity in their notorious *Englandspiel* ('game against England'). Under the command of Major Hans Giskes, the *Abwehr* played the radio sets of captured agents back to Britain and, with the omission of the agent's distinctive security check being ignored, the Germans were able to reel in their opponents, drawing a succession of supplies and, most dreadfully, more than fifty agents straight into their waiting embrace. 'The German *Abwehr* must have laughed their heads off at this deadly and bizarre situation,' commented Freddie Clark of two Dutch operations (*Parsnip 5* and *Lettuce 10*), mounted from Tempsford in the spring of 1943: 'We, their enemy, dropping into their hands, agents, munitions, coffee, chocolate and at the same time exposing our aircrews to real and unnecessary danger'.[232] Clark has alleged that the aircrew losses fell disproportionately upon 138 Squadron as the main service provider to SOE, whereas 161 supported SIS activity (not penetrated to anywhere near the same extent), to a greater degree.

Whatever the designated squadron, however, crews and their passengers flying out of Tempsford and Tangmere were extremely vulnerable. The four man crew of the Hudson FK790 (Flt. Lieut. J. W. 'Ian' Menzies DFC, Sgt. K. Bunney, Sgt. Eric Eliot, Sgt. Denis Withers), were veterans of six previous flights conducted together over the previous eight weeks before they set off on their mission (*Fives 1*) to Holland on the night of 5/6 July 1944. Their crew were four Dutch agents: Pleun Verhoef, a recruit from the remnant of the Dutch Army; Peter Kwint, based at the University of Amsterdam, who escaped occupation via Spain, Portugal and on to Liverpool; Jan Bockma, the twenty two year old son of a leading Dutch Resistance fighter who had made his way to Britain via Spain and the Foreign Legion; Johannes Walter, a recruit from the Dutch Navy, who had married a girl in England and was now expecting their baby. All eight men were killed when their Hudson was shot down over Holland by a Messerschmitt Bf110 night fighter but the agents were probably doubly doomed. According to the Bf110's gunner, far from being congratulated, the crew were taken to task for not allowing the agents to be dropped first (where the Germans were clearly expecting them) before shooting down Menzies' aircraft.[233]

Poor security safeguards were endangering Tempsford's crews, as well as the agents that they were dropping. Even without this, the challenges of clandestine pinpoint delivery and collection in hostile territory were immense, even for the highly skilled pilots of 138 and 161 Squadrons, and efforts were made to assist planes to home-in on the target. Initially

---

[232] Clark, op. cit.

[233] Ibid. See also www.161squadron.org, a website created by Menzies' nephew, Bob Body, in memory of Hudson FK790 and the Tempsford crews. The remains of the plane and its crew were recovered in 1997.

The price of freedom. The four crew and four agents of Hudson FK790, lost over Holland: Flt. Lieut. J. W. 'Ian' Menzies DFC; Sgt. K. Bunney; Sgt. Eric Eliot; Sgt. Denis Withers; Pleun Verhoef; Peter Kwint; Jan Bockma; Johannes Walter (*Photographs courtesy of Bob Body*).

tested at Cranfield airbase in the west of Bedfordshire, one development was the S-Phone, a telecommunications kit that was strapped to the operator and which allowed them to communicate with incoming aircrews. The S-Phone only had a range of six miles, however, and something with greater reach was required. This was the 'Eureka', a portable battery powered radar kit which featured a five foot mast. Eureka's aircraft counterpart was 'Rebecca', installed within the planes. The Eureka/Rebecca system was being tested by Tempsford pilots around mid-summer 1941, according to Clark.

The problem with the system was that once a Eureka set was captured, as it soon was in Holland, it could also be deployed by the Germans. Now, unsuspecting British planes could be drawn to chosen sites to drop their cargo of personnel and equipment, and then attacked by night fighters as soon as they left the area. In theory, coded flash lights ought to have provided an additional safeguard, but on their very first deployment of a captured Eureka set, the *Abwehr* found that the planes just followed the signal, without the need of the flashlights.

SOE's Dutch disaster impacted upon other branches of the services. Tempsford also provided an occasional service for MI9, part of whose job was to arrange the smuggling of allied servicemen (such as surviving aircrew from crashed allied planes) out of occupied Europe and back to safety. The preferred route was via Switzerland, Spain or by specially arranged naval vessels off the French coast, but just occasionally they turned to Tempsford, with Lysanders and Hudsons picking up around fifty air force personnel (out of a total of nearly 3000 who returned). Needing to develop a reliable escape route for the downed allied aircrew in Holland, MI9 turned to SOE to help them parachute in an agent to make contact with local resistance groups. This operation was organised by Airey Neave, himself a celebrated escapee from Colditz Castle, hitherto thought to be a Prisoner of War camp that was escape-proof. The agent concerned was a young woman named Beatrix Terwindt ('Trix'), a former KLM air hostess who had escaped from her occupied homeland, like Neave achieving this in 1942 via Switzerland.

Unaware of the extent to which SOE had been compromised by Giskes, Neave made plans for Trix to be flown out of Tempsford, briefly considering and then rejecting the option of having her face reconstructed with plastic surgery to ward off the possibility that she might be recognised in her native country. With no other suitable volunteer available, Trix had to be dropped into Holland alone for her first (and only) assignment. Nearly forty years later Neave still had to confess that 'I find it difficult to write of what happened to her.'[234] On 13 February 1943 Airey Neave and Trix drove up to Tempsford together, with Neave personally helping her into her parachute harness before handing her some Dutch money and her forged identity papers (as a nurse). Having watched her depart in her Halifax, Neave was later reassured to hear confirmation that the drop had been successful and that a Dutch 'reception committee' had been waiting for Twix, and the accompanying containers full of supplies (including a radio set).

What Airey Neave did not know until later was that these Dutchmen were collaborators and, waiting just out of sight, were also German soldiers. Initially unsuspecting, Trix was taken to a barn and persuaded to provide the name of her immediate contact (a genuine resistance

---

[234] Neave, Airey. *Saturday at MI9* (Hodder & Stoughton, 1969).

Handley Page Halifax (*Imperial War Museum*, MERAF6086).

figure) on the pretext that her identity papers were inadequate and that it would be too dangerous for her to travel until new ones were supplied. She simply thought that these Dutchmen would have better knowledge about the immediate circumstances. Suddenly, German soldiers appeared and she was grabbed from behind, the collaborators swiftly handcuffing her as Trix unsuccessfully attempted to put the poison pill into her mouth.

Beatrix Terwindt was taken to the *Abwehr* headquarters at Dreibergen and interrogated for ninety six hours, virtually without break. She was perturbed to discover that the Germans knew more about SOE than she did, whilst the Germans couldn't understand why the British had dropped a lone girl who evidently was so poorly briefed about her organisation. They failed to suspect that this time they had someone from another covert operations department. The interrogators' puzzlement helped save her life and Nel Lind, a member of the Dutch resistance with whom Trix was briefly incarcerated, later said that she got the impression that the Germans were trying to keep her alive. After a while, they even permitted Trix to have a radio from which she was able to pick up the BBC.[235] For most of the fourteen months that she was

---

[235] Lynn, Vera; Cross, Robin; de Gex, Jenny. *The Women Who Won the War* (Sidgwick and Jackson, 1990).

imprisoned, however, Trix was kept in solitary confinement, apart from a brief spell when they unsuccessfully planted a spy in her cell. She was then sent to Ravensbruck concentration camp, an ordeal which she survived to be liberated at the end of the war, but which nonetheless permanently ruined her health.

In addition to secret agents and supplies for the resistance, Tempsford also provided a third specialist dropping service: pigeons. A pencil and rice paper was attached to the bird, the idea behind this being that the citizens of the occupied countries could write information on to the paper such as news of communication systems, troop placements, collaborators and so on, before sending the trained pigeons back home. There is some indication that more care was taken in the dropping of the pigeons than the 'Joes' but the scheme had only mixed success. Some useful information was returned but if the pigeon was intercepted by a German, a torrent of abuse written in a soldier's vernacular was the least of the dangers inherent in the information.

* * *

Hasells Hall, described by one author as being 'situated on the top of what may be the only serious hill in Bedfordshire', was requisitioned in January 1941.[236] The only occupant of the house by this stage was Frederick Pym, and he died in the same year. Additional outbuildings were added and the premises were first used as a training depot for army officers. Having just left school, Francis Pym was helping out with the harvest at Gibraltar Farm (the last before it became an airfield), and returned to look at what had happened to his former home. 'What a mess they made of the grass!' he recalled thinking as he stared at the tanks and other vehicles (there as part of an army exercise code named 'Bumper'), strewn around the park. Since he was about to join up as a cadet officer in the Royal Armoured Corps, Pym then settled down under one of his family's chestnut trees to observe the goings on.[237] The army didn't stay long at Hasells Hall but then served as the accommodation for the offices of the station commander (for most of this critical period between October 1942 and the end of 1944 this was Group Captain

---

[236] Seebohm, op. cit.

[237] Pym, Francis. *Sentimental Journey* (privately published, 1988).

Edward 'Mouse' Fielden). There was an officer's mess in one of the downstairs rooms, the important task of folding the parachutes was conducted in the library and it was also used by Polish airmen (there were additionally Canadians based nearby).

Hasells was also one of two large houses that were used by the Special Operations Executive. The other, Howbury Hall, to the south of Renhold, was designated as SOE STS 40, under the command of Major P. Tidmarsh, and contained a nominal detachment of five officers and thirty seven other ranks.[238] Appropriately enough, very little is known of this institution other than it was used for RT training, especially the use of S-Phones and Rebecca/Eureka communications that were vital to SOE operations. SOE did not have exclusive use of Howbury Hall; it is possible that the Norwegian Independent Company No 1, Kompani Linge had a base there and as with Hasells Hall, it was also used by Polish airmen. Hasells Hall, was also utilised by SOE, in this case as a last stopover for agents who were due to fly out of Tempsford. There they were looked after by ATS personnel and SOE staff from Baker Street, and attempted to while away the time before the moment came to depart. A good meal was on offer, final briefings and checks were made, and the agents were thoroughly cleansed. This did not mean just a pleasant bath beyond the wartime stipulation of four inches, but a final check to make sure that there were absolutely no traces by which German interrogators might be able to link them to Britain.

The final journey to the where the aircraft would be waiting would be in a car driven by a member of the WAAF. They were given strict instructions not to even look at their passengers in the rear seats (the use of the rear view mirror was prohibited), let alone talk to them. The approximately 240 WAAFs were billeted in a separate camp at Everton – 'the Waafery', approximately 1 1/2 miles from the Tempsford base. Also nicknamed 'the Nunnery' it was reckoned that the perimeter barbed wire was not merely to maintain operational security but to keep the men and women apart.

Operations were frequently aborted at the last minute, sometimes due to weather, sometimes due to local factors. Guy Lockhart, one of Tempsford's outstanding pilots, was sent out on the night of 28/29 May

---

[238] WO 33/2210, National Archives.

to collect former French premier Eduord Daladier and SOE's Andre Simon. The latter had already been arrested and it had proved impossible for the French Resistance to get Daladier to the designated pick-up point. None of this, of course, was known to Lockhart until he became aware that the guidance flares were not in place on the ground. After circling in vain for a signal he was obliged to return home. 161 Squadron's Leading Aircraftsman Doug Scales also had what he later described as a 'close shave'. In the latter stages of the conflict he was scheduled to be flown out to Denmark to make emergency repairs to a plane that had come down in an area that was presumably in a zone that was being contested with the weakening German occupation. At the last moment, the aircraft was stopped from taking off as intelligence had just come through reporting that a German force had managed to move up close to the aircraft and were waiting for the arrival of the Tempsford crew.[239]

If the aircrews had managed to despatch their cargo they normally returned to Tempsford by 04.00-05.00. They would then sleep late before going over to the operations room for further briefing as to the next task that lay ahead. The flights to Norway always seemed to take longer, in part because navigation over the rocky, island strewn coastline was especially difficult. The flights to Poland were invariably taken by the Poles of 138 Squadron, crews from that country having been present in the squadron almost from its very beginning. From an initial five crews, the Polish contribution increased to the extent to which they formed their own independent flight within 138.[240]

The Poles were a group that Frank Griffiths described as a 'magnificent headache':

> They were amazing aviators. Apparently well disciplined, for they were always giving you salutes even if it was their Despatcher handing you a cup of coffee, yet they would smoke when flying, even when surrounded by hundreds of gallons of petrol, the fumes from the overload tanks and the explosives in the cargo! Rebuking a Pole was a waste of time. They would appear to understand, give a magnificent salute and then go away

---

[239] Information from Doug Scales' daughter, Pamela Emms.

[240] Garlinski, Josef. Poland SOE and the Allies (Allen and Unwin, 1969).

and default again …Yet despite the fact that the Polish crews were always in trouble or saluting you couldn't help but like them and admire their aggressive spirit.

Freddie Clark noted one occasion when a Polish aircrew took a two hundred mile diversion in order that they could look down on their home town, a reckless if perhaps understandable action.[241] More seriously, Griffiths was horrified to see one particular example of 'bravery (that) bordered on foolhardiness and a disobedience of orders'. Accompanied on one delivery operation in the vicinity of Crecy by two other Halifax planes, both crewed by Poles, Griffiths suddenly found himself alone as he climbed to a pre-arranged height of 7000 feet in order to avoid the light flak that was known to be situated on the Le Crotoy estuary on the French coast. Looking down, he saw tell-tale tracer fire and suddenly realised that, instead of climbing, the Poles 'had gone in at deck level with guns blazing'. The Halifax's forward Browning machine guns were hardly engaged in an equal contest against the 30mm guns of an anti-aircraft battery and one plane exploded, with another that was so badly damaged that it was forced to turn back to Tempsford. 'It seemed as though it was a loss of face to take evasive action,' concluded Griffiths, with the same sense of exasperated admiration that was shared by most who served with the Poles. Perhaps some of the 'trouble' that Griffiths referred to concerned the WAAFs. The Poles seemed to be drawn to them 'like flies round a jam pot and I fear that the WAAFs were not lacking in the art of encouraging them' he observed. It was the reckless Poles who were apparently the most successful in breaching the perimeter defences of the 'Waafery'.

Four of Tempsford's WAAFs: 'Tibbs' Turner, 'Red' Humble, 'Babs' Chapman and Audrey Caistor. Taken from Frank Griffiths' *Winged Hours*, with the WAAFs, in Griffiths' words, 'all illegally wearing borrowed aircrew insignia.' (*Provenance unknown*).

---

[241] Clark, op. cit.

There was no doubt, however, that the Poles made a brilliant contribution to Tempsford's operations. On 13/14 April 1943, 138's Polish Flight made one round trip of more than ten hours to deliver two 'Joes' and several containers to a number of sites around South West France, flying at heights that were often less than 500 feet. One of these agents was Harry Rée, a Captain in the Intelligence Corps who had been attached to SOE. Like many subsequent heroes Rée followed a chequered path to service, initially being rejected four times before he was even successful in obtaining an interview, and then received mixed assessments, ('rather disappointing' concluded his instructor at the STS at Hatfield). Rée's initial task was to make contact with Resistance forces that were very strong in the Lons-le-Saunier/Jura region, helping to build up the *Stockbroker* circuit, and to co-ordinate sabotage attacks against the Germans. This he did, but Rée also had an assignment that differed from the usual: he had to persuade the owners of the Peugeot factory at Sochaux to help blow up parts of their own premises.[242] This was not as difficult as it might seem as Rudolphe Peugeot was by no means a collaborator, even though compelled to comply with German demands to produce tank turrets and vehicles for the occupying power. The task was made even easier by the fact that the alternative to SOE's scalpel that Rée was able to present to Peugeot, was the RAF's sledgehammer.

Having effectively presented his case to Rudolphe Peugeot, Rée was introduced to key Resistance fighters from within the Peugeot plant, and together they successfully blew up several key installations in a simultaneous attack which put the factory out of action. Attempts by the Germans to replace destroyed equipment proved to be easy pickings for Rée and the Resistance who ambushed them *en route*, thereafter Rée's luck ran out. Betrayed by the traitor, Pierre Martin, Rée found himself cornered in a house by an armed Sergeant of the German *Feld Polizei*, with the Gestapo on their way. Attacking his temporary captor with a bottle, Rée escaped after a desperate fight in which he was shot three times. Thanks to the Resistance's excellent network of hideouts, Rée was smuggled to Switzerland and then home via Spain.

---

[242] MIM file, 5776A (original documents held by National Archives). E. H. Cookridge, E. H. *Inside SOE. The First Full Story of Special Operations Executive in Western Europe, 1940-45* (Arthur Barker, 1966).

Even when piloted by more cautious crews than the spontaneous Poles, the return journey could still be a hazardous one. Just getting off the ground could be difficult enough, as Guy Lockhart found in March 1942 when he was sent to collect Gilbert Renault, a local SOE/resistance network chief, known as 'REMY'. Landing his small Lysander aircraft at the designated location, Lockhart found that a combination of the weight of an additional passenger plus soft ground was sufficient to prevent take off. It took seventeen minutes for Lockhart, with the assistance of men on the ground to get himself airborne, a seventeen minutes that must have seemed like an age with the Lysander's engines continually running and a road not far away. Once up in the air, the hazards became German night fighters and the fire from anti-aircraft guns. Battered by flak, Halifax L316 (regarded by its crew as an 'unlucky' plane), limped back to Tempsford. The wounded were evacuated and the ground crew started to clean out the debris strewn fuselage only to find 'the major part' of a human ear that belonged to an agent who had already been sent off to the hospital at Henlow. The ear was packed off after the patient and successfully sewn back on.

One of these 'Joes' who were given overnight accommodation near Tempsford, SAS Captain John Tonkin, described what it was like to wait around in Hasells Hall. He found himself in Hasells' lounge in the company of other agents – including two 'surprisingly beautiful girls' – and the Baker Street personnel, amongst whom was the redoubtable Vera Atkins. Described as possessing 'steel-trap intelligence' and a force of personality that could be like a 'sledgehammer', it was Atkins' responsibility to ensure that all the agents were thoroughly prepared for their mission – and she was very, very thorough. Vera Atkins would be the key person with whom an agent would deal upon completion of a successful application and training with the secret service, and she would often be the last person that they would see before leaving, escorting them to the steps of the plane and waving them off, invariably with an expletive uttered in French.

Vera Atkins
(Provenance unknown).

Yeo-Thomas' biography did not explicitly state whether he was entertained in Hasells Hall although it did describe how, on one of his aborted missions, he was driven to Tempsford from London, arriving at around 17.00. He was greeted with 'piping hot tea', undertook an equipment check and then dined with the Commanding Officer 'who produced a bottle of excellent burgundy'. It was then time to put on the extensive kit before being driven out to the waiting Halifax bomber 'whose shape loomed up eerily through the mist'. The accompanying officer (presumably Atkins) waved him and his fellow agent off by calling 'merde alors'.[243]

The role of Captain Tonkin was to parachute into France at the launch of the D-Day invasion to lead *Operation Bulbasket*. The job of this team was to attack German communications in the area around Poitiers. Unfortunately, the delay in the landings due to the inclement weather also grounded the agents: 'We had checked and rechecked everything and packed our enormous rucksacks about fifty times. Finally, there was nothing more to do, so we spent the time very profitably with the girls, doing jigsaw puzzles.'[244] Once parachuted into France by a Halifax of 161 Squadron, Tonkin's SAS team got to work, attacking German run trains that were ferrying men and supplies up to the Normandy beachheads, as well as hacking out a 3,000 foot long landing strip. They were joined by 'Dee' Harper, an American P-38 pilot who had been smuggled away by French locals after his plane had crash landed nearby, and who volunteered to give the SAS a hand. It was after Harper had been evacuated that the SAS soldiers at Verriers were surrounded by a much larger German unit including a number from the SS. Tonkin and a handful of SAS men (plus yet another pilot) managed to break out but those who were captured were murdered by the Germans. Amongst those killed was another who had been at Hasells Hall with John Tonkin, Lieutenant Richard Crisp.

One of the beautiful women that made such an impression on Tonkin at Hasells Hall was Violette Szabo, two years older than Tonkin at 24 but already a mother and widowed by the war. Born Violette Bushell, and

---

[243] Marshall, op. cit.

[244] Quoted in Hastings, Max. *Das Reich. The March of the Second Panzer Division Through France, June 1944* (Pan Books, 2000) and also in Binney, Marcus. *The Women Who Lived for Danger* (Hodder and Stoughton, 2000).

Violette Szabo (*Courtesy of Rosemary Rigby and the Violette Szabo, G.C., Museum*).

raised in an Anglo-French home in south London (although she spent part of her childhood in Paris), bilingual Violette married Etienne Szabo in 1940, a French officer who was based in England. Unfortunately, their married life did not last long as Etienne was killed at the Battle of El Alamein in 1942, and thus never saw his daughter, Tania, who was also born that year. Violette applied to join SOE, largely in a desire to exact revenge, apparently expressing a specific determination to kill Germans. Although a superb shot, her daredevil nature was reckoned to be more of a liability for field work and she received mediocre assessments. These were overruled by the head of SOE, Maurice Buckmaster, and she was prepared to be sent to France. It was whilst being trained to learn the crucial codes that she met code master Leo Marks. Marks later recalled that his first impression was of a 'dark haired slip of mischief ... (with) a cockney accent, which added to her impishness'.

For her first mission Violette Szabo accompanied Philippe Liewer (codenamed 'Hamlet') to Paris to investigate the potential of resistance activity around Rouen. Although briefly detained by suspicious French police, the mission was successfully accomplished but, as Susan Ottaway has described, it also ended very uncomfortably.[245] The Lysander, piloted by Flight Lieutenant Bob Large, had to weave its way through anti-aircraft fire on the way home and then had to make a very bumpy landing at Tempsford on tyres that had been shredded by the flak. Violette was bounced around in the back to such an extent that she had no idea where she was, assuming that they had crash landed whilst still over France. In the near darkness, therefore, the tall blonde man, wearing an indistinguishable uniform, was not her heroic pilot but a German captor. Poor Bob got 'an angry tirade in rapid French' and later reflected that he was glad that Mrs Szabo was not carrying a gun. Instead, when she realised her error, Lieut. Large got a pair of arms thrown around his neck and a kiss.

In her recollection of the night of what was just her second operation, Vera Atkins concurred with Tonkin's assessment of Violette, remembering that she 'looked incredibly beautiful, in white marguerite earrings and a marguerite clip that she had bought in Paris on her last mission'. Violette was part of a team coded *Salesman 2* comprising herself, Liewer, the formidable Bob Maloubier and a nineteen year old American wireless operator, Jean-Claude Guiet. As with Tonkin and Crisp, the *Salesman 2* team found their departure hindered by bad weather. On 4 June their plane was actually taxiing for take off when the mission was postponed, obliging Violette and her comrades to return to Hasells Hall, but at least giving them a chance to spend a day in Cambridge on 5 June. On D-Day itself, 6 June 1944, the team were flown to their destination but were unable to find the reception committee and so were obliged to return once again to kick their heels at Hasells Hall. Apparently they missed seeing the vast allied armada crossing the channel below them in the opposite direction. On the night of either 6/7 June or 7/8 June *Salesman 2* was at last successfully deployed to France, being taken out by a B-24 Liberator aircraft sent down from the USAAF 'carpetbagger' base at Harrington in Northamptonshire.[246] Before jumping, Violette kissed each member of the crew and her team in turn.

---

[245] Ottaway, Susan. *Violette Szabo. The Life That I Have* (Leo Cooper, 2002).

[246] Max Hastings states that Szabo flew out of Tempsford in a Halifax whereas Binney, O'Connor, Ottaway and Clark claim that it was in the B24 sent on from Harrington.

Violette Szabo's assignment in France was in much the same region as Tonkin and the SAS. It also took her into the path of the vicious SS 2nd Panzer Das Reich Division as it butchered its way across France towards the advancing Allies. Although precise details are not absolutely clear, a reasonable account of Violette's last hours of freedom can be reconstructed. Liewer was attempting to make contact with the disparate resistance groups in the region, to co-ordinate their activity in an effort to slow up the German reinforcement of its Normandy defenders. Violette was assigned to make contact with one group approximately 100 miles away, being expected to cover half the distance on bicycle but given a lift for the first part in a black Citroen by a young resistance member, Jacques Dufour. Although her fake identity was as the widow of an antique dealer, Violette opted to undermine this cover by taking a sten gun and two magazines of ammunition.

Unfortunately, Szabo and Dufour were intercepted by an impromptu German roadblock set up as part of a hunt for an SS officer recently captured by the *Maquis*. They fought it out, hitting one of the sentries but were forced to flee as reinforcements arrived. There then followed a desperate dash through a wheat field in the direction of a wood, Dufour and Szabo giving each other covering fire as more and more Germans closed in. Although Dufour was able to hide in a farmyard, an exhausted Violette was captured in the wood, possibly after being wounded in the ankle. Now a prisoner, she was interrogated by the Gestapo at their Parisian headquarters at 84 Avenue Foch, before being incarcerated in Fresnes prison. She eventually left here, in chains, to be sent to Ravensbruck concentration camp. Yeo-Thomas, also a prisoner at this time, met her briefly as they were being transported as prisoners on a train that halted after it was attacked by allied aircraft: she crawled to him in manacles to bring him water.

At Ravensbruck Violette was reacquainted with Yvonne Baseden, with whom she had trained in the UK. A WAAF wireless operator, Baseden had also flown out from Tempsford, being been dropped over the Toulouse area in the spring of 1944. After just a few weeks in the field, she was captured by the Gestapo. Taken seriously ill at Ravensbruck, she was rescued from the concentration camp by the Swedish Red Cross. Although she survived, like Yeo-Thomas and Trix Terwindt, the experience had taken its toll on her health. When she returned to

Britain she spent eighteen months in hospital. Violette Szabo was not so lucky, being executed shortly before the liberation of the camp in the spring of 1945, amongst a group of prisoners that included fellow SOE agents, Denise Bloch and Lilian Rolfe.

Possibly the most successful of the female agents that flew from Tempsford was Pearl Witherington. Born in Paris to British parents, she and her family escaped France after the invasion in a seven month adventure that, like so many others, took them via Spain and Portugal. After working for two years in the Air Ministry, Pearl Witherington approached and was accepted by SOE in June 1943, feeling that she wished to take a more active role in the war effort. Her brief, intensive training marked her out as proficient with explosives, although markedly less able with signalling and the physical side of her training. Amongst her instructors there were differences of opinion as to whether she possessed leadership qualities.[247]

Pearl was given an honorary commission in the WAAF and three months later, on the night of 22/23 September 1943, Flt. Sgt. Cole took off from RAF Tempsford to make two drops over France. The first was a number of packages and containers for a circuit in the vicinity of Tours, the second was Pearl Witherington, making her third attempt to reach France. She was parachuted, alone, into the Auvergne region from a height of just 300 feet. There she was to serve as a courier for the *Stationer* circuit leader, Maurice Southgate, but when Southgate was briefly recalled to London Pearl took over the leadership of the circuit in his absence.

Back in France Southgate was lured into a trap by the Gestapo and their *Milice* collaborators, and promptly arrested in May 1944. He was fortunate to survive the subsequent interrogation and incarceration at Buchenwald. Unfortunately, Southgate was carrying false identity cards at the time, incriminating both himself and Pearl Witherington. The Germans now had an idea who they were looking for.

With Southgate gone *Stationer* was divided into two smaller circuits with Pearl becoming the leader of the northern part, codenamed *Wrestler*. Overcoming a fair measure of male prejudice, she worked here with

---

[247] Binney, op. cit.

her fiancée, Henri Cornioley, whilst the *Maquis*' numbers swelled to between 1500 and 2700 (estimates vary), as it harried and challenged Nazi authority. Attempts by the Nazis to reinforce their collapsing hold on northern France were hampered as Pearl organised numerous ambushes, inflicting far greater losses upon the Germans (up to 1000) than they received, with Pearl placing herself in danger on numerous occasions. Throughout this she constantly fed information back to SOE in London and committed numerous acts of sabotage – the *Wrestler* circuit cut the railway line to Paris no fewer than 800 times.

After Pearl's withdrawal from the field in September 1944, she married Henri and, as Madame Cornioley, ultimately settled in France, a country that she loved. Back in the UK she made a number of recommendations for awards from her former comrades that officialdom ruled ineligible as they were technically civilians. Pearl was personally cited for an MC, something that she was also refused on similar grounds as she too was regarded as nominally a non-combatant, and a female one at that. Instead she was offered the consolation of an MBE, which she refused pointing out that she hadn't spent the war behind a desk. This absurd oversight was rectified when, on 11 April 2006, the ninety two year old Pearl Cornioley was at last awarded her parachute 'wings' by the RAF in a ceremony at her French home.

* * *

Tempsford's pilots also delivered the agents who carried out what was arguably the outstanding SOE operation of the war, perhaps the finest example of covert operations ever seen blending intelligence, ingenuity, durability and courage. 'Of the 36 trips that I did with 138 Squadron,' observed one its air crew 'this was the most memorable because of its importance, although we were not aware of that at the time.' Its origins began in a developing race between Germany and the western allies to develop the as yet unknown potential of an atomic bomb. The two sides had chosen different paths. The allies had opted for the enrichment of uranium in reactors in order to produce the critical weapons grade plutonium (Pu^{239}). The Germans opted to manufacture Pu^{239} via the production of deuterium oxide ($D2O$), more commonly known as heavy water. The largest European manufacturer of heavy water was Norsk Hydro, at their Vemork hydroelectric plant in Norway. Following their successful invasion of that country in 1940, the Germans had now got their hands on the means of its manufacture.

From inside the Norsk Hydro plant one worker, Einar Skinnarland, sent messages endeavouring to provide information on the German's efforts to extract deuterium oxide. These messages were sent in a code so complex that no-one could unravel them, save one: Leo Marks. Like the rest of the decoders, Marks didn't fully understand the content of Skinnarland's messages (he recalled wondering what exactly *was* 'heavy water'?). As the significance of these reports began to sink in, however, it was to Marks that all Skinnarland's communications were passed on. Eventually, given the immense complexity of matters, it was necessary for Skinnarland to travel to Britain to make a report in person. This he achieved by being part of a group of Norwegians resistance fighters who daringly commandeered a small ship (*D/S Galtesund*) on 15 March 1942 and escaped to Aberdeen. After just eleven days' debriefing and instruction (including a crash course in parachuting), Skinnarland was returned to his native country by 138 Squadron's P/O W. Smith, a veteran of six months, positioning first to Kinloss (in order to shorten the range), and then flying out in a Whitley. With a bare minimum of parachute training Skinnarland was understandably reluctant to jump at first, the delay consequently resulting in his landing some two or three miles away from the scheduled point. Skinnarland covered his absence from work by reporting that he'd been ill.

The next stage of the operation was *Operation Grouse*, a team of Norwegian commandos whose job it was to reconnoitre the area and make necessary preparations for a party of British Royal Engineers who were to carry out the attack upon the plant. The Norwegians were members of Norwegian Independent Company No. 1, or better known as *Kompani Linge*, named after their founder Martin Linge, a soldier and actor who had been killed during a raid on the Norwegian coast in 1941. *Kompani Linge* was a special operations unit based in the Scottish Highlands, by now under the leadership of Leif Tronstad. In the Norwegian team were its leader, 2nd Lieut. Jens Anton Poulsson, together with Radio Operator Knut Haugland, Sgt. Claus Helberg and Arne Kjelstrup, but getting them to their target was no simple matter. The first attempt at a drop failed when the Halifax developed engine trouble, the second also being thwarted by fog. Eventually, on 18 October 1942,

138s highly experienced W/Cdr R. C. Hockey dropped them onto the Flarfeit Mountain plateau, together with supplies encased within two packages and six containers. Helberg later described the sensation of that drop:

> *Its hard to describe my state of mind just before jumping. A few hours earlier, I had been soaking up the sun on a lawn in England. The joy of returning home blended with the excitement of the jump itself. As the plane descended from 4000 meters to 300 meters, the terrain no longer looked so fine and flat. "Action Station!" The sharp command gave us something else to think about, and a few seconds later I was floating down to the plateau.*[248]

Helberg's impression was correct: although Hockey had dropped them over the plateau, they were approximately nine miles west of their target, landing in rough terrain strewn with 'boulders and rocky mountain slopes'. This was significant as the commandos had to hump the contents of their twelve containers (in repeat journeys) towards the target over ground upon which the snow was too wet for skis. Calories were burnt up at a faster rate than their rations (having to be stretched further than planned), could replace them. It was only upon landing that Poulsson had told his comrades about their mission.

Making contact with Torstein Skinnarland, Einar's brother, the *Grouse* team made their preparations and waited for the next phase, *Operation Freshman*, to arrive. Unlike their Norwegian counterparts, the British were not skiers, and so part of *Grouse's* brief was to find a suitable landing site for the gliders that would be carrying the Engineers. Exactly a month after *Grouse* had been despatched, the demolition teams of *Operation Freshman*, flew out. Tempsford pilots did not fly this stage of the mission which required a different sort of skill, two Halifax bombers each towing a Horsa glider. The hazards of covert operations over such hostile territory in poor weather were amply illustrated by what happened next. The attempts at making Rebecca/Eureka contact failed and one Halifax crashed into a mountain with its glider also going down almost immediately afterwards. Although the second glider successfully

---

[248] Claus Helberg's testimony of the Vemork raid, first published in the 1947 Yearbook of Norwegian Tourist Association, and now available on the internet.

separated from its tow, it was unable to locate the landing ground and it too crashed. Not knowing of Hitler's Commando Order of 18 October 1942 (ordering that all allied commandos were to be immediately executed, even if in uniform, a deliberate break with the Geneva Convention), the survivors surrendered where they were soon after murdered by the Gestapo in a variety of sadistic ways.

The *Grouse* team had little choice but to hang on, enduring the Norwegian winters in one of the most extraordinary survival stories of all time.[249] The last remnant of rations were augmented by boiling moss dug out from under the snow until, on Christmas Eve, Poulsson – 'tall, gaunt and a good hill-man' – shot a reindeer that had come down from the higher reaches of the mountain. For the next few weeks Poulsson, Kjelstrup, Haugland and Helberg ate nothing but a succession of bagged reindeers, including the stomach contents in an effort to offset scurvy. Meanwhile, the suspicious Germans strengthened their guard at Norsk Hydro and SOE reconsidered its options.

The result was *Operation Gunnerside*, which carried just six Norwegian commandos: Briger Stromsheim, Hans Storhaug, Kasper Idland, Frederick Kayser, Knut Haukelid and their leader, 2nd Lieut. Joachim Ronneberg. Their task was to land, make contact with the *Grouse* team, infiltrate the plant and destroy the heavy water production facilities. They were to be conveyed there by Tempsford's 138 Squadron. Although the bulk of the Norwegian's training had been based in Scotland, terrain that most closely resembled that of their native land, the *Gunnersides* had moved south prior to departure. They certainly spent three months at STS 61, Audley End in Essex ('a severe trial to our nerves' recollected Haukelid).[250] The team also received specialist training at STS3 (Southampton), the parachute centre STS 51(Manchester), and possibly RT training at STS 40, Howbury Hall – although Haukelid makes no mention of it.

The first attempt to drop *Gunnerside* was made on 23 January 1943, in a Halifax piloted by Squadron Leader Christopher Gibson. The operation was hampered by fog and low cloud, being forced to turn back when they

---

[249] For example see Mears, Ray. *The Real Heroes of Telemark* (Hodder and Stoughton, 2003).

[250] Haukelid, Knut. *Skis Against the Atom* (North American Heritage Press, 1989).

failed to locate the *Grouse* team's DZ lights. With evenings shortening as winter turned to spring, and *Grouse's* survival skills being tested far beyond original expectations, time was of the essence. The RAF decided, therefore, that if no contact could be made with the ground *Gunnerside's* commandos would have to be dropped 'blind'.

The second attempt, again piloted by Gibson, was made on the night of 16/17 February 1943. The plane's navigator, Flt. Lieut. John Charrot noted that it

> *really was a beautiful night, the moon was bright, the clouds were light and fluffy and we were flying low. At one time the rear gunner suggested that perhaps they were not pretty fluffy clouds, but the tops of the mountains we were scudding over – he may well have been right.*[251]

Once again, no DZ lights could be located so the load was just dropped in the following sequence: six containers; three men; three packages; three men; two packages. 'The rear gunner reported all parachutes had opened and we set off on the long haul to Tempsford' concluded Charrot.

What the rear gunner didn't see was that Haukelid somehow landed amongst the descending containers, being fortunate not to be hit one of them. A few days later *Gunnerside* made contact with a delighted *Grouse* team. After these trials, all that remained to be achieved was to infiltrate the Norsk Hydro complex which was approached by a single 75m bridge, 200m above a deep ravine. To avoid the guards, the commandos went down one side of the ravine, forded an icy river swollen with melted snow, climbed the other side and broke into the building without alerting the German guard. Small explosives destroyed the electrolysis chambers, releasing the heavy water, something that they accomplished without the defenders being aware of their presence until after they had escaped the factory. No shot was fired, no-one was injured. The saboteurs now went their separate ways, discarding enough of their British equipment and uniform to distract the Germans from their usual habit of inflicting savage reprisals upon local civilians.

---

[251] BBC *People's War* website. Article id. A5302810, contributed on 24.8.2005.

After a series of adventures that included a frantic chase on skis exchanging pistol fire with a German pursuer, Helberg made his way to the UK via Sweden. With Leif Tronstad he was parachuted in again in October (Einar Skinnarland guided them in with DZ lights), to co-ordinate the intensification of resistance activity against the Germans. This was part of an immense undertaking from Tempsford, made in appalling weather conditions. Already, on the night of 4/5 October alone, 138 Squadron had flown three operations – *Withers1*, *Stirrup2*, *Saddle7*- to Norway, delivering agents, packages and containers. 'Almost every moonlit night,' recalled Helberg, 'large Stirling planes came with guns, ammunition, food, uniforms and radio equipment.' Freddie Clark noted that planes from 138 and 161 Squadrons made twenty one despatches to Norway on the night of 1/2 November, and another twenty four just over a week later. The dreadful weather contributed to difficulties that, in Clark's words, 'decimated' the sorties. Two planes were hit by lightning (although made it back) but two Stirlings simply disappeared over the North Sea.

The Germans were slowly able to resume production, but subsequent attacks by bombers of the USAAF persuaded them to shift facilities back to Germany. One of the *Gunnersides* hadn't yet finished with them, however. On the night of 20 February 1944, with the assistance of two locals, Knut Haukelid got on board the ferry *Hydro* as it prepared to convey the barrels of heavy water across Lake Tinnsjo. Gaining access to the bilges, Haukelid placed 19lb of explosives 'in the form of a sausage' – possibly an example of one of Nobby Clarke's creation – inside the vessel. They were detonated when the ferry was underway, sinking both it and its cargo in the deep water of the lake, where the wreck still lies.

* * *

With the modesty that is characteristic of most heroes, the RAF aircrew were self-deprecatory when comparing their assignments with that of the agents that they were delivering – 'we the aircrews were there to help them on their way' said John Charrot. They would point out that they flew to 'quiet areas' not the heavily defended installations that were the destination of Bomber Command and, unlike the agents, they had a warm bed to which to return. Remembering the despatch of the *Gunnerside* team over Norway, Charrot noted 'I can remember thinking,

The Secretary of State for the Air, Sir Archibald Sinclair, makes a formal if, by the look of things, relaxed visit to RAF Tempsford on 22 April 1943. Wing Commander Pickard is introducing him to 161s Flight Officers Broadley and Cocker. J. A. Broadley was killed alongside Pickard during the Amiens raid less than a year later. He was just twenty three years of age (*Imperial War Museum, HU60540*).

as we watched the chutes going down onto this frozen wasteland, what courage they had. We were returning to base for bacon and beans, but what lay in store for them?' Frank Griffiths noted his pleasure at being woken by blackbirds and jays, sounds of the Bedfordshire countryside that penetrated his consciousness ahead of the 'cacophonous crackle of four throttled back Merlins ... as a Halifax came into land'.

Their comrades in the RAF knew better. Referring to the sentiments expressed by crews whose job it was to deliver aircraft to the station, Peter Churchill noted 'the crew looked upon Tempsford as a suicide circus... to go hunting for trouble every night when the moon was shining seemed to them about the most pixilated form of madness they could conceive and they raised their veteran's hats to the gentlemen of Tempsford'.[252] The Tempsford planes flew alone, without the protection afforded by a formation and, to deliver and collect, they flew lower. In

---

[252] Churchill, Peter, op. cit.

many of their missions they flew further: flights to Poland, for example, were routed over Denmark and Sweden to avoid German anti-aircraft fire. Such operations pushed the aircraft and their frozen crew to the very limits of their capabilities.

Should an east Bedfordshire villager have happened to be in the vicinity of the airbase late at night, they might have been startled to find one of the young 'gentleman' creeping furtively around the perimeter area. These young men were attempting to evade detection by the camp's security guards but they weren't playing a game: the villager would have been witness to part of the training peculiar to the sort of work required of the Tempsford pilots. Those same pilots who might be later found cheerfully drinking in Sandy's pubs had been preparing for the moment where they too might find themselves behind enemy lines, but without the preparation and protection given to an SOE agent. Hugh Verity, one of the most celebrated pick-up pilots of 161 Squadron, wore a mixture of uniform and civilian clothes in his flights in case of a sudden need to blend into French surroundings. Squadron Leader Guy Lockhart took a large quantity of French cash with him in his escape kit, something for which he was doubtless grateful when a careless Resistance contact laid the landing flares over the line of a ditch, causing Lockhart's Lysander to break its back. Setting fire to his wrecked plane and bolstering his wad of cash with more francs supplied by an apologetic *Maquis*, Lockhart set off on the long trek back to Bedfordshire with something in the region of 80,000F in his pockets. He eventually returned, via Gibraltar, with a suntan and a considerable stock of sherry and cigarettes purchased with the money.[253]

In truth, the pressure of the war took a toll upon men who were far younger than they appear in contemporary photographs. Hugh Verity recalled meeting his Commanding Officer, Wing Commander Charles. Pickard: 'a big man, rather heavily built, with a pointed nose and very fair hair. He smoked a pipe ... He was still in his twenties but he seemed ten years older. One got the impression that he was driving himself hard and burning himself up.'[254] An outstanding leader of 161 Squadron, in succession to 'Mousie' Fielden, 'Pick' was dead at twenty eight.

---

[253] Verity, op. cit.
[254] Ibid.

A combination of fatigue and superstition could be debilitating, as another of 161s pilots, Flight Lieutenant Colin Woodward, emphasised in recalling the traumatic impact that an accident had upon the crew of his Stirling. The crash-landing at Tempsford, which occurred at the end of a training flight dropping leaflets over central France, occurred in part because of damage to the aircraft caused by a previous pilot and the failure of the ground crew to notice it prior to Woodward's inexperienced crew taking over. Although no-one was killed, the crash, not surprisingly, damaged everyone's confidence, leading Woodward to briefly doubt his competence as a pilot. This sentiment he knew was shared by his crew and he noted that they were suddenly 'uncomfortable in my presence'. Until the real culpability was located, Woodward even underwent the humiliation of being made an example of by summarily dismissal to a 'Bad Boys' course at Sheffield (too many Stirlings were being crash-landed, in the opinion of the squadron's leader, Wing Commander Alan Boxer). According to Woodward, the greatest impact was upon Sgt. Jimmy Brooks, placed in the vulnerable position as rear

VE Day celebrations at Tempsford. Standing centre left is Leading Aircraftsman Doug Scales with his arm round Joan Bond (wearing the dark dress). Doug and Joan met at a local dance, subsequently marrying at Southill Church in 1945 (*Courtesy of Pamela Emms*).

gunner, for whom the accident began an irreversible erosion of his morale.[255] The bond between Bedfordshire and the partisans in occupied Europe was summed up by the writer Josef Garlinski thus: 'If anyone was close, very close to those fighting in the underground forces, it was those boys from 138 and 161 Squadrons, from the airfield at Tempsford'.[256]

* * *

The American equivalent to SOE was OSS, Office of Strategic Service, led by the charismatic General William 'Wild Bill' Donovan. The bulk of this work was based in the neighbouring counties of Cambridgeshire and Northamptonshire, but some spilled over into Bedfordshire. The OSS programme of liaison and supply to resistance movements in Europe fell under the heading of the 'Carpetbagger' programme. As the Americans developed this scheme from October 1943, their personnel

---

[255] See testimony posted via link from www.wartimememories.co.uk/airfields/tempsford. Testimony dated 13 December 1994. A photograph of Woodward's crew and their Stirling can be found on p.282 of Freddie Clark op. cit. The unidentified navigator in the photograph is possibly the Australian, Les Gibbs.

[256] Garlinski, op. cit.

from the 801st (Provisional) Bomb Group were trained by the experienced members of the RAF 138/161 Squadrons at Tempsford, many acquiring experience as their British counterparts had done – the hard way. In 1943 the Americans took over the tenancy of Milton Ernest Hall, turning it into a base for the Communications Section of the VIII Air Force Service Command Headquarters. The function of this unit was to provide navigational assistance and radio counter measure support for the USAAF, and approximately 120 Americans with various support staff (some local) plus RAF liaison officers living in the mansion and a cluster of Nissen huts in the grounds around the house.[257] Although this aspect was fairly straightforward and not subject to special classification, it has been recently suggested that there were more clandestine communications services provided by Milton Ernest Hall, that it was yet another SOE 'stately 'ome', and that the full purpose, function and workings of the place have still not yet been made public.[258]

Milton Ernest Hall (*Luton and Bedfordshire Archives*).

[257] Memoirs of Captain Bob Seymour (www.mboss.f9.co.uk/twinwood/seymour/index.htm).

[258] Bowman, op. cit.

Conclusion: How Effective was the Secret War?

Whilst covert manoeuvres have always been part of military strategy, the technical developments in broadcasting ensured that World War Two marked a new departure. Ritchie Calder's son, Angus, expressed this aspect most succinctly in his 1969 book, *The People's War*:

> This was the first war in which it was technically possible for one combatant power to relay its propaganda directly into the homes of the citizens of another, and the British did not neglect the opportunity. Every twenty-four hours, the Political Wartime Executive broadcast a hundred and sixty thousand words over the air in twenty three languages, and nearly a quarter of this went to Germany itself.[259]

On the face of it this is an impressive picture, especially given the belated adaptations that were involved all round. Yet the detractors of the conduct of psychological warfare, as well as other clandestine operations, have also been pretty trenchant in their criticism. One example, quoted by Ellic Howe in *The Black Game*, is this damming indictment from George Martelli, the head of PWE's Italian Section: '...the whole of the Woburn Abbey set-up was a gigantic waste of human effort and public money which could have been much better employed in other ways more conducive to winning the war.'[260]

Given Martelli's role this is an astonishing assertion, although Howe points out that Martelli is referring to 'white' rather than the 'black' operations at Woburn. In fact, Martelli's comments are a reminder of the bile and jealousy that punctuated the myriad sectors of the Secret War (Calder also noted '"white" British propagandists prized the BBC's reputation for objectivity ... and the "Black" propagandists, who ran their own studio, resented this characteristic heartily'). Nonetheless, Howe was indirectly acknowledging that there were profound doubts as to its effectiveness, notwithstanding the immense amount of resourcefulness and courage that went into this, and all the other myriad manifestations of covert operations. M. R. D. Foot, whilst also

---

[259] Calder, Angus. *The People's War. Britain 1939-45* (Jonathan Cape, 1969).

[260] Quoted in Howe, op. cit.

appreciative of the efforts made by SOE, efforts that were distinguished by enormous heroism, was similarly cautious when he concluded that 'SOE provided a large number of lessons on how to conduct – and how not to conduct – clandestine and underground war.'[261]   A younger generation of historians have been even more biting in their criticism, focusing upon the careless amateurism of SOE command and control, as well as the confusion and in-fighting that bedevilled overall activity in the Secret War. This was serious enough in Western Europe, but in the eastern half of the continent, so the argument controversially runs, it critically weakened the establishment of democratic institutions, easing the path for post-war Soviet domination. As Nigel West expressed it:

> Based on the evidence available at present, both SIS and SOE stand indicted of prosecuting an undeclared war against each other with the same, if not more venomous enthusiasm as the official conflict waged against the common enemy. Nor was this some minor, bureaucratic sideshow. It was to help ensure that much of Eastern Europe remained under totalitarian domination for a further 45 years after the Nazi defeat.[262]

Without doubt, there were many within senior military and government circles at the time that were sceptical as to SOE's value. Having been smuggled into Switzerland by the Maquis following a crash-landing in France, Frank Griffiths sent back a report from the safety of the British consulate in Geneva before returning home. He was later gratified to hear that the circulation of his report in government circles had been used to defend the effectiveness of clandestine activities against Bomber Command's criticism that it was a waste of resources. Griffiths had demonstrated that there existed an effective resistance network in France that was worth supporting as part of the preparations for the allied invasion of Europe.

The same infighting bedevilled weapons research also. Neither the War Office nor the Ministry of Supply were particularly happy accommodating the free thinkers of MD1, with their casual observance

---

[261] Foot, op. cit.

[262] West, Nigel. *Secret War. The Story of SOE, Britain's Wartime Sabotage Organisation* (Hodder and Stoughton, 1992)

Partisans gather round a Lysander *(provenance unknown)*.

Winston Churchill, during a visit to Luton *(Luton Museum Service/Luton News)*.

of strict procedure. At least one contemporary put its early survival down to the fact that each Ministry didn't want another to have it, as much as to the interventions of MD1's 'fairy godfather', Prof. Lindemann: 'without his support we should undoubtedly have disappeared as a department long ago.'[263] Churchill may have instinctively appreciated the virtue of 'crackpots and geniuses' at this desperate time, but the creation of the Ministry of Economic Warfare really just served to throw another assertive ferret into an already overcrowded sack.

* * *

In a review of Delmer's *Black Boomerang* that was published in the *New Statesman*, Richard Crossman singled out black propaganda as the weak link. He argued that for all Delmer's ingenious stratagems, the war was not shortened by a single day. The cantankerous Crossman was, of course, responsible for a significant part of the white propaganda and was also in any case given to bitterness and jealousy: 'he does not mind contradicting those friends and admirers who are most disposed to agree with him, even if this means making enemies of them'.[264] Since Crossman was also on record as dismissing all propaganda leaflets as 'a very wasteful way of getting information to the enemy when the radio could do it so much better', one would be obliged to deduce that the only form of propaganda that he thought worthwhile were white broadcasts of the BBC. Certainly both he and Hugh Carleton Greene (whose relations with Delmer became very strained in 1942-43), thought that black propaganda was fun for those who produced it but made very little difference to the conduct of the war. Delmer would only share this view perhaps with regards to the blackest of his black stuff, certainly believing that the limited amount of pornography did more to cheer up the perpetrators than demoralise the recipients. Nonetheless, Crossman raised a serious question (perhaps inadvertently) that still warrants an answer, especially when one notes that even Robert Bruce Lockhart was sceptical as to the value of what he called 'stunts' from Bedfordshire's RUs and Ellic Howe's forgers.

---

[263] Correspondence with C. V. Clarke, 14 December 1941. Private collection.

[264] Barman, op. cit.

Even when specifically praising the contribution of psychological warfare 'from early and humble beginnings' through to 'vigorous maturity', the Allied Supreme Commander Dwight D. Eisenhower made this acknowledgement:

Dwight D. Eisenhower
(The Dwight D. Eisenhower Presidential Library).

> *The exact contribution of psychological warfare toward the final victory cannot, of course, be measured in terms of towns destroyed or barriers passed. However, I am convinced that the expenditure of men and money in wielding the spoken and written word was an important contributing factor in undermining the enemy's will to resist and supporting the fighting morale of our potential allies in the occupied countries … Without doubt, psychological warfare has proved its right to a place of dignity in our military arsenal.*[265]

Eisenhower was to liken SOE's contribution to the equivalent of fifteen divisions but his assessment is essentially just that: psychological warfare was one of *corresponding* strength. This was echoed by Sefton Delmer, perhaps the most effective exponent of psychological warfare, who, in his farewell address to the staff at MB, emphasised the pre-eminence of the military effort, underlining that psychological warfare was 'purely subsidiary'. This chimed with Bruce Lockhart's assessment of the feeble nature of early British propaganda: it wouldn't have made a great deal of difference to the state of affairs even if it had been well run. In fact, one of the reasons that Delmer wanted his team to say nothing at all about their efforts was so that the Germans could not argue that they had been tricked into defeat, as many had done after World War One. With his characteristic generosity and shrewd judgement, Sefton Delmer emphasised that all types of propaganda had a vital role to play within the overall effort, with Howe arguing that rather than being a 'war winner', psychological warfare was essentially a means of softening up an already weakened enemy. As Duff Cooper, a former Minister of Information expressed it:

---

[265] SHAEF Psychological Warfare Division report, quoted in Erdman, op. cit.

The power of propaganda, as of all other weapons, must depend very largely upon the time when it was used. In the early stages of a war its weight is not so great as in the last stages, when it can prove decisive. There is no dispute about the fact that ...when victory in arms is on your side, propaganda can press the results of victory miles further.[266]

Cooper's assessment was vindicated by his German opposite number. On 23 March 1945, with the Third Reich collapsing, Joseph Goebbels noted in his diary:

Enemy propaganda is beginning to have an uncomfortably noticeable effect on the German people. Anglo-American leaflets are no longer carelessly thrown aside but are read attentively; British broadcasts have a grateful audience. By contrast our propaganda has a difficult time making an impact...I am now increasingly switching our propaganda on to low-level activity...Propaganda by sticker and chain letter will also be stepped up. What things one does at this critical time to keep people in a good mood![267]

Wider events had reduced the German master of the dark arts of persuasion to the same enfeebled position as his British counterparts in the early stages of the conflict. It is also appropriate to note that both *Atlantiksender* and *Soldatensender Calais*, the two most highly regarded black propaganda stations, were running during the latter part of the war, when the tide had already begun to turn against Germany.

In his discussion of psychological warfare Cruikshank was sharply critical of attitudes in Whitehall, concluding that propaganda 'was a dirty word' and that 'the real failure was ... their inability to see the manifold advantages of a single department concerned with subversion in all its aspects'.[268] Anthony Eden was of this view, as was Bruce Lockhart with specific regards to propaganda, but the latter's favoured candidate, Hugh Dalton, although doubtless flattered, was not of the same mind as such a move would have meant giving up MEW and SOE: 'I should have hated

---

[266] Cruikshank, op. cit.

[267] Trevor-Roper, Hugh (ed.). *The Goebbels Diaries. The Last Days* (Secker and Warburg, 1978).

[268] Cruikshank, op. cit.

this,' he concluded.[269] Whilst there was no over-arching command, there were nonetheless simultaneous overlaps that were spontaneous rather than structured. Dr Leslie Beck served as both a Chief Intelligence Officer and a French Research Unit housemaster in Bedfordshire, whilst Leonard Ingrams added scriptwriting and broadcasting to his many duties. 'It would have been a great loss had his work been confined to that of providing PWE intelligence from MEW,' noted David Garnett, who shared Robert Walmsley's view that intelligence and propaganda ought to go together.[270] In his mammoth history of British broadcasting, Asa Briggs echoes Cruikshank's criticism, contrasting the diverse and unco-ordinated situation in Britain with Dr. Goebbels' unity of command over all aspects of the German media, a feature that contributed to Thomas Barman's failed mission to Moscow in 1943.[271] 'I believe the Russians lost all interest in the co-operation,' reflected Barman 'when they discovered that the British Government did not control all forms of public expression in Britain, including the newspapers. They could not understand how propaganda could be effective unless everybody told the same story.' To a large extent, however, such criticism is irrelevant: Germany (and for that matter the USSR) was a monolithic state in which a single party tried to control all aspects of life, including the media. Britain's propaganda, by contrast, sprang from a free, pluralistic society, and this was reflected not only in its lack of co-ordination, but also in its ingenuity and flexibility – virtues that contrasted very favourably with the plodding German rigidity that was so ruthlessly exploited in their different ways by PWE, PID and the BBC.[272]

Delmer always believed that black propaganda could be dovetailed to strategic requirements but in truth it also has to be acknowledged that, in Robert Bruce Lockhart's words, 'the importance of our work was never fully appreciated in certain government circles'.[273] The striking exception to this attitude was provided by the Royal Navy, where Ian Fleming and Donald McLachlan, under Godfrey's leadership, provided

---

[269] Dalton, op. cit.

[270] Garnett, op. cit.

[271] Briggs, op. cit., Barman, op. cit.

[272] Trevor-Roper, op. cit. As late as 3 April 1945 Goebbels was issuing a precise six point directive for the German news agencies, for all the good it did him.

[273] Bruce Lockhart, op. cit. p.144.

every assistance. On the other hand, the Royal Air Force saw far less value in clandestine warfare, making it clear as early as 1938 that they were unwilling to risk air crews in leaflet drops and, once war commenced, rebuffed attempts by the Woburn propagandists to make contact. David Garnett, PWE's historian, accompanied Valentine Williams to just one meeting with the officers of Air Intelligence's German Section after which it was made clear by the RAF that no further links would be necessary. Furthermore, Garnett alleged that the fact that the Air Ministry could actually exercise editorial control was 'tacitly accepted until late in the war', claiming the right to reject any leaflet on the grounds that it could endanger captured pilots (a very real threat), damage morale or even on the grounds of good taste.[274] This is an important point to be borne in mind by those inclined to believe that pornography comprised a significant proportion of British anti-German propaganda, and might also explain why it was the USAAF in the main that dropped the editions of *Nachrichten*. It is surely no coincidence that although German pilots listened in to the Milton Bryan broadcasts, there

Charles Portal (*Imperial War Museum,* 13020).

Arthur 'Bomber' Harris (*Imperial War Museum, CH13020*).

---

[274] Garnett, op. cit.

were never any black propaganda programmes aimed directly at the *Luftwaffe* on the scale of *Kurzwellensender Atlantik*, or *Radio Livorno* (aimed at the Italian Navy). This was despite the physical proximity of so many RAF facilities and specialist personnel to Woburn/Milton Bryan.

In respect of the work of SOE, the Chief of the Air Staff, Sir Charles Portal, was on record as saying that he regarded some of its activities as ethically dubious, claiming that he was not happy at dropping what he called 'assassins'. As far as Bomber Command were concerned, deploying heavy aircraft for the supply of resistance organisations in occupied Europe were of only potential benefit, whereas the offensive against targets in Germany produced an immediate result – and there were those who believed that bombing alone would bring Hitler's Reich to its knees. It is possible, therefore, that not only was the sabotage value of SOE underdeveloped, but so too was its reconnaissance value on behalf of the bombing campaign. As for psychological operations, the disparaging views of Arthur 'Bomber' Harris were well known: in his opinion the allies total printed propaganda effort did no more than satisfy the enemy's requirements for toilet paper for the duration of the war. Harris' interpretation of Total War was pretty straightforward: he didn't object to the dropping of leaflets just as long as they tumbled out of a Lancaster's despatch bays in the wake of a shed load of high explosives.

Additionally it needs to be stressed that there was a stark lack of co-operation between government departments even within the specialised area of intelligence gathering. Commenting upon the relationship between the Foreign Office's SIS on the one hand and the Admiralty's NID on the other, the latter's Lt. Col. R. M. Cordeaux made this observation:

> *I don't think SIS thought much about NID at all, any more than they thought much about the corresponding departments in the War Office and Air Ministry. They thought that their own organisation was the only collector of information that was worth talking about, though they had to accept the fact, much to their annoyance, that SOE collected intelligence also … They didn't realise that there were other forms of intelligence which might discredit and contradict their own.*

> *One of the reasons for this lack of appreciation, or knowledge of, the NID and other Service Intelligence Departments was that only two, or*

at most three, members of SIS had any contact with NID and they were not the people who collected the intelligence.[275]

Cordeaux added that, within NID the feeling was reciprocated. This lack of co-operation, especially the unwillingness on the part of longer established departments – such as the Foreign Office – to share in its expertise was irksome in the work of propaganda, damaging in the sphere of intelligence but could be fatal in the operations of SOE. In his introduction to Garnett's history of PWE, historian Andrew Roberts summarised that the 'tale of inter-departmental wrangling and empire building ... is little more than shameful ... various government departments seemed to expand far more energy in outwitting and undermining one another than in trying to confuse and demoralise the enemy'.[276] This echoes the criticism of other historians of this field, such as John Keegan and Nigel West. At one level, therefore, it is reasonable to conclude that the experience provided by Bedfordshire's contribution suggests that World War Two was perhaps a little less 'total' than some of the protagonists imagined at the time. Looking at it another way, if Cordeaux's conclusions were indeed the case, then the activities carried out by key members of the teams at Woburn and Milton Bryan were a tribute to a remarkable degree of personal co-operation and common sense.

* * *

Without doubt, the six years between 1939-45 marked a decisive change in the conduct of warfare, reinforcing developments that were apparent in World War One, but amplifying these elements to a far greater degree and to an extent that some found uncomfortable. When Sir Stafford Cripps complained to Bruce Lockhart (amongst others), about the crude content of GS1 he also declared that 'even if good propaganda he would rather lose (the) war than win by such methods...'[277] Cripps' outraged incomprehension at the evolving nature of this aspect of Britain's clandestine warfare was echoed in Powell and Pressburger's 1943 film,

---

[275] McLachlan papers, op. cit. MLBE 6/2.

[276] Garnett, op. cit.

[277] Young, op. cit. 23.6.1942. Cripps later became a Labour Chancellor of the Exchequer, succeeding Dalton and preceding Gaitskell. The embodiment of post-war austerity, it was said that Cripps was like other men in that he was in favour of short skirts for women, but unlike them in that this was because it saved on textile supplies.

The Life and Death of Colonel Blimp. As the story reaches World War Two, the movie's central figure, General Sir Clive Candy, is abruptly confronted with the painful truth that the principles of soldiering upon which he had based the last forty years of his life had become largely outmoded in this new age. Bewildered that just moments before he was due to go on air, censors at the BBC had blocked a scripted talk that he had been about to deliver to the nation, Sir Clive returns home raging 'Does my knowledge count for nothing, eh? Experience? Skill? You tell me!' It takes one of his house guests (by neat irony, a German) to tell him. The wonderfully named Theo Kretschmar-Schuldorff, at various times Sir Clive's duelling rival, Great War enemy and now his best friend, quietly and firmly explains to his host how warfare has changed, deftly hinting also that whilst methods may look superficially similar, the values that underpin the combatants are profoundly different:

> *I read your broadcast up to the point where you describe the collapse of France. You commented on Nazi methods …by saying that you despised them, that you would be ashamed to fight on their side and that you would sooner accept defeat than victory if it could only be won by those methods … Clive! If you let yourself be defeated by them, just because you are too fair to hit back the same way that they hit at you, there won't be any methods but Nazi methods! If you preach the Rules of the Game while they use every foul and filthy trick against you, they will laugh at you! They'll think you are weak, decadent!*

In this respect then, Bedfordshire can also be held up as a paradigm of Total War. No longer did this small, landlocked and largely rural county just provide its quota of recruits to the Army and Royal Navy. No longer was the impact of war manifested just in high taxes and disruptions to trade, employment and food supplies, with occasional unemployment and rioting as a consequence. Now, amongst its other contributions, Bedfordshire listened in to the enemy; it lied to the enemy; it dropped civilian men and women from the skies to spy upon and to fight that enemy. Its printers kept quiet, its landladies asked no questions, its aniseed balls went missing. Colonel Blimp wouldn't have been alone in finding all this just a little unsettling. 'Nazi methods', perhaps, but as a means to an end rather than an end in itself, Bedfordshire successfully played host to a Secret War and claims the title of The Spy Capital of Britain!

Selected Further Reading

Audric, Brian. *The Meteorological Office, Dunstable and the IDA Unit in World War Two* (Royal Meteorological Society, 2000).

Barman, Thomas. *Diplomatic Correspondent* (Hamish Hamilton, 1968).

Bilham, E. G. 'The Central Forecasting Office, Dunstable.' *The Meteorological Magazine*, vol. 76, no. 898, (April 1947).

Binney, Marcus. *The Women Who Lived for Danger. The Women Agents of SOE in the Second World War* (Hodder & Stoughton, 2002).

Bowman, Martin W. *The Bedford Triangle. US Undercover Operations in World War Two* (Sutton, 2003).

Boyce, Frederic and Everett, Douglas. *SOE. The Scientific Secrets* (Sutton, 2005).

Boyle, Andrew. *Poor Dear, Brendan. The Quest For Brendan Bracken* (Hutchinson, 1974).

Briggs, Asa. *The History of Broadcasting in the United Kingdom. Volume III. The War of Words* (OUP, 1995).

Burian, Michal; Krížek, Ales; Rajlich, Jiří; Stehlík, Eduard. *Assassination. Operation Anthropoid 1941-42* (Prague, 2002).

Calder, Angus. *The People's War. Britain 1939-45* (Jonathan Cape, 1969).

Churchill, Peter. *By Moonlight* (Brown, Watson Ltd.).

Churchill, Peter. *The Spirit in the Cage* (The Elmfield Press, 1974).

Clark, Freddie. *Agents by Moonlight. The Secret History of RAF Tempsford During World War II* (Tempus Publishing, 1999).

Clarke, Peter. *A Question of Leadership. From Gladstone to Thatcher* (Penguin, 1992).

Cookridge, E. H. *Inside SOE. The First Full Story of Special Operations Executive in Western Europe, 1940-45* (Arthur Barker, 1966).

Cruikshank, Charles. *The Fourth Arm: Psychological Warfare, 1939-45* (1977).

Delmer, Sefton. *Black Boomerang* (Secker and Warburg, 1962).

Delmer, Sefton. *Trail Sinister* (Secker & Warburg, 1961).

Dalton, Hugh. *The Fateful Years. Memoirs 1931-45* (Frederick Muller, 1957).

Erdman, James M. 'Leaflet Operations in the Second World War' (unpublished typescript, 1969).

Fadden, Kevan J. 'Archaeological Evaluation of a World War 2 Air-raid Shelter at the Old Rectory, Hills End, Eversholt, Bedfordshire, 1997', (Ampthill & District Archaeological & Local History Society).

Foot, M. R. D. *SOE. The Special Operations Executive 1940-46* (UPA).

Foot, M. R. D. *SOE in France* (Frank Cass, 2004).

Garlinski, Josef. *Poland SOE and the Allies* (Allen and Unwin, 1969).

Garnett, David. *The Secret History of PWE: The Political Wartime Executive. 1939-45* (St Ermin's Press, 2002).

Grayson, William C. *Chicksands. A Millennium of History* (Shefford Press, 1994).

Griffiths, Richard. *Fellow Travellers of the Right. British Enthusiasts for Nazi Germany 1933-39* (OUP, 1983).

Grisewood, Harman. *One Thing At A Time. An Autobiography* (Hutchinson, 1968).

Hastings, Max. *Das Reich. The March of the 2nd SS Panzer Division Through France, June 1944* (Pan Books, 1983).

Haukelid, Knut. *Skis Against the Atom* (North American Heritage Press, 1989).

Hills, R. J. T. *Phantom Was There* (Arnold, 1951).

Hinsley, F. H. and Stripp Alan (eds.). *Code Breakers. The Inside Story of Bletchley Park* (OUP, 1993).

Howard, Anthony. *Crossman. The Pursuit of Power* (Jonathan Cape, 1990).

Howe, Ellic. *The Black Game. British Subversive Operations Against the Germans During the Second World War* (Michael Joseph, 1982).

Jarvis, Sue. *Captain Oswald Tuck R. N. and the Bedford Japanese School* (The Bletchley Park Reports, Report no.19, June 2003).

John, Otto. *Twice Through the Lines* (Futura, 1972).

Jones, Michael. *Colworth in Context. A History of Colworth Estate, Bedfordshire, 1720 to 1947* (Published by the author, 1997).

Keeble, Harold. *Alphabet and Image* (Shenval Press, 1947).

Langhorne, Richard (ed.). *Diplomacy and Intelligence During the Second World War. Essays in Honour of F. H. Hinsley* (CUP, 1985).

Lockhart, Robert Bruce. *Comes The Reckoning* (Putnam, 1947).

(Luton News) *Luton At War* (Home Counties Newspapers, 1947).

Luke, Doreen. *My Road to Bletchley Park. The Memoirs of WAAF LACW 2068978 Doreen Gertrude Spence 1941 to 1946.* (M & M Baldwin, Kidderminster, 2005).

Lycett, Andrew. *Ian Fleming* (Weidenfeld and Nicolson, 1995).

Lynn, Vera, Cross, Robin and de Gex, Jenny. *The Women Who Won the War* (Sidgwick and Jackson, 1990).

McLachlan, Donald. *Room 39. Naval Intelligence in Action 1939-45* (Weidenfeld & Nicolson, 1968).

Macrae, Col. R. Stuart. *Winston Churchill's Toyshop* (Roundwood Press, 1971).

Marks, Leo. *Between Silk and Cyanide. A Codemaker's Story 1941-45* (Harper Collins, 2000).

Marshall, Bruce. *The White Rabbit* (Evan Bros., 1966).

Martel, Gordon (ed.). *The Times and Appeasement. The Journal of A. L. Kennedy 1932-39.* Camden 5th Series, vol. 16, Royal Historical Society (CUP, 2000).

Mears, Ray. *The Real Heroes of Telemark* (Hodder and Stoughton, 2003).

Meulstee, Louis and Staritz, Rudolf F. *Wireless for the Warrior. Vol. 4, Clandestine Radio* (A Radio Bygones publication, 2004).

Neave, Airey. *Saturday at MI9* (Hodder & Stoughton, 1969).

Ottaway, Susan. *Violette Szabo. The Life That I Have* (Leo Cooper, 2002).

Pearson, John. *The Life of Ian Fleming* (Arum, 2003).

Morley, Sheridan. *The Life of David Niven. The Other Side of the Moon* (Weidenfeld and Nicholson, 1985).

Pether, John. *Black Propaganda. Bletchley Park Reports, no. 13.* (Bletchley Park Trust, 1998).

Pether, John and White, Peter. 'Political Warfare in Bedfordshire' *Bedfordshire Magazine* vol. 26, no. 208.

Pike, William S. 'Weather Notes on 15 December 1944, With Particular Reference to the Disappearance of Glenn Miller's Aircraft into the English Channel.' *Journal of Meteorology*, vol. 25, no. 254, (December 2000).

Pimlott (ed.) *The Second World War Diary of Hugh Dalton 1940-45* (Jonathan Cape, 1986).

Pym, Francis. *Sentimental Journey* (privately published, 1988).

Rees, Neil. *The Czech Connection. The Czechoslovak Government in Exile in London and Buckinghamshire* (Neil Rees, 2005).

Roach, Arthur W. *They Also Serve* (self published, 1987).

Roucoux, Omer. 'The Meteorological Office in Dunstable During World War Two.' *Weather*, vol. 56, no. 1 (January 2001).

Rosenberg, Bruce A. & Ann Harleman Stewart. *Ian Fleming* (Twayne, 1989).

Sebag-Montefiore, Hugh. *Enigma. The Battle for the Code* (Phoenix, 2001).

Seebohm, Caroline. *The Country House. A Wartime History 1939-45* (Weidenfeld and Nicholson, 1989).

Skefko Ball Bearing Co. Ltd. *A Factory Went to War* (1946).

Smith, Graham. *Hertfordshire and Bedfordshire Airfields in the Second World War* (Countryside Books, 1999).

Smith, Michael. *The Emperor's Codes* (Bantam, 2000).

Spark, Muriel. *Curriculum Vitae. Autobiography* (Constable, 1992).

Stripp, Alan. *Codebreaker in the Far East* (OUP, 1995).

Stuart, Campbell. *Opportunity Knocks Once* (Collins, 1952).

Taylor, John A. *Bletchley Park's Secret Sisters* (Book Castle, 2005).

Thompson, Harry. *Richard Ingrams. Lord of the Gnomes* (Heinemann, 1994). This book contains some useful background information on Richard's father, Leonard.

Tibbutt, H. G. 'The Cloak and Dagger Squadrons of RAF Tempsford in World War Two' *Bedfordshire Magazine* Vol. XII, pp 269-73.

Trevor-Roper, Hugh (ed.). *The Goebbels Diaries. The Last Days* (Secker and Warburg, 1978).

Turner, Des. *Aston House. SOE Station XII. SOE's Secret Centre* (Sutton, 2006).

Underwood, Andrew. *'Home Rule for Ampthill'* (Ampthill Urban District Council, 1974).

Verity Hugh. *We Landed By Moonlight. Secret Landings in France, 1940-44* (Crecy Publishing, 1998).

West, Nigel. *Secret War. The Story of SOE, Britain's Wartime Sabotage Organisation* (Hodder and Stoughton, 1992).

Way, Chris. *Glenn Miller in Britain. Then and Now* (Battle of Britain Prints/After the Battle, 1994).

Williams, Philip M. *Hugh Gaitskell* (OUP, 1982).

Willis, R. V. *The Coming of a Town. The Story of Leighton Buzzard and Linslade* (published by the author, 1984).

Wright, Wilbur. *Millergate. The Real Glenn Miller Story* (published by author, 1990).

Young, Kenneth. *The Diaries of Sir Robert Bruce Lockhart. Volume II, 1939-65* (Macmillan, 1980).

Selected websites

There are a number of excellent websites on the internet that are very informative. There are also a number that should be treated with caution, a number that are dominated by uncorroborated conjecture and conspiracy theory, and some that are frankly rubbish.

Amongst the very best are the following:

www.64-baker-street.org
Principally devoted to the women agents of SOE.

www.clutch.open.ac.uk/schools/emerson00/home
A fine guide to activities in the Milton Keynes region.

www.harringtonmuseum.org.uk
The duties of both the American 'Carpetbagger' and Tempsford squadrons are covered on this site.

www.members.aol.com/fqurk202/index.html
Devoted to Tempsford and surrounding area.

www.psywar.org
Lee Richards' outstanding site, conveying the full history of psychological warfare.

www.psywarrior.com
A superb American site, also covering recent conflicts.

www.seftondelmer.co.uk
Maintained by Felix Delmer, this remains the best source for material relating to his father's work.

www.161squadron.org
The website created by Bob Body, in memory of Hudson FK790 (piloted by his uncle), and all the Tempsford crews.

Places to Visit

Violette Szabo G. C. Museum,
Cartref House, Wormelow,
Hereford, HR2 8HN
For further details contact:
Rosemary E. Rigby MBE
(01981 540477).

Woburn Abbey
01525 290333
www.woburnabbey.co.uk

306th Bomb Group Heritage Museum
Thurleigh, Bedfordshire
01234 708715
www.306museum@ncsmh.fsnet.co.uk

The Glenn Miller Museum
Clapham, Bedfordshire
01234 350413
www.twinwoodevents.com

The Shuttleworth Collection
Old Warden, Bedfordshire
01767 627927
www.shuttleworth.org

Bletchley Park
Bletchley, Buckinghamshire
01908 640404

The Barn
Tempsford Airfield
by owner's permission only
01767 650251

The Museum of Military Intelligence
Chicksands Bedfordshire
01462 752896
www.army.mod.uk/intelligencecorps/chicksands

Bedford Museum
01234 353323
www.bedfordmuseum.org

Cecil Higgins Art Gallery
01234 211222
www.cecilhigginsartgallery.org

Luton Museums Service
Wardown Park
Luton
01582 546722

**Bedford Tourist
Information Centre**
The Old Town Hall
St Paul's Square
Bedford
MK40 1SJ
01234 215226
www.bedford.gov.uk/tourism

Index
(numbers in **bold** refer to entries with illustrations)